D0207695

Lawlessness and Economics

The Gorman Lectures in Economics

Series Editor, Richard Blundell

A series statement appears at the back of the book

Lawlessness and Economics
Alternative Modes of Governance

Avinash K. Dixit

Princeton University Press

Princeton and Oxford

Copyright © 2004 by Princeton University Press

Published by Princeton University Press,
41 William Street, Princeton, New Jersey 08540

In the United Kingdom: Princeton University Press,
3 Market Place, Woodstock, Oxfordshire OX20 1SY

Library of Congress Cataloguing-in-Publication Data

Dixit, Avinash K.
  Lawlessness and economics: alternative modes of governance / Avinash K. Dixit.
    p.cm. — (The Gorman lectures in economics)
  Includes bibliographical references and index.
  ISBN 0-691-11486-2 (cl: alk. paper)
    1. Economic policy. 2. Corporate governance. 3. Contracts. 4. Rights of property.
5. Corporation law. 6. Business enterprises—Law and legislation. 7. International cooperation.
8. Developing countries—Economic policy. 9. Corporate governance—Developing countries.
10. Contracts—Developing countries. 11. Right of property—Developing countries.
12. Corporation law—Developing countries. 13. Business enterprises—
Law and legislation—Developing countries. I. Title. II. Series.

HD87.D588 2004
330.1—dc22   2003068992

British Library Cataloguing-in-Publication Data

A catalogue record for this book is available from the British Library

This book has been composed in Times and typeset by T&T Productions Ltd, London
Printed on acid-free paper ⊗
www.pup.princeton.edu

Printed in the United States of America

10 9 8 7 6 5 4 3 2 1

Contents

Preface

A multidisciplinary research area, to which I have given the attention-grabbing name "Lawlessness and Economics," has emerged within the social sciences during the last two decades. It studies the alternative institutions that support economic activity when a government is unable or unwilling to provide adequate protection of property rights and enforcement of contracts through the machinery of state law. Research in this field has accelerated in recent years, partly as the underlying conceptual framework has developed, and partly as the importance as well as the difficulties of institution-building in less-developed countries and transition economies have been recognized.

Those who like to see unity in the social sciences could not wish for a better field. It contains ethnographic studies by anthropologists and sociologists, case studies by lawyers and economic historians, and formal modeling and data analysis by economists and political scientists. Moreover, these distinct approaches have not developed in isolation from one another. Practitioners of each have learned from the work of others, and have built on it in their own way.

This research has accumulated to the point where the time seems ripe to pull some of the threads together, to help insiders make some connections they might have missed, and to alert outsiders to the existence of new, interesting, and challenging research opportunities. As a recent arrival in the field, I have mixed qualifications for undertaking this task. I cannot hope to be as comprehensive or authoritative as those who were present at the creation, but can hope to provide a fresh perspective and bring a somewhat different toolkit for analysis. Specifically, in my capacity as an applied game theorist, I can contribute some modeling motivated by case studies and empirical evidence, thereby hoping to improve and deepen our understanding of the issues and phenomena.

The opportunity to make such a contribution came to me in the form of an invitation to deliver the Gorman Lectures at University College London in December 2002. As I said in the preface to *The making of economic policy: a transaction-cost politics perspective* (Dixit 1996), which was based on my Munich Lectures in Economics, books based on a short series of lectures offer the author a delightful vehicle. He can expand the discussion beyond the confines of a journal article, but the limits on length and the short deadlines relieve him of the responsibility of being comprehensive, as would be required in a full-fledged book. I am lucky to get a similar opportunity for a second time, and have chosen to repeat the formula and be highly selective. Think of this book not as a menu from which you can order and consume, but as a prospectus inviting you to invest.

In this instance, attempting a comprehensive treatment would be difficult for another reason, namely the "lemming effect" identified by Robert Solow in his Ely Lecture (Solow 1974). In the course of his research on the economics of exhaustible resources, he found that

> every time the mail came it contained another paper by another economic theorist on [this subject]. It was a little like trotting down to the sea, minding your own business like any nice independent rat, and then looking around and suddenly discovering that you're a lemming.

In the case of institutions of governance, not only economic theorists but also theoretical, empirical, and field researchers from all the social sciences are in the game. (And now the papers come by email, more than once a day.) Search engines find hundreds of thousands of web pages, and thousands of scholarly articles, related to governance. I have no choice but to be highly selective, and have made the selection idiosyncratically to fit with my immediate interests. I apologize in advance to all those fellow lemmings who are left out, either because I did not know of their work or arbitrarily judged it to be outside my current scope.

My primary reaction to the invitation to give the Gorman Lectures was, of course, one of feeling honored. My early research on public economics and international trade owes much to Terence Gorman's foundational work on consumer theory and aggregation. I had the privilege of meeting him on several occasions during the 1970s and 1980s, and greatly admired his combination of seriousness of purpose and infectious enthusiasm for the subject. The economics profession is richer for having had him in our midst for the last half-century, and poorer for his passing in early 2003. I hope these lectures constitute a small tribute to him.

If Terence's writing had one flaw, it was his tendency to make small slips and leave typos uncorrected. There was never anything seriously wrong, but one had to read through carefully and make sure that the slips did not affect the basic argument. This was actually a very useful learning device for students. I would like to pretend that any typos or slips in my writing are kept there deliberately for this purpose (and hope that there are no serious errors).

I have benefited from opportunities to present large and small parts of the contents of this book at other venues. An early version of the general ideas and the model of Chapter 4 formed my presidential address to the Econometric Society in 2001, and was published in *Econometrica* in March 2003. I gave a one-week course based on this material at the June 2002 workshop of the Netherlands Network of Economics (NAKE), two lectures at the Laszlo Rajk College of the Budapest University of

Economic Sciences and Public Administration in October 2002, and a one-day seminar at the IMF Institute in April 2003. And of course I gave seminars based on individual papers at places too numerous to list. I benefited from comments and questions at all of these occasions.

Two of the chapters in this book contain, with slight changes, substantial portions of two of my previously published journal articles. Material from Dixit (2003b) appears in Chapter 3, and that from Dixit (2003a) in Chapter 4. I thank the publishers—the University of Chicago Press and the Econometric Society, respectively—for permissions to reprint from these articles.

It is a pleasure to acknowledge my debt to many people who facilitated my entry into this field, guided me through the literature, and gave me comments and suggestions on my own writing. Alessandra Casella deserves star billing for her encouragement and constructive criticism throughout the process. Karla Hoff's careful and perceptive reading of many of the papers in their early versions helped me make better contacts with existing literature and saved me from some errors. Oriana Bandiera read the first draft of the complete manuscript and gave me detailed and perceptive comments. Such people who convey large positive externalities on others in the profession deserve special recognition and applause. In the earliest stages of my reading in this area, Oliver Williamson was a source of basic ideas and knowledge for me as for so many others, and I found works by Shuhe Li, Jean Ensminger, Avner Greif, and Diego Gambetta especially interesting and stimulating. For discussions of specific topics and comments on individual papers I am grateful to Dilip Abreu, Daron Acemoglu, Lisa Bernstein, Peter Diamond, David Epstein, Xavier Gabaix, Diego Gambetta, Claudia Goldin, Gene Grossman, Katherine Hefer, Giovanni Maggi, Margaret Meyer, Peter Murrell, Thomas Palfrey, Torsten Persson, Anne Sartori, Andrei Shleifer, Robert Solow, Lars Svensson, Jean Tirole, Robin Wells, Oliver Williamson, and Peyton Young.

Richard Blundell and his colleagues at University College London not only made all this possible by inviting me to give the Gorman Lectures, but also offered wonderful hospitality during my stay there; Jennifer Williams deserves special thanks for the organization of my visit. The first draft of the manuscript was written during a sabbatical year spent as a Visiting Scholar at the Russell Sage Foundation in New York. Social scientists who are familiar with this organization know what I mean when I say that there could not be a more ideal setting for research and writing; others do not know what they have missed. I thank the officers and staff of the foundation—especially Eric Wanner, Madge Spitaleri, Auris Lora, and Jackie Cholmondeley—for their year-long hospitality and support, all my fellow Visiting Scholars for providing a constantly stimulating intellectual environment, and Kari Hodges for her efficient and cheerful research assistance. I also thank the National

Science Foundation for financial support of my research. Sam Clark of T&T Productions Ltd merits special thanks and praise for his thorough and perceptive copy editing and expert typesetting. Finally, Richard Baggaley, Peter Dougherty, and their colleagues at Princeton University Press have my gratitude for their work in smoothing the production process of the book.

Lawlessness and Economics

1

Economics With and Without the Law

1.1 The Need for Economic Governance

Most economic activities and interactions share several properties that together create the need for an institutional infrastructure of governance. First, these activities and interactions are opportunities to create or add value. This includes creation of tangible or intangible property (such as improved land, physical and human capital, reputation, and goodwill) and exchange of goods and services. Second, the activities require input from several individuals. We have known since the birth of economics how division of labor enhances productivity; more recently, we have recognized the importance of creation and preservation of common property resources. Third, the interactions are based on explicit or implicit contracts voluntarily made by all the parties involved; exchanges of a good or service for another good or service or money are the main instances of this. Some actions may be unilaterally undertaken by one party but create costs or benefits for another; examples include accidental or deliberate damage to property, or its opposite, namely positive spillovers that improve another's property.

Everyone can potentially benefit from the creation or addition of economic value. However, each participant in the process usually has available to him various actions that increase his own gain, while lowering the others' gain by a greater amount. The only exceptions are situations involving simultaneous exchange of goods or services of immediately verifiable attributes and qualities, but these are a small subset of all economic interactions. In most situations, the participants have opportunities to supply defective goods, shirk on the job, renege on payment, and so on. Williamson (1979, 1985) has coined the term "opportunism" for this whole class of actions that tempt individuals but hurt the group as a whole.

Problems also arise with property rights. If no mechanisms—governmental or non-governmental—exist to deter theft, then any one person can wait for someone else to create property or produce output and then steal it; this usually takes less effort than creating the property or the product oneself. Some may even extort money from others by making threats of destroying their property. Hirshleifer (2001), Grossman and Kim (1985), and others have focused on these problems.

Anticipation of opportunism, theft, or extortion constitutes a strong disincentive to making potentially valuable investments or entering into mutually beneficial contracts in the first place. Therefore if market economies are to succeed, they need a foundation of mechanisms to deter such privately profitable but socially dysfunctional behaviors, and thereby to sustain adequate incentives to invest, produce, and exchange. In other words, markets need the underpinning of institutions of economic governance.

1.2 Economics Taking the Law for Granted

Economists have always recognized the need for governance. However, until relatively recently they assumed that the government, specifically the institution and machinery of the state's law, provided the needed governance. Criminal law, while it has major non-economic functions, also serves to deter theft and some forms of economic fraud. Civil law has economic aspects centrally in its concerns. Contract law can be said to be mainly for the governance of economic activity; laws of tort and liability pertain to contracts as well as non-contractual relationships, both mainly in the economic sphere.

Even the most libertarian economists, who deny the government any useful role in most aspects of the economy, allow that making and enforcing laws that give clear definitions of property rights, and ensuring adherence to voluntary private contracts, are legitimate and indeed essential functions of government, in addition to national defense. Friedman (1962, p. 2) puts this succinctly:

> [The government's] major functions must be to protect our freedom
> both from the enemies outside our gates and from our fellow-citizens:
> to preserve law and order, to enforce private contracts, to foster competitive markets.

There seems universal agreement in traditional economics that the framework of law is a necessary condition for a market economy to succeed.

Extreme libertarians regard the government's legal framework as not only necessary but also sufficient for markets to function well—the Coase Theorem (Coase 1960, 1988) says that if property rights are well defined, voluntary contracts can achieve all available economic benefits, including the internalization of externalities and the provision of public goods. Most other economists recognize the possibility of market failure even under the aegis of a well-functioning state law; for them, institutions of law are not a sufficient condition to ensure optimal outcomes from markets. For example, McMillan (2002, pp. ix, x) lists three other elements for markets to work well: "information flows smoothly, . . . , side-effects on third parties are curtailed, and competition is fostered." The opposites of these, namely imperfect information, externalities, and imperfect competition, are well-recognized causes of market failure, and they can exist regardless of whether a government adequately protects property rights and enforces contracts.

Thus conventional economic theory does not underestimate the importance of law; rather, the problem is that it takes the existence of a well-functioning institution of state law for granted. It assumes that the state has a monopoly over the use of coercion, and that the state designs and enforces laws with the objective of maximizing social welfare. Moreover, until the last 30 years or so, that is, until economics recognized the ubiquity and importance of information asymmetries and transaction costs, the usual implicit assumption was that the law operated costlessly.[1]

This simple view of the law made it possible to achieve faster progress in the research on the economic forces of supply and demand, and of their equilibration in markets; therefore it was a useful abstraction in its time. However, its shortcomings soon hinder rather than help the economic analysis of markets and limit its usefulness. Only advanced countries in recent times come anywhere near the economist's ideal picture, in which the government supplies legal institutions that are guided solely by concern for social welfare and operate at low cost. In all countries through much of their history, the apparatus of state law was very costly, slow, unreliable, biased, corrupt, weak, or simply absent. In most countries this situation still prevails. Markets with such weak underpinnings of law differ greatly from those depicted in conventional economic theory.

Deficiencies of the law are most acute in less-developed countries (LDCs) and in transition economies. For example, Bearak (2000) reports that there are 25 million cases pending before the courts in India, and even if no new ones are filed, it will take 324 years to clear the backlog. Murrell (1996, p. 34) found that laws in many transition economies were "a facade without a foundation." Recent assessments of the effectiveness of the legal system in post-Soviet Russia differ among Western observers, but a fair assessment is that while the *Arbitrazh* court system created to handle commercial disputes has begun to function reasonably well in handing down verdicts, getting these verdicts enforced remains highly problematic, especially for smaller enterprises (Hendley and Murrell 2001; Hay and Shleifer 1998). McMillan and Woodruff (1999, 2000) and others have found similar situations in other transition economies in Eastern Europe and in Vietnam. Djankov and Murrell (2002) survey this literature.

Of course economic activity does not grind to a halt because the government cannot or does not provide an adequate underpinning of law. Too much potential value would go unrealized; therefore groups and societies have much to gain if they can create alternative institutions to provide the necessary economic governance.

---

[1] Barzel (2002, especially Chapters 1 and 2) criticizes the orthodox economic view of the state as a benevolent and costless monopolist in coercion.

They attempt to develop, and sometimes succeed in developing, such institutions of varying degrees of effectiveness. These include self-protection or hired professional protection for property rights (see, for example, Hirshleifer 2001; Gambetta 1993), networks of information transmission, and social norms and punishments for contract enforcement (see, for example, Greif 1993, 1994; Milgrom, North, and Weingast 1990; Gambetta 1993). Indeed, an extreme version of the Coase Theorem says that everything works out in the best feasible way (Stigler 1988). If governance is costly, the least-cost method will get chosen from among the available institutions, whether it be state law or a private alternative. In this view, the emergence of a state or government is itself endogenous, and will occur if, and only if, it is the most efficient mode of governance. But even without going that far, we can recognize that societies will attempt to evolve other institutions, albeit imperfect ones, to underpin their economic activity when state law is missing or unusable. In other words, governmental provision of legal institutions is not strictly necessary for achieving reasonably good outcomes from markets.

Rodrik (2003, pp. 10–16) summarizes the lessons of case studies of several countries as follows.

> Institutions that provide dependable property rights, manage conflict, maintain law and order, and align economic incentives with social costs and benefits are the foundation of long-term growth. ... State institutions are not the only ones that matter. Social arrangements can have equally important and lasting consequences. ... Modest changes in institutional arrangements ... can produce large growth payoffs ... [but] the required changes can be highly specific to the context.

This yields some general lessons for policy-makers in LDCs and transition economies who are contemplating market-oriented reforms and privatizations, and for their economic advisers from Western countries and international organizations. They must recognize that markets will not succeed unless they are supported by adequate governance institutions. The processes of creating the institutions and the apparatus of state law, and of improving them to the point where they function well, are slow and costly. But it is not always necessary to create replicas of Western-style state legal institutions from scratch; it may be possible to work with such alternative institutions as are available, and build on them. Of course, to do this we must have a good understanding of how various institutions of governance work, and of how they interact with each other and with an imperfect state law where that exists. My aim in this book is to contribute to the improvement of this understanding.

1.3 "Lawlessness and Economics" in Context

Where does the study of alternative institutions for protection of property rights and enforcement of contracts, to which I have given the eye-catching albeit strictly inaccurate title "Lawlessness and Economics," stand in relation to many closely related fields of inquiry? Such demarcation of fields or subfields is always a difficult question. Reality is usually a complex mixture, whereas theoretical analysis usually proceeds faster and goes deeper by identifying pure conceptual categories. In the present context, all countries have governments of some kind, of varying scope, competence, and benevolence. And in all of them, significant aspects or components of economic activity are conducted without direct reference or recourse to the state's law. Isolating pure categories from this reality is a matter of judgment, and any attempt at a precise definition or delineation leaves significant exceptions or overlaps. But an attempt must be made, however imperfect, so that researchers and students in neighboring areas can fit this book into the context of their own work.

Lawlessness and Economics can be regarded as a subfield within the broad conceptual framework of the New Institutional Economics. This large and varied body of research has built upon pioneering ideas of Coase (1937, 1960, 1988), North (1990), Williamson (1985, 1996), and others; Williamson (2000) has given us a good recent overview and assessment.

North distinguishes between institutions and organizations. For him, institutions are the overarching framework of rules and constraints, formal and informal, that govern interactions among individuals; constitutions and social norms are examples. Organizations are groups of individuals that operate within the general framework of institutions, and implement the rules and norms of the institutions; examples are legislatures, political parties, and universities. Of course there are interactions and feedbacks between institutions and organizations. The rules and constraints imposed by institutions do not eliminate all freedom for organizations to act, and since organizations have members with differing interests and abilities, interesting issues of "the play of the game" at this level must be analyzed. Institutions can then evolve to alter the rules of the game so as to achieve better outcomes from the play at the organizational level. Finally, individuals interact within the frameworks set up by both institutions and organizations, and these transactions have their costs of information, commitment, and so on. North (1990, pp. 92–104) argues that institutions and organizations attempt to economize on transaction costs, but usually fall short of optimality, especially when changing economic and technological conditions require changed or new institutions. He gives two categories of reasons for the long lags and bottlenecks in the process of institutional change: first, resistance by powerful special interests with stakes in the old system; and second, multiple equilibria and historical accidents.

Others use the same terms in slightly different senses and draw somewhat different distinctions. For example, in his pioneering game-theoretic analysis, Schotter (1981, p. 11) defines institutions as

> a regularity in social behavior that is agreed to by all members of society, specifies behavior in specific recurrent situations, and is either self-policed or policed by some external authority.

Thus his institutions specify the strategies that the individuals should choose. That is, they include aspects of the play of the game as well as the rules. Calvert (1995a,b) develops this idea further, and interprets it more explicitly as specifying the equilibrium that is to be played. Sobel (2002, p. 147) similarly says that

> an individual's expectation of the response to his action is often an important part of the institutional environment; that is, the institutional environment also serves to coordinate beliefs and select equilibria.

And Greif (2000) defines institutions as

> a system of social factors—such as rules, beliefs, norms, and organizations—that guide, enable, and constrain the actions of individuals.

Thus he includes organizations as an example of institutions, not a separate category. Moreover, the beliefs in his analysis are beliefs about the strategies that others would choose in off-equilibrium situations, and therefore serve to select an equilibrium; this accords with Calvert's view of institutions. I conclude that North's conceptual distinction between the rules and the play of the game, leading to the distinction between institutions and organizations, serves a useful purpose of focusing our attention on the different functions, but there are many feedbacks between the two categories blurring the distinction.

Williamson (2000) draws finer distinctions with a four-level classification scheme. At the first (highest or most basic) level stand informal institutions, such as religion, social customs and norms. These are slow to change, over the timescale of centuries or millennia. At the second level is the institutional environment, consisting of formal rules, such as constitutions and laws. The timescale of evolution of these is measured in decades. The play of the game occurs at the third level, and this includes the choice of appropriate modes of governance for each type of transaction, or organizations in North's sense, the aim being to economize on transaction costs. The idea that transactions and governance modes are aligned in this way is Williamson's (1996, p. 12) famous discriminating alignment hypothesis. Finally, the fourth and lowest level contains routine economic activities such as production, employment, market equilibration.

Williamson places other subfields within this scheme. Positive Political Theory (PPT) operates mostly at the second level, focusing on political institutions such as the executive and the legislature, and their implications for economic performance. Transaction Cost Economics (TCE) is located mostly at the third level. It focuses on economic structures such as firms and on transactions within and across these structures. It studies how the economic structures and transactions respond to the available governance structures and their limitations.

As with all attempts at taxonomy, this leaves some ambiguities and overlaps, and is not universally followed. Most importantly, some other people would locate many informal institutions of social norms at the second rather than the first level. For Williamson, norms and other informal institutions have "mainly spontaneous origins" and "have a lasting grip on the way a society conducts itself" (2000, p. 597). In my opinion this is true of some but not all norms. Societies make conscious efforts to instill some norms into their members, enlisting the help of parents, teachers, media, and leaders of opinion for this purpose. Many of the norms pertain to civic duties such as voting, but others pertain to honesty in economic matters. This process of social conditioning and education can respond to changing needs much faster than the evolutionary timescale. Many of the communities facing collective-action problems that were the subject of Ostrom's (1990) studies created and used such norms. Therefore I will be more flexible in the location of norms in Williamson's scheme. Next, there are important feedbacks from level 3 to level 2, therefore they should be studied jointly.

Where does LLE fit within Williamson's classification? In one sense, it is about what PPT leaves out. LLE asks: if the government's apparatus is absent from the institutional environment of level 2, what takes its place and provides the rules of the game? There is another difference between LLE and PPT. In its relation to economics, PPT is interested in more macro aspects of economic policy and how these are affected by political institutions, for example, how fiscal, monetary, regulatory, and trade policies differ between presidential and parliamentary systems (Persson and Tabellini 2000). The focus of LLE is on the much more microeconomic level of individual transactions. At level 3, LLE shares many concerns with TCE, but it is focused more on the interaction among distinct decision units than on governance within one firm. However, this distinction is not at all clear-cut, as the boundaries of decision units are themselves endogenous and can change in response to changes in transaction technologies and enforcement modes.

Thus the concept of institutions in the New Institutional Economics is somewhat imprecise, and is interpreted differently by different scholars. In my view this is not a serious defect. It is not so important to have a definition that would be valid and rigidly enforced in all contexts; what matters is that we understand what it means in any specific context we are analyzing.

Next I discuss the relationship between LLE and another large and growing field, variously labeled "Institutions and Growth" or "Institutions and Development." This field studies how the institutions and organizations that make and implement government policy affect economic performance, and attempts to identify what constitutes good governance in this sense. The literature is vast and wide-ranging. Pioneering historical and conceptual perspectives such as North (1990) and Olson (1993) have taught us the importance of securing property rights, especially against the government's own predation. Case studies of De Soto (1989, 2000), the compilation of analytical case studies in Rodrik (2003) (and many other case studies), the theoretical modeling of Grossman (2002) and others, and the combination of theory and empirical observation by Shleifer and Vishny (1998), all reinforce this message.

Construction of quantitative indexes of good governance is an active enterprise; a recent example is Kaufman, Kraay, and Mastruzzi (2003). Much empirical work has established positive correlations across countries between various measures of economic performance and various aspects of good governance such as the rule of law in defining and protecting property rights, accountability of policymakers, transparency of policy, lack of corruption, and simplicity and speed of bureaucratic procedures. Examples are Hall and Jones (1999), Sokoloff and Engerman (2000), La Porta et al (1998, 1999), Rodrik (2000), Acemoglu, Johnson, and Robinson (2001), Acemoglu et al (2002), and Kaufman and Kraay (2002). Of course the positive feedback may indicate reverse causation—the demand for good governance rises with incomes—or common effects of third variables on both. Empirical researchers handle this problem using different instrumental variables that are not affected by current economic performance, for example colonial origin (Hall and Jones), historical measures of morality (Acemoglu, Johnson, and Robinson), and an instrumental variable estimation of reverse causation plus direct knowledge of measurement errors to achieve identification (Kaufman and Kraay). In fact Kaufman and Kraay find a negative reverse causation: across countries, higher incomes on average lead to worse governance. This may be because in a country with higher income, especially if the income derives from natural-resource extraction, there is more rent-seeking and greater likelihood of capture of government and policymaking (see Tornell and Lane 1998). However, Sachs and Warner (2001, p. 836) present evidence to the contrary. Overall, the empirical literature gives good support to the proposition that good governance causes higher incomes and growth.

Lawlessness and Economics differs from this literature in two ways, but each of them also points out the need for building better bridges between the two. First, LLE is concerned with micro issues of governance of individual transactions, specifically with property rights and contracts, and not directly with the macro issues of economic growth or development. One can think of LLE as a potential microfoundation for theories of how governance institutions affect macroeconomic performance. Secondly, LLE in its purest form assumes that the government's law is completely absent or ineffective, and examines purely non-governmental alternatives that attempt to perform some of the same functions; therefore the quality of government is not directly an issue. In most of the formal models I develop in this book I focus on this part of LLE, and do not examine in any detail the situation where the government itself is predatory or kleptocratic. This is because I believe that a thorough theoretical analysis of the pure case of non-state economic governance constitutes a useful start for further research on the interactions between corrupt or predatory governments and private institutions of governance. In Chapter 2, I do consider interactions between private arrangements that can use better inside information on the one hand, and a state law that must use worse public information on the other. However, the state in that chapter is assumed to be neither corrupt nor predatory. Predation by the state or its agents has been the essence of the problem in many countries and in the literature on the quality of government, and a start at theoretical thinking has been made, for example by Shleifer and Vishny (1998), Hay and Shleifer (1998), and Grossman (1995, 2002). I make one contribution to this line of research: in Section 5.4 I reinterpret standard theories of optimal income taxation to obtain some characterization of the interaction between a predatory government, and citizens trying their best to evade its attempts to take their assets and outputs. Further analysis of predatory governments should be an important part of the agenda for future theoretical research in LLE.

I hope this discussion of what LLE does and does not attempt will help readers locate my topic in relation with other fields and subfields. However, the unavoidable ambiguities of taxonomy require that such boundaries should be permeable. In this chapter I will indulge in a few more attempts at definition and demarcation. But then, for the rest of the book, I will proceed without any consistent attempt to stay strictly within those confines.

1.4 Law and Economics

The field of Law and Economics became established during the 1960s and 1970s, and continues to grow. It studies the interaction between state law and economic activities and outcomes. Thus "Law and Economics" and "Lawlessness and Economics" can be regarded as two mutually exclusive and jointly exhaustive subfields of the larger field of economic governance; of course in reality there are overlaps and omissions. In this section I mention some of the major concerns of Law and Economics to bring out the contrasts, but do not go into any of them in any detail, merely referring interested readers to Posner and Parisi (1997). This three-volume handbook contains many of the important articles on Law and Economics, along with detailed editorial commentary.

The early contributions to Law and Economics mostly dealt with the implications of law for economics, that is, they considered the effect of legal rules on the economic choices of individuals and firms and on market outcomes. To quote from the survey by Cooter and Rubinfeld (1989, p. 1068), this theory "treats laws, like prices, as incentives for behavior." This work encompassed both criminal and civil laws. Becker's (1968) article on the optimal detection and punishment strategies to deter crime has become classic. Modern theory has added information- and game-theoretic aspects to the analysis. Polinsky and Shavell (2000) survey this literature. Various branches of civil law—liability, tort, contract, property—govern situations where two or more individuals can enter into a contractual relationship, explicit or implicit, as well as ones where one person's actions have spillover effects on others without any voluntary agreement on their side. These legal rules affect the incentives of individuals to take actions, or to refrain from actions, that carry benefits or costs to others, and that in turn affect overall economic outcomes and efficiency. Baird, Gertner, and Picker (1994) discuss many examples of this kind in the course of their exposition of game theory.

Later work took up a reverse causation from economics to law and jurisprudence, namely evaluation of alternative legal rules in the light of the economic concepts of efficiency. This led to issues of design or reform of specific legal rules, and even the concept of the law as a system that can be designed, rather than as a collection of cases and precedents to be studied and applied. Posner (2002) examines the law in this way from an economist's perspective.

1.5 Economics in the Shadow of the Law

Even in modern countries where a well-functioning institution and apparatus of government-provided law exists, economic—or, indeed, non-economic—disputes do not immediately lead to litigation. Recourse to the law is often the last resort, not the first one. People attempt to resolve their disputes using various private methods of negotiation, and only if these fail do they go to the courts. In the context of business, this idea goes back at least as far as Macaulay (1963). Williamson (1996, pp. 10, 122), citing previous legal scholars, says that businessmen "speak of 'cancelling the order' rather than 'breaching our contract'," and that contracts and courts are "a norm of ultimate appeal when the relations cease in fact to work." In matters of personal relationships, too, Mnookin and Kornhauser (1979) cite estimates that less than 10% of divorces are contested in court. All of this has led to the concept of "private ordering in the shadow of the law."

An obvious explanation for the persistence of such private ordering is that resolution of disputes using the formal machinery of state law is far from costless; in fact its costs, especially time costs, often exceed those of alternative methods of private ordering. Sometimes formal law may yield outcomes that are worse for all parties than can private ordering. Therefore the outcome that the parties expect to obtain in the court (net of the costs of using the court system) becomes a backstop or threat point to private negotiation. I will sketch this idea in somewhat greater detail in Section 2.2.

Long-term relationships and arbitration are the most common modes of private ordering. Long-term relationships can be self-enforcing for reasons familiar from the theory of repeated games: the immediate gains from behaving opportunistically can be offset by future losses, because the opportunism leads to a collapse of the relationship and therefore to lower future payoffs. But now we have another possibility. The relationship need not collapse completely; it can be replaced by one based on formal contracts and court enforcement. This is still costly and therefore serves to deter opportunism in the original ongoing relationship. But the cost may be less than that of a total breakdown of interaction. Correspondingly, the deterrence effect falls short of the level possible when total breakdown is the only alternative. Thus availability of court enforcement may, in a seeming paradox, reduce the extent of good behavior that can be sustained in the long-term relationship. I will examine this possibility in Section 2.3.

The official law can interfere with a long-term relationship in another way, namely by agreeing to hear a case filed by one of the parties in such a relationship attempting to overturn an adverse outcome in the implicit contract. However, courts often recognize the merits of implicit contracting in long-term relationships like employment, and refuse to hear such cases. This is the doctrine of forbearance (Williamson 1996, p. 27).

Private arbitration can have cost advantages over the government's courts, but perhaps more importantly, it can have information advantages and therefore provide dispute resolution of higher quality. Arbitration forums specialize by industry, geographic region, and so on, in the range of disputes they take up. They acquire expertise in their special areas. They can adopt procedures and rules of evidence that suit their specific concerns. State courts must stand ready to consider all matters that could arise under the law, and although some attempt can be made to assign cases to judges on the basis of their expertise, the rules and procedures must remain the same for all cases. For these reasons, arbitrators are better able to obtain, interpret, and use information pertinent to the dispute than are the state courts. I will develop a model of such informational advantage in Section 2.4.

Arbitrators lack the coercive powers of the state and therefore cannot ensure compliance with their verdicts. But, as with long-term relationships, the government's courts often recognize the advantages of arbitration for governance of particular classes of transactions. Then they accept the arbitrator's verdict and will not agree to rehear the issue. This is formalized in US laws (Bernstein 2001, footnote 111) and in international agreements (Mattli 2001, p. 939). Given this shadow of the law, if one party refuses to comply with the arbitrator's verdict, the other can enlist the help of the courts for enforcement.

Landes and Posner (1979) describe and analyze private institutions of adjudication historically as well as in the context of modern states. Milgrom, North, and Weingast (1990) describe a specific historical institution, namely the *lex mercatoria* or merchants' law, usually called "the law merchant," in medieval Europe. They and others find that many principles developed by the private judges or adjudicators of the law merchant were later taken over by the state's law. However, Landes and Posner point out that private adjudicators lack the incentives to supply the "public good" of principles and precedents, so we expect it to be underprovided.

1.6   Other Institutions of Economic Governance

Let us turn to an extreme conceptual situation that is the true realm of Lawlessness and Economics, namely an economy lacking any government-provided legal institutions or organizations for protection of property rights and enforcement of contracts. Such a society needs to develop its own alternative modes of economic governance. Two general types of such institutions and organizations are observed. They are parallel to the long-term relationships and arbitration forums mentioned in the previous section, but here the private ordering must operate unsheltered, without the shadow of the law.

The alternative that has been studied most thoroughly is self-enforcing governance through repeated interaction. If the same parties interact with each other repeatedly, and they value the future sufficiently highly relative to the present, then the prospect of a long-term collapse of the relationship can control the temptation to obtain a short-term gain. This is well understood, both in the theory of repeated games and in practice (Axelrod 1984; Abreu 1986; Abreu, Pearce, and Stacchetti 1990; and several others). But many economic activities require dealing with different partners at different times. Even bilateral relationships may get severed, requiring one or both parties to find a different partner in the future. Therefore we must consider situations where there is little long-term relationship with the same person, but stable membership of a whole large group. Self-governance in such a group requires that if any one person cheats his current partner, the news is conveyed to others in the group who might be the cheater's future partners. This loss of reputation can lead to ostracization, or other actions by the group that have the effect of punishing the cheater on behalf of his current victim. In turn, such reputational considerations can deter opportunistic behavior. For this process to work, the society needs good information networks and credible multilateral punishment strategies.

Both of these conditions can be fulfilled in stable and cohesive groups or networks, which might be defined by business ties (Greif 1993; Bernstein 1992, 2001), ethnicity (Casella and Rauch 2002; Rauch 2001), and so on. However, the quality of information and the credibility of punishment both degrade as the size of such a group increases. The case studies of Ostrom (1990) and the contrasting case studies of two merchant groups by Greif (1994, 1997) illustrate this vividly, and numerical calculations on the theoretical models of Kandori (1993) and Ellison (1994) show similar tendencies. Therefore we need a better understanding of the limits of self-governance. What happens if trading opportunities expand beyond the close group? When does some other mode of governance become better? What happens at the interface between the two systems? I will tackle some of these questions in Chapter 3.

Instead of relying on self-governance, the group might attempt to obtain the service for a fee from a private individual or group. One can think of this as a "private government," established to serve just this one function, as opposed to the broader institution we call the government, which performs a multitude of functions. Credit-rating agencies and similar certification intermediaries can collect and disseminate information about a person's history to his prospective partner. Arbitration is another common arrangement of this kind. In the absence of state law, it cannot rely on the courts' forbearance to ensure compliance with its verdicts. But arbitration can use repeated interactions in the group. Thus, if any member of the group defies the arbitrator's ruling, the arbitrator can publicize this information to the whole group, and then the group will not deal with the miscreant. In effect, the arbitrator becomes the hub of an information network. The private judges at trade fairs in medieval Europe functioned in this way (Milgrom, North, and Weingast 1990); Bernstein (1992, 2001) gives examples of modern trade associations that provide similar functions for their members.

Finally, organized crime provides services of information as well as enforcement (Gambetta 1993; Varese 2000; Whiting 1999; and others). In a society without state law, there is no external mechanism to ensure honesty of the arbitrator, the private judge, or the mafioso. That has to be self-enforcing, based on reputation considerations in a long-term relationship. Even though the participants in the economic transactions may not meet the same partners repeatedly, each of them can have a repeated interaction with the person or organization that provides the governance, so an honest equilibrium of this kind is logically conceivable. I will study the operation of such third-party private governance, paying attention to the question of the intermediary's honesty, in Chapter 4.

Thus far I have been concerned with the governance of economic interactions, that is, explicit or implicit contracts between two or more parties, made with mutual consent. Protection of property rights raises some different issues. Violation of property rights is a unilateral action taken by the predator; this differs from contractual relationships, which are based on voluntary consent of both or all parties. Indeed, the owner of a property may not even know the identity of the potential thief or extortionist. Then the potential victim must take unilateral steps to deter the potential invader, and to detect and punish him if deterrence fails. The property owner may try to do this directly, diverting resources from other productive uses into protection, or he may hire a specialized protector—a private guard or, again, organized crime. In some countries and at some times the government or its agents may be the thieves who try to extract as much as they can from the citizens for their own consumption. The citizens cannot hope to resist the government's coercive power with force, but may attempt to hide their assets. Also, the prospect that the fruit of ones's efforts will be taken by the government will be a disincentive to produce or accumulate. I will examine some of these issues in Chapter 5.

Anecdotal evidence suggests that the various alternative institutions of governance can be very effective. Greif (1993, p. 528) found "only a handful of documents contain[ing] allegations of misconduct" in the archives of the correspondence among Maghribi traders. Bernstein (1992) reports that in the numerous transactions that occur every year among the 2000 members of the New York Diamond Dealers' Club and the numerous non-members who trade there, only 30–40 trades result in a judgment from the arbitration system of the club. Exact figures are not available for the total number of transactions or the number of cases where the defendant refuses to pay the judgment, but a safe guess is that the former is in the hundreds of thousands and the latter in single digits.

Some may regard this as evidence for fundamental goodness of human nature. However, the record of failures of other less-well-designed institutions of governance suggests otherwise. Ostrom (1990, Chapter 5) and Liebcap (1989, Chapters 5, 6) discuss cases of failures to define and enforce property rights and to solve common-resource-pool problems. Several studies in Rodrik (2003) show that less-developed countries with poor property-right and contract-enforcement systems fail to attract foreign investment and sustain growth. Thus we should conclude that institutions can be effective deterrents to opportunism, but that in their absence, beneficial economic activity is likely to be hindered by a well-grounded fear of being cheated.

1.7 Some Basic Analytical Apparatus

The need for governance arises because, in its absence, individuals pursuing their own interests would generate an inferior equilibrium outcome. Game theory studies many instances of this, most notably the prisoner's dilemma. In this section I briefly outline three simple games of this kind; in later chapters, some extensions and variants will be developed and applied in greater detail. Readers who are familiar with the theory of repeated games can omit this section.

First consider a situation involving two participants, or players in the sense of game theory. The first player begins the game by choosing whether to take a costly action, here called an investment. Then the second player takes another action that determines how the product of this investment is shared between the two. They have an agreement or understanding on this matter. If the second player follows through

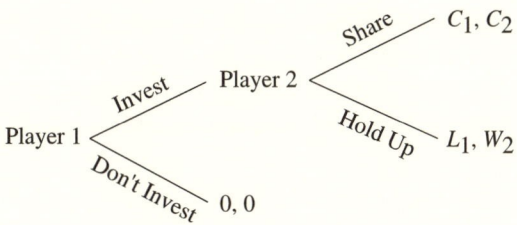

Figure 1.1. One-sided prisoner's dilemma in extensive form.

Table 1.1. One-sided prisoner's dilemma in normal form.

		Player 2	
		Share	Hold Up
Player 1 {	Invest	C_1, C_2	L_1, W_2
	Don't Invest	$0, 0$	$0, 0$

with the agreement, both parties will get a positive outcome or game-theoretic payoff. However, the second player can instead take an opportunistic action, which will yield him a larger payoff but the first player a negative payoff. This is the famous "hold-up problem" (Klein, Crawford, and Alchian 1978; Williamson 1979). It is also the situation of medieval merchants studied by Greif (1993, 1994, 1997a, 2000). These merchants had to consign goods to distant agents, who might then abscond with the goods or the proceeds of the sales.

Figure 1.1 shows the game in its extensive or tree form and Table 1.1 shows the payoff matrix in the strategic or normal form. If Player 1 does not make the investment, the status quo prevails. This is chosen as the origin for measuring the payoffs of both players, so both get 0 in this outcome. If the first player invests and the second takes the sharing action, the resulting positive payoffs are denoted by C_1 and C_2, respectively. If the first player invests and the second engages in opportunistic hold-up, then the first gets a loser's payoff L_1 worse than the status quo ($L_1 < 0$), while the second gets a winner's payoff W_2 better than that from sharing ($W_2 > C_2$).

In the extensive form, the second player's optimal choice at the second node is Hold Up ($W_2 > C_2$), and foreseeing this, the first player's optimal action is Don't Invest ($L_1 < 0$). This is the only outcome of rollback analysis, or subgame-perfect equilibrium. And in the normal form, (Don't Invest, Hold Up) is the only Nash equilibrium; for any other strategy combination, one of the players wants to deviate to a different strategy. In this outcome both players get 0, but both would be better off if they could achieve (Invest, Share). The second player could promise that he will choose Share, but in the absence of some form of governance, the promise is not credible.

This is like a prisoner's dilemma except that only the second player has the opportunity to make an extra private gain, therefore it is often called a one-sided prisoner's dilemma. There are two broad approaches to resolving such dilemmas, although each appears in many different manifestations appropriate for different circumstances.

First, some method can be found for inflicting a direct penalty on the second player if he chooses Deviate. The state law can do this. The two players agree before the fact that (Invest, Share) is the better outcome, so they can sign a formal contract whereby the first player undertakes to choose Invest and the second to respond Share. The court stands ready to enforce this contract, under the threat of sufficiently harsh fines, and ultimately coercion if that proves necessary. Of course this requires that any deviations from the agreement can be proved before the court, or in game-theoretic terminology, are verifiable. If state law is absent or ineffective, private enforcement can perform similar functions to some extent; that possibility was mentioned in Section 1.6 and is the subject of Chapter 4.

Second, if this game is played repeatedly, the prospect that future benefits depend on current performance may suffice to induce the second player to choose Share, and then the first can recognize this and choose Invest. In the strict logic of game theory, repetition must be infinite or at least indefinite, because in any fixed and finite sequence of repetitions, cooperation will unravel from the end. In reality, some cooperation is observed in cases of fixed repetitions or even single play (Camerer 2003, pp. 45, 46, 221–223), but participants in most commercial transactions would be reluctant to rely on this and would insist on the support of some mechanism of governance.

If the same two players continue to interact for the infinite or indefinite future, the good outcome can be sustained as an equilibrium of the repeated game if the interest rate r at which the future is discounted is sufficiently low. Consider the following strategies: Player 1's strategy is "Invest so long as Player 2 has not chosen Hold Up in the past, but stop investing in response to any history of Hold Up." Player 2's strategy is "Share always." Player 1's strategy is called a grim-trigger strategy: it threatens a grim punishment, namely a total breakdown of the relationship, and it is triggered by any action of Player 2 that departs from his specified equilibrium strategy.

For this to be an equilibrium, neither player should stand to gain by deviating from the specified strategy. The key test is for the second player. If he deviates once, he gets W_2 instead of C_2, for an immediate one-time gain of $(W_2 - C_2)$. Then the first player stops investing, so the second player gets 0 for each subsequent period, whereas he would have received C_2 if he had kept to the specified strategy of compliance. If the deviation is to be unprofitable to Player 2, the interest he could earn on the up-front one-time gain should not exceed the future loss in each period.

That is,

$$r\,(W_2 - C_2) \leqslant C_2\,. \tag{1.1}$$

Equivalently, the immediate gain $(W_2 - C_2)$ should not exceed the capitalized value C_2/r of the subsequent per-period loss. This reasoning assumes that the deviating action is immediately detected, and the future cost comes in the form of a permanent collapse of the mutually beneficial arrangement. But the idea can be extended to more complex situations. Detection of a deviation may be less than perfect. In a large population where one player may meet different potential partners in different periods, the news of a deviation may be communicated to others with less than certainty. The population may have people with different preferences or behaviors, and a player's action may convey information about his type. Strategies other than permanent disengagement may be used. However, the general idea of a trade-off between immediate gains and subsequent losses underlies them all. In later chapters I will develop several such applications.

A thematically related but structurally different problem is that of agency. One of the parties to the transaction (the principal) wants the other (the agent) to take some action that will bring the principal some gain but require the agent to expend some cost. The contract specifies how the agent will be compensated for this. But the contract is constrained by information. Some or all of the agent's action and cost and the principal's gain may be observable only to the person in question, or observable to both parties but not provable or verifiable to outsiders, or verifiable to some industry experts but not to the general public including officials of state law. The principal and the agent share a common interest in writing as efficient a contract as the information and institutions allow, but then the agent will behave opportunistically and pursue his own best interest to the extent that the contract allows. This looks like a one-sided dilemma, but it is better handled using different models and techniques. I examine some aspects of such agency problems in Chapter 2.

In many transactions, both sides can engage in opportunism, and their game becomes a conventional (two-sided) prisoner's dilemma. Gambetta (1993, p. 15) gives a nice example. A cattle breeder he interviewed in the course of his research on the Sicilian Mafia told him:

> When the butcher comes to me to buy an animal, he knows that I want
> to cheat him [by giving him a low-quality animal]. But I know that he
> wants to cheat me [by reneging on payment].

The game has the familiar payoff matrix shown in Table 1.2. I label the two actions "Comply (with the explicit or implicit terms of the agreement)" and "Deviate (from the agreement)." In informal discussions, I will sometimes refer to these as honest behavior and cheating, respectively, but Comply and Deviate better capture the idea

Table 1.2. Two-sided prisoner's dilemma.

		Player 2	
		Comply	Deviate
Player 1 {	Comply	C_1, C_2	L_1, W_2
	Deviate	W_1, L_2	D_1, D_2

formally.[2] Each player fares best when he chooses Deviate while the other chooses Comply, and worst when he chooses Comply while the other chooses Deviate. Between these extremes, the payoff is higher when both choose Comply than when both choose Deviate. Thus $W_1 > C_1 > D_1 > L_1$ and $W_2 > C_2 > D_2 > L_2$.

Of course formalization requires simplification of reality. The single action labeled Deviate may in fact stand for a complex set of possibilities. Indeed, the true game of opportunism may consist of seeking and finding actions that are advantageous to oneself, not merely choosing one from a set of already known actions. Another subtlety arises if a formal contract does not constitute the true implicit understanding between the parties, with the result that "Comply" means "comply with the true spirit of the contract," while "Deviate" means "revert to the letter of the formal contract," as in a work-to-rule. Although formalization hides such subtleties, it has its own advantage of giving us a deeper understanding of the mechanisms or processes of the parties' interactions. Therefore formal analysis should be done, and then interpreted in a broader and more flexible manner. That is what I shall attempt.

If the game is played once—or a fixed, finite, and known number of times—each player's dominant strategy is always to play Deviate. The resulting equilibrium with payoffs (D_1, D_2) is worse for both than what they would get if both chose Comply (acted honestly), but that is not achievable given the temptation of each to choose Deviate (cheat).

If the game is repeated infinitely or indefinitely often, the good outcome where both choose Comply can be sustained using grim-trigger strategies for both players, stipulating permanent deviation by both players after the occurrence of even a single deviation by either. When each expects the other to follow this strategy, Player 1 does not want to deviate if the interest $r(W_1 - C_1)$ he could earn on his immediate gain $(W_1 - C_1)$ from choosing Deviate does not exceed the reduction in his payoffs for each subsequent period, $(C_1 - D_1)$. That is,

$$r(W_1 - C_1) \leqslant C_1 - D_1, \tag{1.2}$$

---

[2]Cooperate and Defect are commonly used in game theory, but I want to avoid "Cooperate" because that invites confusion with a "cooperative game" in the technical sense, where the actions are jointly agreed and also jointly implemented. There the substantive issue is the process of reaching an agreement, and deviations are impossible once an agreement has been reached. By contrast, my focus is on how to achieve good or cooperative *outcomes* despite the fact that the players choose *actions* individually (non-cooperatively).

Table 1.3. Two-sided prisoner's dilemma with option not to play.

		Player 2		
		Play, Comply	Play, Deviate	Don't Play
	Play, Comply	C_1, C_2	L_1, W_2	$0, 0$
Player 1	Play, Deviate	W_1, L_2	D_1, D_2	$0, 0$
	Don't Play	$0, 0$	$0, 0$	$0, 0$

and similarly for Player 2. In later chapters I will discuss several variants and elaborations of this game; a general theoretical treatment can be found in Osborne and Rubinstein (1994, Chapter 8), and a survey of the literature in Pearce (1992).

The standard prisoner's dilemma game assumes that both players have already decided to play. However, in many real-life situations the players have the option of not playing, if they calculate that their payoffs in the resulting equilibrium will be less than what they could get in the available alternative opportunities. This is a two-stage game. At the first stage each player decides whether to play the dilemma game. If both choose to play, the second stage occurs and consists of the actual play of the dilemma game. While this could be shown in its extensive form, it is simpler to look at the normal form. Each player chooses one of three strategies: (1) Don't play, (2) Play and choose Comply, and (3) Play and choose Deviate. The payoff scales are chosen so as to make each player's payoff from his outside alternative equal to zero. The other payoffs are as before. Table 1.3 shows the payoff matrix of the game.

The outcome where both players choose "Don't Play" is always a Nash equilibrium of this game, because if one is choosing this action, the other cannot get a higher payoff by choosing anything else. But there can be other equilibria, depending on the signs of D_1 and D_2, that is, whether it is better to play the game even if both are going to Deviate. If D_1 is negative, then there is an equilibrium where Player 1 chooses not to play, and Player 2 chooses Play and Deviate. If D_2 is negative, there is a similar equilibrium with the players interchanged. If both D_1 and D_2 are negative, both of these are equilibria, so there are three equilibria in all. However, since both have to choose to play for the game to take place, the outcome in all these new equilibria is that the game is not played and both players end up with their outside alternative, so these are distinctions without a difference.

If both D_1 and D_2 are positive, we find a genuinely different second Nash equilibrium, where both choose Play and Deviate. The existence of two equilibria is often a nuisance, but it can be a help in sustaining cooperation in repeated games. Specifically, even with a finite and known number of repetitions, cooperation may be sustainable for all but the last few plays. This can be achieved using strategies that specify starting out with the (C_1, C_2) outcome, and switching to the (D_1, D_2) outcome in those last few plays, but switching immediately to the $(0, 0)$ outcome if either player deviates at one of the earlier plays where compliance was indicated.

Benoit and Krishna (1985) develop the general theory of such games; I will have occasion to use a simple specific instance of it in Chapter 3.

The situations studied in each of the following three chapters differ in their specification of players, information, and available strategies. Therefore the models above are not directly applicable merely by a special interpretation of the actions and the payoffs. While they share the schematic structure of the dilemma games, each needs its own reformulation.

All of them have one restrictive feature requiring discussion. All are models of repeated games under stationary conditions. Each can describe how an institution of governance functions, or how two institutions can coexist, once all traders' expectations and actions have adjusted to this fact. However, the process whereby a society changes from one institution to another is dynamic. When I say something about this dynamics, I have interpreted the models beyond their formal results, for example drawing some dynamic inferences from comparative static analysis.

Dynamic games are far more complex than repeated games, and require different approaches and techniques, for example evolutionary theory, stochastic processes, and computer simulations. Some authors, for example Young (1998) and Aoki (2001), have taken this approach to the study of institutions. In comparison with this book, they represent a different choice in the trade-off between a better representation and analytical tractability.

My focus is on the problems of information and enforcement in specific contexts: verifiability and its cost in Chapter 2; localization of communication in Chapter 3; and simultaneous games played between each trader and the intermediary in Chapter 4. To treat these details adequately, I have simplified the dynamics. Others make the opposite choice: they represent the game played each period in a simple or schematic way and focus on the dynamic process. Young (1998, Chapter 9) finds conditions under which the participants in the society will eventually choose efficient contracts. But their actions are limited to offering contracts; no cheating occurs within a contract after it is chosen. For example, in his "marriage game," the prospective partners may both offer a contract under which they will share control, but neither is then allowed to renege and attempt to seize control. Thus issues of interest to Lawlessness and Economics do not arise. Aoki (2001) is concerned with many of the same issues of governance as I am. In his modeling of dynamics in Chapters 7–10, he sets up a general taxonomic scheme, and then interprets several examples of empirical studies in its categories. But he does not go into the details of information or communication in each game, nor does he examine how these aspects will affect the dynamics of each specific case.

Future research may achieve a synthesis that has both the dynamics and the fuller specification of the underlying games, and feedbacks between these two aspects. In

the meantime, I hope that the available approaches serve as complementary inputs to our thinking about the issues.

1.8 Approach of the Book

In the previous three sections, I have outlined the questions I will discuss in the rest of the book, and something of the methods I will use for that purpose. Here I describe and discuss my approach in greater detail.

Each of the following chapters takes up one set of issues within the range of Lawlessness and Economics. Each chapter begins with a selective overview of the literature. The existing body of research is not only multi-disciplinary but also multi-methodology. There is some statistical empirical work, and much more descriptive work consisting of case studies and ethnography. Theoretical research has lagged behind the empirical and descriptive, although the gap is closing rapidly.

This assessment may surprise some who have followed the literature on the New Institutional Economics. For example, Alston, Eggertson, and North (1996, p. 1) say that

> the field is long on theoretical analysis but short on empirical work. It
> is probably true that the stock of knowledge would grow faster if the
> new institutionalists put more emphasis on empirical work.

The difference arises, as usual, due to our different interpretations of the word "theory." A good general conceptual scheme clearly exists, and Eggertson (1996) depicts it in a diagram of boxes and arrows showing connections between institutions, organizations, contracts, and so on. However, I believe that if theory is to be useful in improving our understanding of specific institutions and helping us design or reform existing organizations and institutions, theoretical analysis must go beyond general schemata, and develop more detailed models of the specific situations and problems that concern us. Such modeling is expanding fast, but still has some catching up to do. That is where I hope to make some original contribution in this book.

Empirical research, especially case studies and ethnography, and theoretical modeling have different and complementary merits and drawbacks. Case studies give us rich, detailed description of the facts of each situation. Econometric research establishes correlations among variables across countries or over time. However, both approaches leave basic questions of cause and effect implicit or unexamined. Theoretical modeling more explicitly sets up hypotheses about causes and effects, and examines all the logical consequences of the set of hypotheses under consideration. It brings together some key aspects that are common to many situations and cases, and gives a sharper and deeper understanding of forces and mechanisms that operate. This improved understanding is what justifies theoretical modeling. I would like to steal a line from Casper Gutman in *The Maltese falcon* and claim that formal models are "genuine coin of the realm, sir. With a dollar of this you can buy more than with ten dollars of talk" (Hammett 1930, Chapter 18).

However, for reasons of tractability, such work must abstract from many of the rich details of specific contexts. Thus each theoretical model selects for its in-depth analysis only a narrow subset of the range of facts and situations known to us from empirical and case studies. The aim of theory should be to construct a collection of models that is sufficiently small to be remembered and used, and covers a sufficiently large portion of the spectrum of facts. Overall understanding of the rich arrays of facts will best be achieved by interpreting them in the light of an appropriate model (or a few pertinent models) from this set, and by compiling and comparing the insights they generate. What about one universal model to cover all the facts? Neoclassical economic theorists who admire the generality and the beauty of the Arrow–Debreu model of competitive equilibrium may wish to attempt similar grand theorizing everywhere. But that has not proved to be a fruitful approach in other areas of economics. In the field of Industrial Organization, for example, theoretical progress has come from a toolkit of several models. I believe the same is likely to be true in the emerging field of Lawlessness and Economics. Only a small number of models covering only small patches of the territory have been constructed so far, but that simply means that there is a lot of room for further modeling.

How should one judge such models? I suggest two criteria. First, a model should do more than explain just the simplest and most obvious motivating facts that led one to build that model, it should offer a sharper or deeper understanding of them in terms of more basic economic principles or by connecting them to other seemingly unrelated facts. Second, a theoretical model should not merely reproduce as results the factual observations of case studies that the model was constructed to explain in the first place; it should yield some new results or hypotheses that can then be compared with other facts. Conversely, case study or empirical research should not treat each case as a mere narrative or description of an isolated situation; it should attempt to place it in an overall framework of other cases and theories. Ultimately progress must come from a dialogue and feedback between the different modes, not from any one of them on its own.

My comparative advantage is in theoretical modeling, so I spend more time and space on that. By way of background and motivation for the theory to come, I begin each chapter with a selective look at the literature—concepts, descriptions and case studies of some institutions and organizations, and surveys. Then I pick up some aspects of the findings of the case studies, and construct one or more theoretical models of them. I attempt to live up to the self-imposed criterion of asking the models to deliver more than just the facts they were rigged to explain; sometimes I even succeed.

In the concluding section of each chapter I assess where the modeling of that chapter gets us, what it leaves out, and what the prospects are for future research. In each chapter the readers will find several interesting empirical observations that my models do not touch at all. I do not apologize for that. This book is at best an interim stock-taking of a field in its infancy. The omitted dimensions need other models. Readers should take the frequent and large gaps and flaws I point out as challenges for further research, and an invitation to join the band of lemmings who form the field of Lawlessness and Economics. Very fittingly, no property rights to ideas are staked out or enforced in this field; everyone is free to take any idea and to run with it.

2

Private Ordering in the Shadow of the Law

2.1 Issues and Empirical Research

Even in modern advanced economies where the state promulgates and enforces laws bearing on economic conduct, these laws rarely govern all detailed aspects of transactions and contracts. Most business transactions between, as well as within, firms are conducted using various informal arrangements, such as handshakes and oral agreements, ongoing relationships, and custom and practice. If disputes arise, the parties first attempt to resolve them by direct negotiation. The law is available if these attempts at private settlement fail, but recourse to it is usually the last step, not the first, and often signifies the end of an ongoing relationship. Evidence bearing on this goes back at least as far as the classic article of Macaulay (1963), and covers many countries with well and poorly functioning legal systems alike, as discussed in Williamson (1985, 1996, pp. 95–100) and Johnson, McMillan, and Woodruff (2002).

Such private ordering in the shadow of the law arises for different reasons, and takes different forms that attempt to respond appropriately to each reason. Perhaps the simplest of these reasons is the cost of using the formal legal system. The cost can arise in many ways. First, even in countries with well-functioning state civil law, obtaining and enforcing a judgment in the court system takes a long time; three years is not uncommon. The court may include interest when calculating damages, but for most traders who are somewhat constrained in access to capital markets, the interest rate used in this calculation is likely to be an underestimate of the rate at which they discount the future. Next, in its calculation of damages, the court may underestimate or even leave out items like lost profit that are speculative and can be overstated by the plaintiff. Third, judges in state courts have to cover all conceivable matters that could arise under civil law, and therefore lack the expertise that insiders would be able to acquire about a specific industry. Therefore their verdicts in commercial disputes can be less predictable than those available in alternative specialized forums. Both parties to a dispute dislike this unpredictability. Finally, courts may require public disclosure of information about business opportunities, costs, and profits that one or both parties to the dispute would prefer to keep secret. Sometimes the parties wish to avoid public knowledge of the mere fact that they were involved in litigation, because potential future transactors may think of them as inflexible and unwilling to renegotiate deals in response to changed circumstances. Bernstein (1992, pp. 134–138, 149) discusses these problems in more detail and illustrates them for the case of the diamond industry.

When the operation of the law is costly, both parties can benefit by resolving their dispute through bargaining or renegotiation, in which the expected outcome of recourse to the legal system constitutes the fallback, or the best alternative to negotiated agreement (BATNA) in Harvard Business School jargon. In turn, their initial contract and economic choices will be affected by this prospect of future renegotiation. This view of bargaining in the shadow of the law is well developed in the Law and Economics literature (see, for example, Shavell (1982) and the survey by Cooter and Rubinfeld (1989)). I sketch a simple model of it in Section 2.2.

Most other reasons for using private ordering pertain to information. In this context we have a threefold key distinction, between private, observable, and verifiable information. Consider a transaction between two parties. Information is private when it is available to one of the parties but not the other. Sometimes the informed party wants to convey the information truthfully to the other party, but must do so in a credible way because the uninformed party will be wary of strategic misrepresentation. If the two parties' interests are well aligned, mere declaration (cheap talk) may work. Otherwise the informed party has to look for a costly action (signal) that credibly conveys the truth of the matter, because that action would not have been optimal had the information been different. Sometimes the uninformed party can devise tests (screening or mechanism design), requiring the informed party to undertake actions that will reveal the truth. The theory of asymmetric information is now a standard part of economic theory; see Dixit and Skeath (2004, Chapter 9) for an elementary exposition, and Rasmusen (2000) for a somewhat more advanced and detailed treatment.

Signaling and screening can be parts of contracts between the two parties. For example, if the seller of a car knows its quality much better than the buyer can find out by inspection, then a warranty may serve as a signal of quality. However, the terms of such a contract cannot specify actions to be taken under circumstances that only one of the parties can observe, because that party would have every reason to misrepresent the circumstances so as to avoid taking a costly action. Thus the warranty cannot specify the circumstances under which a part of the car has to be replaced in such a way that only one party can observe them. If the buyer is the sole judge of whether the transmission operates satisfactorily, he may claim that it is unsatisfactory at the slightest excuse and obtain a new one. Contracts must implicitly or explicitly give each party the discretion to act on the basis of its private information.

Turning to the other two categories, information is called observable when it is available symmetrically to both parties, and verifiable when it can be proved to third parties such as a court. In practice, this is a matter of cost, and the standard of proof required. Contracts that are intended to be enforced in a court of law can only stipulate actions that are conditioned on verifiable information; courts cannot judge whether a breach of the contractual terms has occurred if they cannot verify whether the circumstances that call for an action have actually transpired. However, observable information can be the basis for contracts that are enforced by extralegal or private methods, because the two parties can know fully well whether a breach has occurred. Such extralegal methods of enforcement come in two broad types. One is enforcement by insider third parties with specialized knowledge that enables them to verify information that outsider general courts of law cannot; arbitrators in industry associations are the most prominent enforcers of this kind. The second is based on a relationship or ongoing interaction between the parties; a breakup of this relationship constitutes the punishment that may deter one of the parties from breaching. This covers many possibilities. The same two parties may meet repeatedly; the two may not have a direct repeated interaction with each other, but each may interact with others in a group or network that transmits information about any breach to all members and collectively sanctions the miscreant, using ostracism in business interactions or social relationships or both.

The distinction between observable and verifiable information is standard in the economic theory of contracts. In the legal context, Schwartz (1992, pp. 279, 280) gives a good discussion. Charny (1990) discusses the general concept of extralegal sanctions. All these ideas have been used for explaining the observed contracting forms in many industries; Bernstein's (1992, 2001) studies of the diamond and cotton industries are well-known examples; McMillan (2002, p. 23) describes how the New York Stock Exchange developed its internal rules and procedures for dispute resolution, and (McMillan 2002, p. 46) how intermediaries between Taiwanese shoe manufacturers and Western fashion houses performed dispute-resolution functions in addition to their primary matchmaking ones. McMillan and Woodruff (1999, 2001), and Johnson, McMillan, and Woodruff (2002) analyze and compare various methods of private ordering in transition economies. Using these conceptual discussions and case studies, I construct formal models of relation-based contracts and arbitration, respectively, in Sections 2.3 and 2.4.

One may think that these alternative methods of private ordering must suffer a crippling disadvantage relative to the government's courts, namely their lack of coercive power to ensure that their decisions are obeyed. However, the difficulty is often nonexistent or easily overcome. First, the sanctions available for private ordering are often very effective. Breach of contract can be deterred in ongoing relationships by the threat that the miscreant will be barred from future business with this particular partner or the group; this can be buttressed by social ostracism if the group fosters social ties among its business members. Sometimes this threat may be even more severe than the fines that courts would impose in the matter. If the threat is credible, in the sense of being a part of the strategies in the subgame-perfect equilibrium of the repeated game that constitutes the ongoing relationship, then the contract is self-enforcing. Second, arbitrators may have similar sanctions at their disposal; if they can bar the miscreant from the industry association, they can instantly put him out of business, which can be a more effective sanction than the fines the courts will impose (Bernstein 1992, pp. 148, 149). Of course, the feasibility of such sanctions depends on the availability of the requisite information, and in the case of repeated interactions, on how highly the participants value the future relative to the present. These are central aspects in the formal modeling below.

Finally, courts recognize the informational advantage of the alternative institutions. Therefore when a relational or implicit contract serves such an informational purpose, courts refuse to intervene to modify its terms, or to insert missing provisions, or to overrule the availability of discretion to one party (Schwartz 1992, pp. 282, 283). They also enforce the awards of industry arbitration tribunals, using the government's power of coercion to obtain compliance if the loser in the arbitration attempts to defy the ruling. In the United States, this has been so since 1920 (Bernstein 2001, footnote 111); in the international context, over 100 countries now accede to the 1958 New York Convention on the Recognition and Enforcement of Arbitral Awards (Mattli 2001, p. 939).

Bernstein (2001, p. 1741) explains the nature of the informational advantage of arbitration:

> [B]y providing for the appointment of industry-expert arbitrators, who can make many factual determinations more accurately and less expensively than a judge or jury can, the rules greatly expand the "contractible" aspects of an exchange. The use of stream-lined procedures together with the appointment of expert adjudicators transforms considerations that in the public legal system would have been only observable to the parties ... into considerations that are also verifiable ... thereby encouraging transactors to enter into more complete contracts.

The point is not that arbitrators have access to *more* information. Any relevant information can be elicited and brought before the court by either party to the dispute through the legal process of discovery. Conversely, many arbitration forums do not allow discovery, although the arbitrator can request additional information. The key is how information is used; industry arbitrators can use their expertise to interpret it—make factual determinations—more accurately and at a lower cost than non-specialized courts can (Bernstein 2001, pp. 1729, 1741). This is the sense in which verifiability should be interpreted in this context. My model of Section 2.4 builds on this idea.

Arbitration is used in other contexts for other reasons. In international transactions, each party may suspect that the other country's courts will be biased in favor of its own nationals; this can deter them from entering into contracts that may end up in national courts. Therefore both may agree ex ante to settle any disputes in an agreed international forum of arbitration. Several of these exist, based in London, Paris, Stockholm, etc. They differ in their procedures (degree of formality, time taken, fees charged, etc.) and the range of legal traditions they cover (civil, common, Islamic, etc.). These affect the choice of forum by the parties to each transaction. These forums usually lack the expertise that industry-specific forums can provide. Therefore they are not likely to lower costs or improve verifiability and permit more complete contracts; instead, removing the suspicion of bias may be their most important function. Dezalay and Garth (1996), Casella (1996), and Mattli (2001) describe and discuss several of these institutions of arbitration in international trade. My model does not deal with this aspect.

The different modes of private and official governance can interact in various ways. For example, if an ongoing relationship based on the superior observability of information by the two parties breaks down, the best alternative available to the parties may be recourse to a contract based on verifiable information enforceable in a court of law, not total cessation of transactions. And if an arbitrator's award is not enforceable by direct sanctions such as fines, it may nonetheless form part of a relational arrangement where the arbitrator can terminate the miscreant's access to future trades. I model some of these variants below; the readers can similarly model the others.

To conclude this empirical section, I relate an instance of Williamson's (1996, p. 12) discriminating alignment hypothesis in action. Not only do modes like arbitration evolve and apply to provide governance for transactions where they have an informational advantage and can reduce transaction costs, but also transactions take forms that adapt to the available information and governance. Marin and Schnitzer (2002, pp. 42, 43) explain the emergence and prevalence of barter and countertrade in post-Soviet Russia in this way: "The advantage of paying with goods rather than money is that they can be earmarked as property of the creditor." Money is fungible and liquid; a buyer can hide money easily if he chooses to renege on his promised payment to the seller. Goods in a barter or countertrade contract are more difficult to hide, and therefore can act as deal-specific collateral that mitigates opportunism.

2.2 Bargaining When the Law is a Backstop

Economic and legal scholars who study business disputes (and other events such as accidents where some economic consequences are at issue) recognize that the initial allocation of legal entitlements, the expectation and uncertainty about a court's decision in the matter, and the costs of using the legal system all affect the parties' choice between going to the law and settling the dispute by private negotiation (Shavell 1972; Cooter and Rubinfeld 1989). Rolling back one more step along a game tree, the same considerations also affect individuals' decisions about engaging in activities that can lead to accidents or disputes. In this section I sketch a very simple model that helps us think through such choices and interactions.

Consider two parties involved in an economic dispute. One of them (plaintiff) could sue the other (defendant) in a court of law. Their expectation, for the time being assumed to be commonly held and known, is that the court will award A_P to the plaintiff and A_D to the defendant. (If the defendant is ordered to make restitution or pay a fine, his payoff A_D can be negative.) In addition, each side has to bear some cost for using the court; this can be monetary in the form of court costs and lawyers' fees, or non-monetary in various forms, such as time, mental strain, or damage to reputation. The costs can depend on the legal system; for example, in the American system each side bears its own court and lawyer costs, whereas in the British system the loser bears both sides' costs. Denote the overall monetary equivalent costs by C_P for the plaintiff and C_D for the defendant. Thus the expected net payoffs from recourse to the court are $(A_P - C_P)$ for the plaintiff and $(A_D - C_D)$ for the defendant.

The two parties could negotiate a settlement, either before a suit is filed at all, or after a suit is filed but before trial. Doing so enables them to avoid some or all of the costs of using the law. If the court is expected to levy a fine in addition to mandating some transfer between the parties, and the proceeds of the fine go to the government, then the negotiation avoids the fine and leaves a larger sum of money available for dividing between them. Suppose S is the total available for them to bargain over, and

$$S > (A_P - C_P) + (A_D - C_D).$$

The excess of the left-hand side of this inequality over the right-hand side constitutes the "surplus" that is available for them to negotiate over. Denote the sums they can get through bargaining by X_P and X_D, respectively, then

$$X_P + X_D = S$$

is the bargaining frontier.

Figure 2.1 shows the various payoffs and outcomes. The bargaining frontier is a straight line of slope -1. If the negotiation fails and the plaintiff has to sue, their payoffs in the court will be $(A_P - C_P, A_D - C_D)$. This point is therefore the threat point that lies behind their bargaining. The generalized Nash bargaining solution then says that each party will get its threat-point payoff, plus a share of the surplus equal to its bargaining power. This bargaining power can be explained in terms

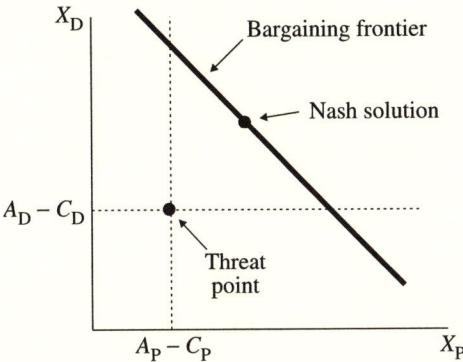

Figure 2.1.   Bargaining with the court outcome as the backstop.

of the two parties' relative impatience, but I will not go into that here, and simply assume that the plaintiff's bargaining power is π and that of the defendant $(1 - \pi)$. Then the outcome of the negotiation is

$$
\begin{aligned}
X_P &= (A_P - C_P) + \pi \left[S - (A_P - C_P) - (A_D - C_D) \right] \\
&= \pi S + (1 - \pi)(A_P - C_P) - \pi (A_D - C_D),
\end{aligned} \tag{2.1}
$$

$$
\begin{aligned}
X_D &= (A_D - C_D) + (1 - \pi) \left[S - (A_P - C_P) - (A_D - C_D) \right] \\
&= (1 - \pi) S - (1 - \pi)(A_P - C_P) + \pi (A_D - C_D).
\end{aligned} \tag{2.2}
$$

These expressions yield several simple implications. For example, they tell us how different rules about the allocation of legal costs affect the outcome of pre-trial negotiation. Suppose the expectation is that the plaintiff will win. Under the American system, each side would pay its own monetary legal costs. Under the British system, the monetary part of the plaintiff's legal costs would be shifted to the defendant. Denote this by M. Then in the British system, as compared with the American, C_P is lower and C_D higher by M. Therefore (2.1) shows that X_P is higher by M, and (2.2) shows that X_D is lower by M, in the British system than in the American. In turn, we can calculate how the expectation of this outcome affects the incentives of the parties to engage in activities that may lead to such disputes. This argument assumes that the expected payoffs A_P and A_D when the parties go to the court are the same in the two systems. If the courts adjusted the payoffs to offset the stipulated allocation of costs, then the threat points of the two systems would be the same, and therefore so would the Nash solution of the negotiation.

However, this simple model has some flaws. Most obviously, in the model the negotiations succeed and the threat of going to court is never invoked. This is less egregious than it may appear at first sight, because only 10% of disputes go to trial (Cooter and Rubinfeld 1989, p. 1070). Simple extensions of the model explain why and which disputes are likely to go to trial. The main cause is the parties' inconsistent expectations about the outcome in court. If the plaintiff expects A_P to be high, and the defendant simultaneously expects A_D to be high, then each may think that there is no surplus to bargain over (Shavell 1982). The simple figure and algebra I have developed here seem promising foundations for formal models of such extensions, but I will leave developments along these lines for future work.

The model can readily be extended to apply to another situation. My discussion of the court that generates the threat-point payoff in this model treated it as a well-meaning but costly system. However, it could easily be a corrupt system, or a predatory or kleptocratic government. Economic activities and transactions in such a country would try to proceed in secrecy. However, the threat of disclosure, and the consequent exposure to extortion by the state's agents, would underlie all negotiations. By interpreting C_P and C_D as the expected amounts the state would extort from the two parties, the model can cover this situation.

2.3 Relational and Formal Contracts

In this section I develop the idea, sketched in Section 2.1, that the parties to an economic transaction can exploit their high-quality inside information using a relational contract, and a formal contract that must be based on lower-quality publicly verifiable information acts as a fallback in the event of cheating within their relationship. Baker, Gibbons, and Murphy (1994, 2002) have constructed such a model of a principal–agent contract. Here I offer an alternative and somewhat simpler model for exposition of the same idea, using the formulation of multi-action agency in Baker (2002). I use a linear-quadratic structure to allow explicit solutions that convey the intuition in a simple way.

The principal has to hire an agent to take some actions that will yield the principal some outcome. The actions are costly to the agent, and observable only to himself. The principal cares only about his own outcome minus his payments to the agent. The principal wants to motivate the agent's actions, but there is some uncertainty so actions cannot be inferred precisely from the outcome. In the standard theory of agency, the principal's outcome is assumed to be verifiable, so outcome-based bonus or incentive payments can be designed and written into a contract that can be enforced in a court of law if necessary. However, in reality the principal's true outcome is rarely verifiable to outsiders, even though the parties may have good information about it. External, legally enforceable contracts then have to rely on some other performance measure that is an imperfect proxy for the principal's outcome, and an even more imperfect proxy for the agent's actions.[1]

---

[1] The traditional economic theory of agency formulated the problem as a trade-off between giving the agent stronger incentives and making him bear more risk (Grossman and Hart 1983). However,

The simplest example of this situation is an employment contract, where the principal is the owner of a firm and the agent a manager or worker. But it can also be interpreted in the context of a firm's outsourcing decision. The principal firm buys from an agent firm a component that is an input to one of the principal's final products. The principal firm's ultimate objective is profit, but the contribution of the component to the final product, and indeed the contribution of the final product to the profit of the firm as a whole, are so thoroughly concealed in the accounts of the firm as to be unverifiable to a court of law. Matters like the quantities and time of delivery of the component are recorded and easily verifiable; therefore a contract that specifies the firm's payment to the component supplier as a function of these matters can be written and enforced by the government's civil courts. But the two firms may have a much better idea of other matters, such as the quality of the work, and can base a relational contract on such inside information.

The Model

The agent's action is a, an n-dimensional vector. This is not observed by anyone else. The agent's cost of performing the action is given by

$$C(a) = \tfrac{1}{2} a' a.$$

The agent's utility outside of the relationship with this principal is u_0, and the principal's outside opportunity (profit) is normalized to 0.

The action gives rise to an outcome y for the principal. This can take on only two values, 0 or 1, for example failure ($y = 0$) or success ($y = 1$) of the project. The probability of success is a linear function of the agent's actions:

$$\text{Prob}\{ y = 1 \mid a \} = y' a,$$

where y is a vector of the same dimension as a. The components of y are the marginal products of the actions with respect to the outcome. The value of y is internal, that is, observed by the principal and the agent, and this fact is common knowledge between them.

The action also gives rise to an external or publicly verifiable performance measure x, which can also take only the two values 0 or 1, and

$$\text{Prob}\{ x = 1 \mid a \} = x' a,$$

where x is another vector of the same dimension as a; the components of x are the marginal products of the actions on the performance measure.

I assume, as do Baker, Gibbons, and Murphy (2002), that all the parameters are such that the probabilities fall in the requisite range (0, 1) for all the relevant levels of

---

Baker (1992) argues convincingly that the imperfectness of verifiable performance measures is a more important problem in reality, and that is the approach I follow.

actions. I also assume that both parties are risk-neutral, but their joint involvement is essential; thus the principal cannot simply sell the whole project to the agent for a fixed fee.

Under the constraints of the available information, the agent's compensation package can consist of three components.

(1) Salary s, which is unconditional and enforceable by recourse to law if needed.

(2) Objective bonus ξ to be paid if $x = 1$. This is enforceable by recourse to law if needed.

(3) Subjective bonus η to be paid if $y = 1$. This has to be self-enforcing in a repeated game between the principal and the agent. The discount rate for this game is r.

Best Responses, etc.

For the moment assuming that everything is enforceable (i.e. temporarily assuming that the internal signal y is also verifiable), the agent's expected payoff is

$$U = s + \xi \, \boldsymbol{x}' \, \boldsymbol{a} + \eta \, \boldsymbol{y}' \, \boldsymbol{a} - \tfrac{1}{2} \, \boldsymbol{a}' \, \boldsymbol{a} \, .$$

The agent chooses $\boldsymbol{a}$ to maximize this. Written out in full, we have

$$U = s + \xi \sum_{i=1}^{n} x_i \, a_i + \eta \sum_{i=1}^{n} y_i \, a_i - \frac{1}{2} \sum_{i=1}^{n} (a_i)^2 \, .$$

Differentiating with respect to any one a_j,

$$\frac{\partial U}{\partial a_j} = \xi \, x_j + \eta \, y_j - a_j \, .$$

Therefore the first-order conditions of maximization yield an immediate solution

$$a_j = \xi \, x_j + \eta \, y_j \quad \text{for } j = 1, 2, \ldots, n \, ,$$

or back in vector notation,

$$\boldsymbol{a} = \xi \, \boldsymbol{x} + \eta \, \boldsymbol{y} \, .$$

The second-order own-partial derivatives are all negative:

$$\frac{\partial^2 U}{\partial a_j^2} = -1 \quad \text{for } j = 1, 2, \ldots, n \, ,$$

and the second-order cross-partial derivatives are all zero, so the second-order conditions are satisfied.

Substituting for the agent's optimal $\boldsymbol{a}$ into the utility expression, we find his maximized or indirect utility

$$U = s + \tfrac{1}{2} \, (\xi \, \boldsymbol{x}' + \eta \, \boldsymbol{y}') \, (\boldsymbol{x} \, \xi + \boldsymbol{y} \, \eta)$$
$$= s + \tfrac{1}{2} \, (\boldsymbol{x}' \, \boldsymbol{x} \, \xi^2 + 2 \, \boldsymbol{x}' \, \boldsymbol{y} \, \xi \, \eta + \boldsymbol{y}' \, \boldsymbol{y} \, \eta^2) \, .$$

At this point, much notation can be saved by choosing units such that

$$\boldsymbol{x}' \, \boldsymbol{x} = 1 = \boldsymbol{y}' \, \boldsymbol{y}$$

and then defining the parameter K by

$$K = \boldsymbol{x}' \, \boldsymbol{y} \, .$$

Geometrically, if we visualize $\boldsymbol{x}$ and $\boldsymbol{y}$ as vectors of unit length in the n-dimensional Euclidean space, then K is the cosine of the angle between them. Therefore $|K| \leqslant 1$. More formally, by the Cauchy–Schwarz inequality, $K^2 \leqslant 1$. Note that if the agent's action $\boldsymbol{a}$ were scalar, then K^2 would necessarily equal 1. Thus the assumption that the agent's action is multidimensional is essential to the analysis. However, this assumption is very realistic; in fact the opposite assumption of first-generation principal–agent theory that the agent performs a single scalar action is what has been unrealistic. See Baker (2002) for a fuller discussion.[2] As there, K^2 will play a crucial role. It measures the correlation between the marginal effects of the agent's actions on the outcome y and public performance measure x, and therefore can be thought of as a measure of the accuracy of the external signal x.

With this notation, the agent's maximized utility is

$$U = s + \tfrac{1}{2} \, (\xi^2 + 2 \, K \, \xi \, \eta + \eta^2) \, . \tag{2.3}$$

The principal finds it optimal to satisfy the agent's participation constraint $U \geqslant u_0$ by setting

$$s = u_0 - \tfrac{1}{2} \, (\xi^2 + 2 \, K \, \xi \, \eta + \eta^2) \, .$$

Then the principal's expected payoff will be

$$\Pi = \boldsymbol{y}' \, \boldsymbol{a} - s - \xi \, \boldsymbol{x}' \, \boldsymbol{a} - \eta \, \boldsymbol{y}' \, \boldsymbol{a} \, .$$

Substituting the expression for the optimal action and simplifying, we obtain

$$\Pi(\xi, \eta) = (K \, \xi + \eta) - \tfrac{1}{2} \, (\xi^2 + 2 \, K \, \xi \, \eta + \eta^2) - u_0 \, . \tag{2.4}$$

---

[2] So we have a fortunate coincidence where a technically necessary assumption is also realistic. An added advantage is that it makes unnecessary the complication in Baker, Gibbons, and Murphy (1994) that the agent privately observes an efficiency parameter of the external signal before taking his action.

First Best

Continue for a while with the assumption that everything is enforceable. The principal chooses ξ and η to maximize Π as defined in (2.4), where the agent's incentive compatibility (action choice) and participation constraints have already been incorporated. The first-order conditions for this maximization are

$$K - \xi - K\,\eta = 0\,,$$
$$1 - K\,\xi - \eta = 0\,.$$

The second-order necessary condition requires the matrix

$$\begin{pmatrix} -1 & -K \\ -K & -1 \end{pmatrix}$$

to be negative semi-definite. This amounts to requiring $K^2 \leqslant 1$, which is true as was discussed above.

The first-order conditions have the solution $\xi = 0$, $\eta = 1$, which is unique if $K^2 \neq 1$. The intuition is that the subjective measure y is a fully accurate (in fact direct) indicator of the principal's outcome, so it is used by itself if it is credible.[3]

In this hypothetical first best, the principal's payoff is

$$\Pi^{\text{FB}} = \tfrac{1}{2} - u_0\,,$$

and the total social surplus is

$$W^{\text{FB}} = \Pi^{\text{FB}} + u_0 = \tfrac{1}{2}\,.$$

If $\tfrac{1}{2} < u_0$, then the two parties do better in their outside opportunities than even the first best within their interaction with each other, and the whole analysis becomes irrelevant. Therefore I assume in all that follows that $\tfrac{1}{2} > u_0$, or $2\,u_0 < 1$.

Purely Formal Contract

Now suppose that the agent's compensation can be based on only the external measure x. Thus the principal sets $\eta \equiv 0$ and chooses ξ to maximize Π in (2.4). This yields the first-order condition

$$\xi = K\,.$$

The principal's payoff under this purely external contract is

$$\Pi^{\text{Ext}} = \tfrac{1}{2}\,K^2 - u_0\,,$$

---

[3] If $K^2 = 1$, both measures are equally and perfectly accurate, and can be used in suitable combinations without any loss. Mathematically, in this case the solution for ξ, η is not unique, but the non-uniqueness is harmless.

and the total social surplus is

$$W^{\text{Ext}} = \tfrac{1}{2} K^2 .$$

The fact that the optimal external bonus ξ equals the correlation K between the marginal products of action on the true outcome and the external performance measure is very intuitive. The bonus serves the purpose of motivating the agent to take those actions which increase the performance measure. If the same actions, on the whole, also increase the true outcome, then the bonus is a good way to motivate the agent, and therefore the principal uses it more. Observe that the magnitude of K matters, not its sign. If K is close to -1, then by making ξ negative one can motivate the agent to take actions that reduce the performance measure and thereby increase the true outcome. A lack of correlation, or K being close to 0, would make the external performance measure useless for the purpose of incentive design. See Baker (2002) for a more detailed discussion. In the next section, I offer an alternative intuition for the same result, using the idea of information or signal extraction.

If $\tfrac{1}{2} K^2 > u_0$, or $K^2 > 2 u_0$, then the external contract will be offered in the absence of better alternatives. In particular, it will constitute the reversion situation if the principal cheats in an ongoing relationship. If $\tfrac{1}{2} K^2 < u_0$, the agent's outside opportunity will play this role. The question of interest here is how the relational contract operates in the shadow of the formal one, for which the case $K^2 > 2 u_0$ is the one of interest. Therefore I focus on it, and merely mention in the appendix (Section 2.6.1) what happens in the opposite case.

When Is the First Best Self-Enforcing?

Now remove the previous temporary assumption about enforceability of the contract based on y. Therefore, when $y = 1$, the principal is tempted to renege on his agreement to pay η. In the implicit or relational contract, the cost of such cheating is that in all future periods the game between the principal and the agent will revert to a worse outcome. However, in the case I am considering, where $\tfrac{1}{2} K^2 > u_0$, dealing with each other on the basis of the external formally enforceable measure alone is Pareto-better than breaking off the relationship altogether. Therefore a threat of reversion to the latter is not credible, and the formal contract based on the purely external signal is the reversion scenario.

In the first best, the principal's immediate gain from cheating is 1, and the subsequent loss of profit each period is

$$(\tfrac{1}{2} - u_0) - (\tfrac{1}{2} K^2 - u_0) = \tfrac{1}{2} (1 - K^2).$$

Therefore the condition for the principal's adherence to the relational contract is that 1 be less than the capitalized value of these subsequent losses, or $1 \leqslant (1 - K^2)/(2 r)$, or

$$1 - K^2 \geqslant 2 r . \tag{2.5}$$

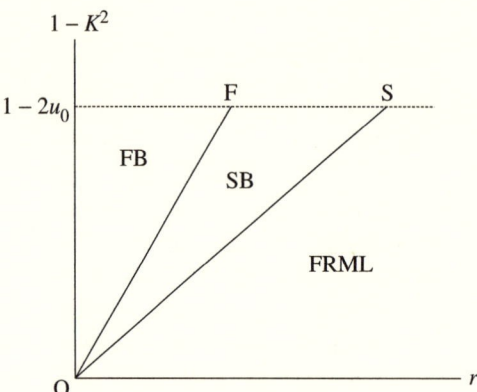

Figure 2.2.   Accuracy of external measure and success of relational contract.

Figure 2.2 shows the discount rate r on the horizontal axis, and $(1 - K^2)$, which measures the *inaccuracy* of the external measure x, on the vertical axis. Note that the vertical axis variable is bounded above by $(1 - 2u_0)$, reflecting my assumption that the external contract is better than a total breakdown of the interaction. The line OF has slope 2. The first best is self-enforcing at all points to the northwest of this line, that is, in the region labeled FB. In this region, a sufficient increase in K^2 (the *accuracy* of the external signal), which means a move vertically downward in the figure, eventually makes the first best infeasible. It does this by increasing the principal's payoff from the reversion to formal contracting, and thereby increasing his temptation to renege on the relational contract.

Second Best

Following the same logic as in the previous section, but now for a general (ξ, η), the principal's gain from reneging on the agreement to pay the relational bonus is η, and the loss is $\Pi(\xi, \eta) - \Pi^{\text{Ext}}$ each future period. Therefore the no-cheating condition is

$$\eta \leq [\Pi(\xi, \eta) - \Pi^{\text{Ext}}]/r,$$

or

$$\Pi(\xi, \eta) - r\,\eta - \Pi^{\text{Ext}} \geq 0. \tag{2.6}$$

The principal chooses (ξ, η) to maximize $\Pi(\xi, \eta)$ subject to this constraint. This yields the second-best relational contract for the agency. I leave the details for the appendix (Section 2.6.1), and merely state the results here. These can be summarized in terms of the ratio $(1-K^2)/r$ of the *inaccuracy* of the external signal to the discount rate, and the regions of Figure 2.2. The line OF in the figure has slope 2, so long as the ratio equals 2. The line OS has slope 1, so along as the ratio equals 1.

Region FB: Ratio > 2. This is the region in Figure 2.2 to the northwest of the line OF. Here the external measure is relatively inaccurate, and the future is relatively important (the discount rate is relatively low). Then a purely relational contract based on the accurate internal performance measure is self-enforcing and achieves the first best. The resulting social surplus equals $\frac{1}{2}$.

Region SB: Ratio Between 1 and 2. This is the middle region, between the lines OF and OS. Here the alternative opportunity of reversion to the formal contract becomes a binding constraint on the relational contract. The best feasible relational contract is a second best, with a mixture of the formal and relational bonuses. An increase in the accuracy of the external signal tightens the principal's no-cheating constraint and therefore reduces the ability to rely on the fully accurate internal measure, and therefore lowers the total surplus.

Region FRML: Ratio < 1. This is the region to the southeast of the line OS. Here the discount rate is high, and the external measure accurate. Both these factors tighten the principal's incentive constraint to the point that no relational bonus is feasible. Only the external contract can be used. The social surplus is $K^2/2$, which increases as the accuracy of the external measure increases. Finally, in the limit as we approach the horizontal axis, K^2 goes to 1, the outcome goes to the first best, but now achieved using the increasingly accurate external measure.

Some of the structure of these results is quite intuitive. The finding that relational contracts work best when the parties value the future highly and when the external performance measure is of very poor quality is hardly surprising. However, one result is not so immediately obvious, and repays further thought. This is the finding that when the incentive constraint is binding and the relational contract yields a second best, a partial improvement in the external performance measure worsens the outcome of the relational contract. This reminds one of various "second-best" propositions in economics: when an economy has two or more distortions, a reduction in the size of one distortion may aggravate the overall distortion and reduce economic welfare. In this instance the explanation is tied to a general property of tacitly cooperative equilibria of repeated games. The harsher is the punishment that faces a deviator, the better the equilibrium that can be achieved. In this model, the punishment consists of having to fall back on the formal contract based on the external performance measure. The more accurate is that measure, the better is the payoff from the formal contract and therefore the weaker the punishment.

Similar results appear in other contexts. For example, Kranton (1996) models self-governing repeated interactions with well-matched partners, when the consequence of cheating is having to go to an anonymous arms-length market with inferior matching but enforceable contracts. A partial improvement in the quality of matching in the market then tightens the incentive constraint on self-governance and worsens its outcome. In Kranton's context this leads to a cumulative process leading to an equilibrium where one or the other of the modes survives.

More generally, one can argue that cooperation within a group is better sustained if the consequences of deviation are made worse, which requires worse outcomes from dealing with people outside the group. This is a trade-off: better within-group cooperation may require worse cross-group relations. In starker terms, a beneficial sense of "us" may be fostered only by sharpening the sense of "us versus them" hostility. Dugatkin (1999, Chapter 4) discusses these larger issues in the context of group selection in evolutionary biology.

In the economic context, the result has potentially serious implications for less-developed countries and transition economies that are attempting to install a formal system of contract law or to improve an existing one. The new institution of governance cannot be expected to leapfrog to perfection. The organizations and people are sure to need a period of trial and error, of experimentation and learning. The above result says that the process of gradual improvement of state law may inflict an interim cost on the economy, by worsening the outcomes of the currently used relation-based system. Therefore it is important to explore the result in greater depth, and look for empirical evidence bearing on it. Johnson, McMillan, and Woodruff (2002, p. 260) report a finding that bears on this: "In an established bilateral relationship it is the relationship itself that determines the degree of cooperation, regardless of whether the courts are effective." This is encouraging for the prospects of improving the courts gradually without causing short-term harm. But the finding runs contrary to the theoretical result. If the theoretical model is broadly right, effectiveness of the courts would be irrelevant to the outcome of the relational contract only if the parameters put the equilibrium in the region FB of Figure 2.2, that is, the relational contract is achieving the first best. That seems unlikely. A second possibility, formally explored in the mathematical appendix (Section 2.6), is that the accuracy of the external measure is so poor that the alternative to a relational contract is not recourse to the courts but a total breakdown of the interaction. (This happens if $K^2 < 2u_0$, corresponding to the top strip of Figure 2.3 in the appendix.) That may be more likely. The third possibility, of course, is that the theoretical model is missing some key aspect of reality; that provides a challenge and an opportunity for future research.

2.4 Arbitration and Information

The theme of this section is similar to that of the previous one. A mode of private ordering has an information advantage over court-based formal governance, and the operation of the private mode in the shadow of the law is the object of analysis. Here the private mode is arbitration. Its informational advantage (better verifiability) was discussed in the introductory section, Section 2.1, as was the question of its enforcement (punitive sanctions or backup enforcement by courts). For the model of this section, I assume that the courts will enforce the arbitrator's award if one of the parties tries to renege. I leave to interested readers the analysis of the alternative where the arbitrator's award has to be self-enforcing in a relationship; this will combine features of the model of the previous section and this one.

The Model

Much of the set-up and the notation is the same as in the previous section. The interaction needing enforcement is between a principal and an agent. The agent takes an action $\boldsymbol{a}$, an n-dimensional vector. The agent's cost of taking the action is

$$C(\boldsymbol{a}) = \tfrac{1}{2}\,\boldsymbol{a}'\boldsymbol{a}\,.$$

The outcome for the principal is a binary variable y, which can equal 0 or 1 (denoting failure and success, respectively), and the probability of success is given by

$$\text{Prob}(\,y = 1 \mid \boldsymbol{a}\,) \equiv Y(\boldsymbol{a}) = \boldsymbol{y}'\boldsymbol{a}\,.$$

The new feature is that only the principal observes the outcome y. Thus not even a relational contract can be based upon it. Instead, all contracts have to be based on other verifiable measures to be specified soon. The agent's reservation utility is u_0 and the principal's reservation profit is 0.

First Best

The joint surplus from the relationship is

$$S = \boldsymbol{y}'\boldsymbol{a} - \tfrac{1}{2}\,\boldsymbol{a}'\boldsymbol{a}\,.$$

The first-order condition defining the first-best action $\boldsymbol{a}^{\text{FB}}$ to maximize S is $\boldsymbol{y} - \boldsymbol{a} = 0$.[4] This immediately yields the solution

$$\boldsymbol{a}^{\text{FB}} = \boldsymbol{y}\,, \tag{2.7}$$

and the resulting total surplus is

$$S^{\text{FB}} = \tfrac{1}{2}\,\boldsymbol{y}'\boldsymbol{y}\,. \tag{2.8}$$

The first best could be achieved if y were verifiable, by offering the agent a contract consisting of a salary s plus a bonus equal to 1 to be paid if $y = 1$. Then the agent's expected utility would be

$$U = s + 1 \times \boldsymbol{y}'\boldsymbol{a} - \tfrac{1}{2}\,\boldsymbol{a}'\boldsymbol{a}\,.$$

---

[4]The procedure of writing out the inner products in full and differentiating with respect to each component of $\boldsymbol{a}$ was explained for the agent's optimization problem in the previous section, Section 2.3, and readers who are not familiar with differentiation with respect to vector independent variables, for example from the theory of likelihood maximization in econometrics, may want to repeat those steps here. Also, second-order conditions are easy to verify for all the linear-quadratic maximization problems in this section, so I omit their details.

Then the first-order condition for the agent's choice of a is the same as the joint surplus maximization condition (2.7). The salary s is calculated to meet the agent's participation constraint $U \geqslant u_0$.

Performance Measures and Their Verifiability

My focus is on a situation where only the principal can observe y. Therefore any contract conditioned on y is infeasible, even on a relational basis. I assume that there are two other performance measures x and w that can serve as a basis for contracts. Both are binary variables, taking values 0 or 1. I assume that x is publicly verifiable, but w can be verified only by an arbitrator with specialized skill. So explicit or formal contracts based on x can be enforced in a governmental court of law. Contracts based on w as well as x can be adjudicated by the arbitrator. In this section I assume that the government's courts stand ready to enforce the arbitrator's judgment if necessary. In Section 4.3 I take up an alternative where a profit-motivated third party gathers and provides information about cheating, which then forms the basis for a relational arrangement in the group of traders.

The structure of information is special in two respects: there is only one performance measure of each kind (publicly verifiable and verifiable only by the specialized arbitrator), and each is binary. Relaxing both merely complicates the algebra without any significant change in the economic content or the results, therefore I have opted for the simplicity afforded by my assumptions.

In this section I follow Baker, Gibbons, and Murphy (2002) and assume that x and w are stochastically independent. In the appendix (Section 2.6.2) I consider the more general case, and examine the implications of dependence for the possible set of contracts.

Each of x and w can take on two values; therefore four distinct realizations of the state of the world are possible. We need to specify probabilities for these. The most relevant ones are those outcomes on which the payments to the agent can depend. The public courts can verify x but not w. The arbitrator can verify both, and the most significant new item of information for him is if his indicator w shows success while the public x shows failure. In the text of the paper, for analytical simplicity, I make both these probabilities linear functions of the agent's action a; thus

$$\text{Prob}(x = 1 \mid a) \equiv X(a) = x'a,$$
$$\text{Prob}(x = 0, \ w = 1 \mid a) \equiv W(a) = w'a,$$

where x and w are constant vectors that denote the marginal effects of actions on the respective performance measures. In the appendix (Section 2.6.2) I consider more general functions. Also, to simplify later notation and without loss of further generality, I choose units so that the vector x has unit length, that is,

$$x'x = 1. \tag{2.9}$$

Court-Enforced Contract

The state legal system or governmental court can verify only x. Then the most general available form of the formal or court-enforceable contract will stipulate payment to the agent in the form of an unconditional salary s, and a bonus ξ to be paid if $x = 1$. Then the agent's utility is

$$U = s + \xi \, \boldsymbol{x}' \boldsymbol{a} - \tfrac{1}{2} \, \boldsymbol{a}' \boldsymbol{a} \, .$$

The agent's utility-maximizing choice of action $\boldsymbol{a}$ is characterized by the first-order condition

$$\xi \, \boldsymbol{x} = \boldsymbol{a} \, .$$

Here I have stated the outcome of differentiating U with respect to all components of the vector $\boldsymbol{a}$ directly in vector form. Readers who are unfamiliar with this can do the component-by-component differentiation and then gather the results together as was done in the previous section for relational contracts.

The principal chooses s and ξ to induce effort $\boldsymbol{a}$ so as to maximize his expected profit

$$\Pi = \boldsymbol{y}' \boldsymbol{a} - [s + \xi \, \boldsymbol{x}' \boldsymbol{a}] \, ,$$

subject to the agent's participation constraint $U \geqslant u_0$. To meet this, the principal sets

$$s = u_0 - \xi \, \boldsymbol{x}' \boldsymbol{a} + \tfrac{1}{2} \, \boldsymbol{a}' \boldsymbol{a} \, .$$

Substituting for s, the principal's objective function becomes

$$\begin{aligned} \Pi &= \boldsymbol{y}' \boldsymbol{a} - \tfrac{1}{2} \, \boldsymbol{a}' \boldsymbol{a} - u_0 \\ &= (\boldsymbol{y}' \boldsymbol{x}) \, \xi - \tfrac{1}{2} \, (\boldsymbol{x}' \boldsymbol{x}) \, \xi^2 - u_0 \\ &= (\boldsymbol{y}' \boldsymbol{x}) \, \xi - \tfrac{1}{2} \, \xi^2 - u_0 \, , \end{aligned}$$

where the second line uses the agent's first-order condition and the second uses the normalization (2.9). The choice of ξ to maximize this, namely the bonus coefficient in the optimal contract with enforcement by governmental courts of law, is therefore

$$\xi^{\mathrm{CRT}} = \boldsymbol{y}' \boldsymbol{x} \, . \tag{2.10}$$

Then the agent's action is

$$\boldsymbol{a}^{\mathrm{CRT}} = (\boldsymbol{y}' \boldsymbol{x}) \, \boldsymbol{x} \, . \tag{2.11}$$

The resulting joint surplus is

$$S^{\mathrm{CRT}} = \tfrac{1}{2} \, (\boldsymbol{y}' \boldsymbol{x})^2 \, . \tag{2.12}$$

This is of course smaller than the first-best surplus in (2.8), formally this is because of the Cauchy–Schwarz Inequality.

The intuition for this result comes from Baker (2002); it also appeared in Section 2.3. The size of the bonus is positively related to the correlation between two vectors of marginal effects of the multiple dimensions of the agent's efforts: the first consists of the marginal effects on the principal's payoff, and the second, on the verifiable indicator. Here I develop an alternative interpretation by analogy with information or regression theory, which may be more familiar to some readers. The principal induces the agent to take a vector of actions that is just the projection of the vector $\boldsymbol{y}$ (the coefficients of the principal's benefits of action) on $\boldsymbol{x}$ (the effects of actions on the verifiable performance measure). The shortfall of action below the first best, namely

$$\boldsymbol{a}^{\mathrm{FB}} - \boldsymbol{a}^{\mathrm{CRT}} = \boldsymbol{y} - (\boldsymbol{y}'\boldsymbol{x})\,\boldsymbol{x}\,, \tag{2.13}$$

is orthogonal to $\boldsymbol{x}$:

$$\begin{aligned}
(\boldsymbol{a}^{\mathrm{FB}} - \boldsymbol{a}^{\mathrm{CRT}})'\boldsymbol{x} &= \boldsymbol{y}'\boldsymbol{x} - (\boldsymbol{y}'\boldsymbol{x})\,\boldsymbol{x}'\boldsymbol{x} \\
&= 0\,,
\end{aligned}$$

using the normalization of the length of $\boldsymbol{x}$. Thus the information contained in the indicator is used to the full extent possible. This will be important when we study the properties of the optimal arbitration contract. Of course this simple interpretation of information in terms of projections and orthogonality is specific to the linear-quadratic structure; in the appendix (Section 2.6.2) I consider more general functional forms.

Arbitration

Now introduce an arbitrator who can verify the outcome of w. Since x remains publicly verifiable, the two players can condition their contract on the realizations of both x and w. Now four states of the world are distinguishable, therefore in addition to the salary s, there can be three distinct bonus payments. To allow direct comparison with the contracts of the previous section enforced in courts where only x was verifiable, I make one bonus contingent only on x. A second bonus is paid in the event of special interest in the context of arbitration, namely where the arbitrator's measure indicates success while the public one indicates failure. The bonuses are denoted by

$$\begin{aligned}
\xi \quad &\text{if } x = 1, \\
\omega \quad &\text{if } x = 0 \text{ and } w = 1\,.
\end{aligned}$$

Baker, Gibbons, and Murphy (2002) use a similar two-bonus contract for expository simplicity. In principle one can consider a separate bonus for a third contingency:

$$\beta \quad \text{if } x = 1 \text{ and } w = 1\,.$$

I do this in the appendix (Section 2.6.2). It turns out that the third bonus can be expressed as a linear combination of the first two if the two performance measures x and w are stochastically independent conditional on $\boldsymbol{a}$. I am assuming this in the text, so the two-bonus restriction on contracts involves no additional loss of generality here.

Recall that I am assuming that the official legal system is available to enforce the arbitrator's decision, backed by the power to levy sufficiently large penalties. Therefore such contracts are binding. We can find the optimal contract following the same steps as in the section on court-enforced contracts above.

The agent's expected utility is

$$U = s + \xi\, \boldsymbol{x}'\boldsymbol{a} + \omega\, \boldsymbol{w}'\boldsymbol{a} - \tfrac{1}{2}\,\boldsymbol{a}'\boldsymbol{a}\,.$$

The agent's choice of action is characterized by the first-order condition

$$\xi\, \boldsymbol{x} + \omega\, \boldsymbol{w} = \boldsymbol{a}\,.$$

The principal chooses s, ξ, and ω to induce effort $\boldsymbol{a}$ so as to maximize his expected profit

$$\Pi = \boldsymbol{y}'\boldsymbol{a} - [\,s + \xi\, \boldsymbol{x}'\boldsymbol{a} + \omega\, \boldsymbol{w}'\boldsymbol{a}\,]\,,$$

subject to the agent's participation constraint $U \geqslant u_0$. To meet this, the principal sets

$$s = u_0 - \xi\, \boldsymbol{x}'\boldsymbol{a} - \omega\, \boldsymbol{w}'\boldsymbol{a} + \tfrac{1}{2}\,\boldsymbol{a}'\boldsymbol{a}\,.$$

Substituting for s, the principal's objective function becomes

$$\Pi = \boldsymbol{y}'\boldsymbol{a} - \tfrac{1}{2}\,\boldsymbol{a}'\boldsymbol{a} - u_0\,.$$

Substituting for $\boldsymbol{a}$ from the agent's first-order condition and collecting terms into suitable vectors and matrices, we have

$$\Pi = \begin{pmatrix} \boldsymbol{y}'\boldsymbol{x} & \boldsymbol{y}'\boldsymbol{w} \end{pmatrix} \begin{pmatrix} \xi \\ \omega \end{pmatrix} - \tfrac{1}{2} \begin{pmatrix} \xi & \omega \end{pmatrix} \begin{pmatrix} \boldsymbol{x}'\boldsymbol{x} & \boldsymbol{x}'\boldsymbol{w} \\ \boldsymbol{w}'\boldsymbol{x} & \boldsymbol{w}'\boldsymbol{w} \end{pmatrix} \begin{pmatrix} \xi \\ \omega \end{pmatrix}\,.$$

The first-order condition to maximize this is

$$\begin{pmatrix} \boldsymbol{y}'\boldsymbol{x} \\ \boldsymbol{y}'\boldsymbol{w} \end{pmatrix} = \begin{pmatrix} \boldsymbol{x}'\boldsymbol{x} & \boldsymbol{x}'\boldsymbol{w} \\ \boldsymbol{w}'\boldsymbol{x} & \boldsymbol{w}'\boldsymbol{w} \end{pmatrix} \begin{pmatrix} \xi \\ \omega \end{pmatrix}\,. \tag{2.14}$$

This is a pair of simultaneous linear equations with the two bonus coefficients under arbitration, ξ and ω, as the unknowns, and it yields the following solutions:[5]

$$\left. \begin{aligned} \xi^{\mathrm{ARB}} &= \frac{(\boldsymbol{w}'\boldsymbol{w})\,(\boldsymbol{x}'\boldsymbol{y}) - (\boldsymbol{w}'\boldsymbol{x})\,(\boldsymbol{w}'\boldsymbol{y})}{(\boldsymbol{x}'\boldsymbol{x})\,(\boldsymbol{w}'\boldsymbol{w}) - (\boldsymbol{w}'\boldsymbol{x})^2}\,, \\[2mm] \omega^{\mathrm{ARB}} &= \frac{(\boldsymbol{x}'\boldsymbol{x})\,(\boldsymbol{w}'\boldsymbol{y}) - (\boldsymbol{w}'\boldsymbol{x})\,(\boldsymbol{x}'\boldsymbol{y})}{(\boldsymbol{x}'\boldsymbol{x})\,(\boldsymbol{w}'\boldsymbol{w}) - (\boldsymbol{w}'\boldsymbol{x})^2}\,. \end{aligned} \right\} \tag{2.15}$$

---

[5] I use the normalization $\boldsymbol{x}'\boldsymbol{x} = 1$ later; for now I keep the more general form to bring out the symmetric structure of the solutions.

This is again interpretable as regressing $\boldsymbol{y}$ on $\boldsymbol{x}$ and $\boldsymbol{w}$ jointly, and the resulting action $\boldsymbol{a}^{\text{ARB}}$ is just the projection of $\boldsymbol{y}$ on the plane spanned by $\boldsymbol{x}$ and $\boldsymbol{w}$.[6] The algebraic expression for the action is not especially insightful so I omit it.

The solution is valid if the denominator is non-zero. This will be so unless the vectors $\boldsymbol{x}$ and $\boldsymbol{w}$ are perfectly collinear. If the marginal effects of actions $\boldsymbol{a}$ on the probabilities of the two indicators x and w are mutually proportional, the w indicator does not carry any extra useful information, and the two equations in (2.14) collapse to one. Thus, if $\boldsymbol{w} = \lambda\,\boldsymbol{x}$ for a scalar λ, then the two equations reduce to one:

$$(\boldsymbol{x}'\boldsymbol{x})\,(\xi^{\text{ARB}} + \lambda\,\omega^{\text{ARB}}) = (\boldsymbol{x}'\boldsymbol{y})\,,$$

which determines only the combination $\xi^{\text{ARB}} + \lambda\,\omega^{\text{ARB}}$. The agent's action also depends only on this combination,

$$\boldsymbol{a}^{\text{ARB}} = (\xi^{\text{ARB}} + \lambda\,\omega^{\text{ARB}})\,\boldsymbol{x}\,.$$

Therefore the outcome can be achieved using the ξ bonus alone, without arbitration, relying only on the official civil courts and their ability to verify x.

Now suppose that the vectors of marginal effects of action on the two indicators are linearly independent. Then the denominator in (2.15) is positive by the Cauchy–Schwarz inequality. Substituting these bonuses into the expression for the agent's action and then into the principal's payoff, the expression for the total surplus from arbitration becomes

$$S^{\text{ARB}} = \frac{1}{2}\,\frac{(\boldsymbol{w}'\boldsymbol{w})\,(\boldsymbol{x}'\boldsymbol{y})^2 - 2\,(\boldsymbol{x}'\boldsymbol{w})\,(\boldsymbol{x}'\boldsymbol{y})\,(\boldsymbol{w}'\boldsymbol{y}) + (\boldsymbol{x}'\boldsymbol{x})\,(\boldsymbol{w}'\boldsymbol{y})^2}{(\boldsymbol{x}'\boldsymbol{x})\,(\boldsymbol{w}'\boldsymbol{w}) - (\boldsymbol{w}'\boldsymbol{x})^2}\,. \qquad (2.16)$$

How does this compare with the surplus, found in (2.12), achievable using the state civil law alone? The difference provides an upper bound to the extra cost the parties would be willing to pay for having access to the arbitration forum. After some tedious algebra, we find

$$S^{\text{ARB}} - S^{\text{CRT}} = \frac{1}{2}\,\frac{[\,(\boldsymbol{x}'\boldsymbol{w})\,(\boldsymbol{x}'\boldsymbol{y}) - (\boldsymbol{x}'\boldsymbol{x})\,(\boldsymbol{w}'\boldsymbol{y})\,]^2}{(\boldsymbol{x}'\boldsymbol{x})\,[(\boldsymbol{x}'\boldsymbol{x})\,(\boldsymbol{w}'\boldsymbol{w}) - (\boldsymbol{w}'\boldsymbol{x})^2\,]}\,. \qquad (2.17)$$

This is always non-negative, and can be zero only if the expression in the square brackets in the numerator is zero. To understand this benefit of arbitration a little further, use (2.15) to note that

$$S^{\text{ARB}} - S^{\text{CRT}} \sim (\omega^{\text{ARB}})^2\,.$$

Thus arbitration yields a positive benefit when, and only when, the optimal contract governed by arbitration uses the bonus payable upon realization of the indicator

---

[6]This also tells us how the procedure can be generalized to allow multiple performance measures of each kind.

verifiable only to the arbitrator at a non-zero level. This seems trivial except for one word, namely non-zero: ω does not have to be positive. Using the normalization (2.9), we see that the sign of ω is the same as the sign of

$$\boldsymbol{w}'\,[\,\boldsymbol{y} - (\boldsymbol{y}'\boldsymbol{x})\,\boldsymbol{x}\,] = \boldsymbol{w}'\,[\,\boldsymbol{a}^{\mathrm{FB}} - \boldsymbol{a}^{\mathrm{CRT}}\,]\,,$$

using (2.13). Thus the extra bonus instrument available to the principal under arbitration is useful to the extent that the vector of effects of actions on the newly verifiable measure w is aligned with the vector by which action under court enforcement alone would fall short of the first best. If the two vectors are positively aligned, a positive bonus in the event $w = 1$ serves to move action in the right direction; if negatively aligned, negative. Only if $\boldsymbol{w}$ is orthogonal to the action shortfall is arbitration no better than court enforcement.

The intuition can be completed by asking how the availability of the new performance measure w changes the bonus awarded on the basis of the publicly verifiable measure x. Using (2.10) and (2.15), we find

$$\xi^{\mathrm{ARB}} - \xi^{\mathrm{CRT}} = -(\boldsymbol{w}'\boldsymbol{x})\,\omega^{\mathrm{ARB}}\,.$$

If the effects of action on the two variables are positively aligned, then the two measures are substitutes—for example, if the new bonus is used with a positive magnitude, its availability reduces the magnitude of the old bonus. This is again similar to the theory of omitted variables in econometrics.

When the gain in surplus from arbitration is positive, the size of this gain is an upper bound on the cost of arbitration that would still leave a positive net gain. Of course it remains to structure a game with fully specified moves and division of the net gains that will lead the parties to choose this route, but that is quite easy to do so I omit it.

The general finding is that arbitration based on its information advantage works well in conjunction with the formal legal system; the two may be said to be complementary to each other. This may explain why the law takes such a benign view of arbitration, respecting its verdicts and even standing ready to enforce them. It may also offer a good approach to the development of formal institutions in less-developed countries and transition economies. These can start with a minimal state law that promises to enforce the judgments of arbitration tribunals. At the early stages of this process, the government should encourage such forums to develop rules and procedures using their information advantage. Gradually, the state law can take over these rules and the courts can take over some of the functions of the arbitrators. The emerging systems of commercial law in European states similarly adopted and enforced the practices evolved by the private adjudicators of "the law merchant" (Milgrom, North, and Weingast 1990). This seems to have occurred despite the fact that private arbitrators do not have the incentive to provide a public good to society, or even to their own profession, by creating rules and precedents (Landes and Posner 1979). Rubin (1994) discusses and advocates such a process for former socialist countries.

2.5   Assessment and Prospects

This chapter has considered methods of private ordering of contractual interactions, and the relationship between these private methods and state law. The general idea was that private methods can better use information that is available to the parties but cannot be proved in a state court at an acceptably low cost.

The chapter opened with a brief overview of some empirical studies of such private ordering institutions and organizations; later sections built mathematical models to study specific aspects of them in greater depth. Now we can look back on the chapter as a whole, assess what the modeling has accomplished, and identify the needs of future research.

I modeled two types of private ordering: self-enforcing long-term relationships, and arbitration by specialized third parties. Modeling always involves making assumptions—who takes what action and with what information, the payoffs as functions of the actions, and so on. Many of these are harmless simplifications. For example, I considered a principal–agent type of interaction, but this can encompass many business relationships including outsourcing and employment. Some results of the models depended crucially on the agent's actions being multidimensional, but this is a desirable feature taking the models closer to reality, not farther from it.

An important purpose of the modeling was to relate the methods of private ordering to state law and to each other. The link between relational and formal contracts arises because recourse to the courts offers an alternative if the relationship breaks down. This led to the unfortunate result that a partial improvement in the functioning of the state law made it more attractive to renege on the relational contract and thereby worsened the outcome of private ordering. By contrast, arbitration could supplement or complement state law by allowing more complete contracting without detracting from the ability of the courts to resolve issues based on publicly verifiable information.

I did not model the interaction between arbitration and relationships, but that is not a hard exercise for interested readers. One model of this kind in a somewhat different setting will appear in Section 4.3; another is in Milgrom, North, and Weingast (1990).

The modeling also yields some useful byproducts. The model of relational contracts in Section 2.3 is a simplification of the well-known model of Baker, Gibbons, and Murphy (1994, 2002). This may enable others to use it to model other or more complex questions on relational contracting. The model of Section 2.4 shows the relationship between additional verifiable information and the realizable surplus in a principal–agent interaction. In many contexts, verifiability of information is endogenous. For example, an auditing or monitoring system can be installed or improved at a cost, to make verifiable some information that was previously only observable to the insiders or even private to one of the parties.[7] The model allows us to compute the benefit from this, and also identifies the precise kind of information that would be most useful, namely, the information that is best correlated with the residual left after using the previously available information. This can help the state law, or any alternative private governance method, improve its information structure and therefore its usefulness.

Formal modeling has thus deepened and sharpened our understanding of each of these modes of private ordering, and of their connections with state law. However, illustrating the general point made in Section 1.8, these advantages come at a cost. Each institution has a rich and multidimensional structure. Theoretical models, to be tractable, must select a narrower set of issues and dimensions to analyze in depth, and simplify or even ignore others. For example, in the model of relational contracts in Section 2.3, the two parties were involved in only one interaction. In reality, such pairs often simultaneously interact in several dimensions, including not only business dealings but also social meetings. Private governance can sometimes advantageously use this multiplicity to create punishments in one dimension to deter cheating in another. Bernheim and Whinston (1990) developed the theory of such games, and we see them in action among the industries studied by Bernstein (1992, pp. 140, 141; 2001, p. 1750).

My model of arbitration involved even more drastic narrowing and simplification. I focused on just one aspect of this institution, namely the ability of specialized industry arbitrators to interpret information at lower cost, making more information verifiable and allowing more complete contracting. However, arbitration occurs in other contexts for other reasons, most importantly in international trade to avoid suspicions of the bias of national courts; my model did not cover this at all. Neither did the model incorporate the variety and other prominent features of arbitration that have been observed. For example, Bernstein (2001, p. 1733) observes that the rules of arbitration are of the simple "bright-line" kind, avoiding general terms of common law like "reasonable". Mattli (2001) emphasizes that the institutions of arbitration differ in the degrees of centralization and formality. At one extreme, arbitration can be institutional or centralized, using a preexisting organization or arbitration center with formalized rules and procedures that guide the conduct of, and supervise, the arbitrators. At the other extreme, arbitration can be ad hoc, not relying on such a formal administration or center, and using adjudicators chosen for the purpose by the parties to the dispute. The latter offers more flexibility, but less accuracy

---

[7]Endogeneity of verifiability can go in the opposite direction in other contexts. For example, a blackmailer can be regarded as making a promise to the victim, in exchange for a payment, to make a compromising item of information unverifiable.

and enforceability. So disputes that have a greater degree of uncertainty about the traders' behavior have to go to more centralized forums. But disputes in areas where the underlying circumstances change rapidly may benefit from more flexible ad hoc forums. Centralized forums also have the advantage of better enforceability, because they can disseminate information about any misbehavior more quickly and widely, and can better arrange sanctions such as denial of future trading opportunities. Therefore parties to disputes with serious potential problems of enforcement have to use more centralized methods. Parties with long-term ongoing relationships can more easily use flexible and ad hoc methods. Such issues of the relative merits of different kinds of arbitration, and of the choice among different forums, will need other models.

There is always the risk that the aspects simplified or omitted in theoretical modeling interact in significant ways with those the model is trying to focus on. Therefore modeling involves judgment, which may turn out to be wrong. This calls for continued testing of the results, both by looking for empirical evidence supporting or contradicting the results, and by enlarging the scope of the model. In the latter activity, the understanding of concepts and techniques gained from the original model play an important part. In other words, known or suspected deficiencies of a model should be regarded, not as arguments for condemning modeling as such, but as opportunities and challenges for further research. I hope the readers will be stimulated to undertake some of this.

2.6 Mathematical Appendix

This gives details of some arguments sketched in the body of the chapter, and generalizes some of the modeling.

2.6.1 Relational and Formal Contracts

This subsection contains the mathematical details that were omitted in Section 2.3. These pertain to the principal's choice of the formal and relational bonus coefficients ξ and η to maximize his profit subject to the incentive constraint. The Lagrangian is

$$
\begin{aligned}
\mathcal{L} &= \Pi(\xi, \eta) + \lambda \, [\, \Pi(\xi, \eta) - r\,\eta - \Pi^{\text{Ext}} \,] \\
&= (1 + \lambda) \, \Pi(\xi, \eta) - \lambda\,r\,\eta - \lambda\,\Pi^{\text{Ext}} \\
&= (1 + \lambda) \, [\, \Pi(\xi, \eta) - \mu\,r\,\eta - \mu\,\Pi^{\text{Ext}} \,] ,
\end{aligned}
\tag{2.18}
$$

where I have defined $\mu = \lambda / (1 + \lambda)$. Given the direction of the inequality in the constraint, the Lagrange multiplier λ must be non-negative. Therefore μ must satisfy $0 \leqslant \mu \leqslant 1$.

The first-order conditions for the maximization can then be written as

$$K - \xi - K \eta = 0 \,,$$

$$1 - K \xi - \eta - \mu r = 0 \,.$$

These yield

$$\left. \begin{array}{l} \xi = \mu r K / (1 - K^2) \,, \\[2mm] \eta = (1 - K^2 - \mu r) / (1 - K^2) \,. \end{array} \right\} \qquad (2.19)$$

Note that this is not quite the solution, because the μ on the right-hand side has still not been solved for. For that, we first substitute for ξ and η to express the constraint in terms of μ. After some algebraic simplification, this becomes

$$\frac{(1 - 2r)(1 - K^2) + (2\mu - \mu^2) r^2}{2(1 - K^2)} - \frac{K^2}{2} \geqslant 0 \,. \qquad (2.20)$$

The derivative of the left-hand side with respect to μ equals $r^2 (1 - \mu)/(1 - K^2)$, which is positive for all $\mu \in (0, 1)$, so the left-hand side is an increasing function of μ throughout its range.

When $\mu = 0$, the left-hand side equals $(1 - 2r - K^2)/2$. This is non-negative if $1 - K^2 \geqslant 2r$, that is, in region FB of Figure 2.2. Therefore in this region, the Kuhn–Tucker conditions are automatically satisfied when the multiplier on the incentive constraint equals zero. That corresponds to the first best, confirming our previous analysis of the credibility of the first best.

Next consider the case where $1 - K^2 < 2r$, which corresponds to the set of points to the right of OF in Figure 2.2. Evaluate the left-hand side of (2.20) at $\mu = 1$. This simplifies to

$$(r + K^2 - 1)^2 / (1 - K^2) \,,$$

which is always non-negative, and zero only if $1 - K^2 = r$. Thus the constraint is just met at $\mu = 1$ when $1 - K^2 = r$, which is shown as the line OS in Figure 2.2. This line divides the area to the right of OF into two regions, which are labeled SB and FRML. In both of these regions, the expression on the left-hand side of (2.20) is strictly positive when $\mu = 1$. Since the expression is negative at $\mu = 0$ in these regions, and increasing for $\mu \in (0, 1)$, it equals zero for exactly one μ in this range. That positive μ, together with the constraint satisfied as an equation, fulfills the Kuhn–Tucker conditions and completes the solution.

The constraint equation can be written as

$$r^2 (\mu^2 - 2\mu) = (1 - K^2)^2 - 2r (1 - K^2) \,.$$

Adding r^2 to both sides completes squares:

$$r^2 (\mu - 1)^2 = (1 - K^2 - r)^2 \,.$$

The signs of the square roots must be chosen differently in the two regions SB and FRML to ensure $0 < \mu < 1$ in each. This gives

$$\mu = \begin{cases} (2r + K^2 - 1)/r & \text{if } r < 1 - K^2 < 2r \text{ (region SB)}, \\ (1 - K^2)/r & \text{if } 1 - K^2 < r \text{ (region FRML)}. \end{cases} \tag{2.21}$$

Finally, the solution for μ can be substituted into the expressions in (2.19) to complete the solutions for ξ and η. In region SB we have

$$\left. \begin{aligned} \xi &= K\,(2r + K^2 - 1)/(1 - K^2), \\ \eta &= 2\,(1 - K^2 - r)/(1 - K^2). \end{aligned} \right\} \tag{2.22}$$

As K^2 the accuracy of the external signal increases, which corresponds to a movement vertically downward in Figure 2.2, it is easy to see that η decreases and ξ increases. At the northwest extreme of region SB (along the line OF), where the first-best relational outcome just stops being feasible, $1 - K^2 = 2r$. Substituting this in (2.22), we do indeed get $\eta = 1$ and $\xi = 0$. At the southeast extreme, along the line OS, we have $1 - K^2 = r$. Substituting this in (2.22), we get $\eta = 0$ and $\xi = K$, which is the best purely external contract.

The intuition is the same as the previous explanation in region FB of why an increase in K makes the first best infeasible: by increasing the value of the reversion situation, it tightens the incentive constraint on the relational part of the contract based on the accurate internal measure. This has an implication for the payoffs, too. Writing Π^{SB} for the principal's payoff and $W^{SB} = \Pi^{SB} + u_0$ for the social surplus in the second best of region SB, we have

$$\begin{aligned} \frac{dW}{dK} &= \frac{d\Pi^{SB}}{dK} \\ &= \frac{\partial \mathcal{L}}{\partial K} \text{ at the optimum, by the envelope theorem} \\ &= (1 + \lambda)\,\frac{\partial}{\partial K}[\,\Pi(\xi, \eta) - \mu r \eta - \mu \Pi^{\text{Ext}}\,] \\ &= (1 + \lambda)\,\frac{\partial}{\partial K}[\,(K\xi + \eta) - \tfrac{1}{2}\,(\xi^2 + 2K\xi\eta + \eta^2) - \mu r \eta - \tfrac{1}{2}\mu K^2\,] \\ &= (1 + \lambda)\,[\,\xi - \xi \eta - \mu K\,], \end{aligned}$$

where I have used the expressions for the Lagrangian in (2.18) and for the principal's payoff in (2.4). Substituting the expressions for ξ and η in terms of μ from (2.19) into this, the sign of the derivative we seek is the same as the sign of

$$\mu K \left[\mu \left(\frac{r}{1 - K^2} \right)^2 - 1 \right],$$

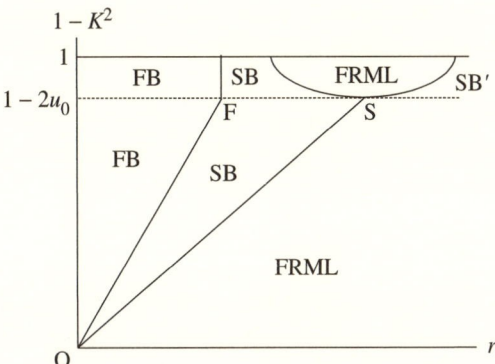

Figure 2.3. Optimal formal and relational contracts—general cases.

which is negative since $0 < \mu < 1$ and $r < 1 - K^2$ in region SB. Thus an increase in the accuracy of the external measure reduces the payoff from the incentive-compatible second-best contract that uses the internal measure.

In region FRML, substituting the solution for μ into (2.19) yields $\eta = 0$ and $\xi = K$; thus the best purely external contract is used throughout this region. The resulting payoffs—$\Pi^{\text{Ext}} = \frac{1}{2} K^2 - u_0$ to the principal and $W^{\text{Ext}} = \frac{1}{2} K^2$ for the social surplus—of course increase as K increases, finally reaching back to the first-best levels on the bottom boundary of region FRML, the horizontal axis, where $K = 1$.

I conclude this section with a brief statement of what happens when $K^2 < 2 u_0$, omitting the mathematical details. In this case, if the principal refuses to pay the relational bonus η, the relationship collapses and the parties revert to their outside opportunities, where the principal's payoff is zero. Therefore his incentive constraint is no longer (2.6), but instead

$$\Pi(\xi, \eta) - r \eta \geqslant 0.$$

Carrying out the same kind of constrained optimization as before, we find different outcomes for various combinations of r and $1 - K^2$. These are shown in Figure 2.3, and the new cases are in the horizontal strip that gets added above the regions replicated from Figure 2.2. If $r < \frac{1}{2} - u_0$, the first-best relational contract is incentive compatible. To the right of this region we have a second-best outcome, with a mixture of formal and relational bonuses. To its right comes a region where no relational bonus is feasible, and the formal contract is used. However, for very high discount rates, a new and different kind of second best, labeled SB$'$, emerges. It becomes possible to sustain a relational contract where the relational bonus is negative and the formal bonus is large and positive. This leaves the principal with no incentive to renege, and the combination is sufficiently attractive to the worker that he does not wish to walk out. Since the formal bonus is based on an inaccurate measure, such a payment scheme would not be desirable in general. But if the outside opportunity is sufficiently bad, it may be a poor second best, and that appears to be the case here. However, I think this is not of much practical significance. Note that a similar possibility does not arise when $1 - K^2 < 1 - 2u_0$, when the formal contract provides a better outside alternative.

2.6.2 Arbitration and Information

This subsection extends the arbitration model of Section 2.4 to allow more general functional forms for the probabilities and a more general structure of bonuses, to clarify the role of stochastic independence of the two performance measures and the nature of the extra information that can be used under arbitration.

The agent's action $\boldsymbol{a}$ is an n-dimensional vector as before. But now the agent's cost of action $C(\boldsymbol{a})$ is a general function, as are the probabilities for the principal's outcome

$$\text{Prob}(\, y = 1 \mid \boldsymbol{a}\,) = Y(\boldsymbol{a})\,,$$

and the performance measures

$$\text{Prob}(\, x = 1 \mid \boldsymbol{a}\,) = X(\boldsymbol{a})\,,$$
$$\text{Prob}(\, x = 0,\ w = 1 \mid \boldsymbol{a}\,) = W(\boldsymbol{a})\,,$$
$$\text{Prob}(\, x = 1,\ w = 1 \mid \boldsymbol{a}\,) = B(\boldsymbol{a})\,,$$
$$\text{Prob}(\, x = 0,\ w = 0 \mid \boldsymbol{a}\,) = 1 - X(\boldsymbol{a}) - W(\boldsymbol{a})\,.$$

These functions are assumed to be twice-differentiable and subject to all the second-order conditions of maximization in the calculations below.

A special case of some interest is when, conditional on $\boldsymbol{a}$, the two indicators x and w are stochastically independent. The condition for this stipulates that, given $\boldsymbol{a}$,

$$\text{Prob}(\, w = 1 \mid x = 1\,) = \text{Prob}(\, w = 1 \mid x = 0\,)\,,$$

or

$$\frac{B(\boldsymbol{a})}{X(\boldsymbol{a})} = \frac{W(\boldsymbol{a})}{1 - X(\boldsymbol{a})}\,.$$

This simplifies to

$$B(\boldsymbol{a})\,[1 - X(\boldsymbol{a})] = X(\boldsymbol{a})\,W(\boldsymbol{a})\,. \tag{2.23}$$

(Equating the two probabilities for x conditioned on different realizations of w leads to the same condition.)

First Best

The joint surplus from the relationship is

$$S = Y(\boldsymbol{a}) - C(\boldsymbol{a}) \, .$$

The first-order condition defining the first-best action $\boldsymbol{a}^{\text{FB}}$ to maximize S is

$$\nabla Y(\boldsymbol{a}) = \nabla C(\boldsymbol{a}) \, , \tag{2.24}$$

where ∇ denotes the gradient of a function—the (column) vector of its partial derivatives. I assume that the resulting first-best joint surplus S^{FB} exceeds the sum of the two parties' reservation payoffs, namely u_0; otherwise the whole relationship would be irrelevant.

As in the linear-quadratic case of the text, the first best can be achieved if y is verifiable, by offering the agent a contract consisting of a salary s plus a bonus equal to 1 to be paid if $y = 1$.

Court-Enforced Contract

The state legal system or official court can verify only x. Then, as in the linear-quadratic case of the text, the most general available form of the contract stipulates payment to the agent in the form of an unconditional salary s, and a bonus ξ to be paid if $x = 1$. Then the agent's utility will be

$$U = s + \xi \, X(\boldsymbol{a}) - C(\boldsymbol{a}) \, .$$

The agent's utility-maximizing choice of $\boldsymbol{a}(\xi)$ is characterized by the first-order condition

$$\xi \, \nabla X(\boldsymbol{a}) = \nabla C(\boldsymbol{a}) \, . \tag{2.25}$$

To find the comparative static derivative of $\boldsymbol{a}(\xi)$ to ξ, differentiate (2.25) totally:

$$[\, \nabla^2 C - \xi \, \nabla^2 X \,] \, \mathrm{d}\boldsymbol{a} = \nabla X \, \mathrm{d}\xi \, ,$$

or

$$\frac{\mathrm{d}\boldsymbol{a}}{\mathrm{d}\xi} = [\, \nabla^2 C - \xi \, \nabla^2 X \,]^{-1} \, \nabla X \, , \tag{2.26}$$

where the operator ∇^2 applied to a function denotes the n-by-n matrix of the second-order partial derivatives of that function, and the points of evaluation $\boldsymbol{a}(\xi)$ are omitted for brevity. The matrix within the square brackets on the right-hand side of (2.26) is positive definite by the second-order condition of the agent's utility-maximization problem.

The principal chooses s and ξ to induce effort $\boldsymbol{a}$ so as to maximize his profit

$$\Pi = Y(\boldsymbol{a}(\xi)) - [\, s + \xi \, X(\boldsymbol{a}(\xi)) \,] \, ,$$

subject to the agent's participation constraint $U \geqslant u_0$. To meet this, the principal sets

$$s = u_0 - \xi \, X(\boldsymbol{a}(\xi)) + C(\boldsymbol{a}(\xi)).$$

Substituting for s, the principal's objective function becomes

$$\Pi = Y(\boldsymbol{a}(\xi)) - C(\boldsymbol{a}(\xi)) - u_0. \tag{2.27}$$

Observe that when s is chosen as a function of the principal's other instruments to satisfy the agent's participation constraint, the principal's objective becomes fully consistent with social optimality. The only question is how well the available instruments can affect the agent's action. This is the theme of much of the later analysis.

The first-order condition for the choice of ξ to maximize Π is

$$0 = [\nabla Y - \nabla C]' \, d\boldsymbol{a}/d\xi$$
$$= [\nabla Y - \nabla C]' \, [\nabla^2 C - \xi \, \nabla^2 X]^{-1} \, \nabla X. \tag{2.28}$$

The right-hand side in (2.28) is an n-by-1 (column) vector. If $n = 1$ (effort $\boldsymbol{a}$ is a scalar), the right-hand side of (2.28) reduces to a product of three scalars, of which the last two are non-zero. Therefore the condition becomes $\nabla Y = \nabla C$, which is the first best. The intuition is that the single bonus variable ξ suffices to control the scalar effort $\boldsymbol{a}$. At least it does so locally. There remains the question of global controllability, namely of whether the range of the function $\boldsymbol{a}(\xi)$ includes the first best $\boldsymbol{a}^{FB}$. Very little that is useful can be said about this with general functional forms; therefore I do not pursue this.

Arbitration

Now introduce an arbitrator who can verify the outcome of w. Since x remains publicly verifiable, the two players can condition their contract on the realizations of both x and w. This opens up the possibility of three distinct bonus payments in addition to the salary s:

$$\xi \quad \text{if } x = 1,$$
$$\omega \quad \text{if } x = 0 \text{ and } w = 1,$$
$$\beta \quad \text{if } x = 1 \text{ and } w = 1.$$

Let $\boldsymbol{v}$ denote the 3-by-1 column vector of the bonus payments ξ, ω, and β in that order.

I assume that the official legal system is available to enforce the arbitrator's decision, backed by the power to levy sufficiently large penalties. Therefore such contracts are binding. An alternative would be to leave the arbitrator's decision subject to relational governance in a repeated interaction, along the lines of the analyses in Baker, Gibbons, and Murphy (1994, 2002). I leave this case for future research.

With this, the agent's expected utility is

$$U = s + \xi\, X(\boldsymbol{a}) + \omega\, W(\boldsymbol{a}) + \beta\, B(\boldsymbol{a}) - C(\boldsymbol{a}).$$

The agent's choice of action is characterized by the first-order condition

$$\xi\, \nabla X(\boldsymbol{a}) + \omega\, \nabla W(\boldsymbol{a}) + \beta\, \nabla B(\boldsymbol{a}) = \nabla C(\boldsymbol{a}). \tag{2.29}$$

This can be written in the form

$$\left(\nabla X(\boldsymbol{a}) \;\vdots\; \nabla W(\boldsymbol{a}) \;\vdots\; \nabla B(\boldsymbol{a}) \right) \boldsymbol{v} = \nabla C(\boldsymbol{a}),$$

where the partitioned matrix on the left-hand side is n-by-3 (consisting of three horizontally stacked n-by-1 column vectors), and the vector multiplying it is 3-by-1, yielding an n-by-1 matrix to match the size of the vector on the right-hand side. The condition defines the agent's action as a function $\boldsymbol{a}(\boldsymbol{v})$ of the vector of bonuses $\boldsymbol{v}$. Its comparative static derivative can be found by total differentiation:

$$\frac{d\boldsymbol{a}}{d\boldsymbol{v}} = \left[\nabla^2 C - \xi\, \nabla^2 X - \omega\, \nabla^2 W - \beta\, \nabla^2 B \right]^{-1} \left(\nabla X \;\vdots\; \nabla W \;\vdots\; \nabla B \right). \tag{2.30}$$

The matrix in the square brackets on the right-hand side is n-by-n, and is positive definite by the second-order condition of the agent's utility-maximization problem. The left-hand side, being the derivative of an n-dimensional function of a three-dimensional variable, is an n-by-3 matrix. All the gradients, etc., are evaluated at $\boldsymbol{a}(\boldsymbol{v})$.

The principal must now choose s and $\boldsymbol{v}$ to maximize Π. Subsuming the agent's optimal choice of $\boldsymbol{a}$, the participation constraint yields

$$s = u_0 - \xi\, X(\boldsymbol{a}(\boldsymbol{v})) - \omega\, W(\boldsymbol{a}(\boldsymbol{v})) - \beta\, B(\boldsymbol{a}(\boldsymbol{v})) + C(\boldsymbol{a}(\boldsymbol{v})).$$

Then

$$\begin{aligned} \Pi &= Y(\boldsymbol{a}(\boldsymbol{v})) - [\, s + \xi\, X(\boldsymbol{a}(\boldsymbol{v})) + \omega\, W(\boldsymbol{a}(\boldsymbol{v})) + \beta\, B(\boldsymbol{a}(\boldsymbol{v})) \,] \\ &= Y(\boldsymbol{a}(\boldsymbol{v})) - C(\boldsymbol{a}(\boldsymbol{v})) - u_0. \end{aligned}$$

The first-order condition for the choice of $\boldsymbol{v}$ to maximize this is

$$\begin{aligned} 0 &= [\, \nabla Y - \nabla C \,]'\, d\boldsymbol{a}/d\boldsymbol{v} \\ &= [\, \nabla Y - \nabla C \,]' \left[\nabla^2 C - \xi\, \nabla^2 X - \omega\, \nabla^2 W - \beta\, \nabla^2 B \right]^{-1} \\ &\qquad\qquad\qquad\qquad \times \left(\nabla X \;\vdots\; \nabla W \;\vdots\; \nabla B \right). \end{aligned} \tag{2.31}$$

The third factor on the right-hand side is an n-by-3 matrix. Suppose $n = 3$ (the agent takes three actions). Suppose also that the partitioned matrix

$$\left(\nabla X \ \vdots \ \nabla W \ \vdots \ \nabla B \right),$$

which is now 3-by-3, is non-singular. The inverse matrix in the middle of the right-hand side is positive definite. Therefore the condition (2.31) reduces to $\nabla Y = \nabla C$, which is the condition for the first best. Subject to the problem of global controllability, about which little useful can be said for general functional forms, we see that in this case the first best is attainable. Thus arbitration can expand the range of principal–agent interactions for which the first best is feasible.

The partitioned matrix

$$\left(\nabla X \ \vdots \ \nabla W \ \vdots \ \nabla B \right),$$

is non-singular if the vectors ∇X, ∇W, and ∇B are linearly independent, and in the present context these derivatives should be evaluated at the first-best action a^{FB}. How does this linear independence relate to the stochastic independence of the indicators x and w? The condition for the latter is (2.23). Taking logarithms and differentiating, we have

$$\frac{1}{B} \nabla B - \frac{1}{1 - X} \nabla X - \frac{1}{X} \nabla X - \frac{1}{W} \nabla W = 0. \qquad (2.32)$$

For any given $\boldsymbol{a}$ where all these functions and gradients are evaluated, this gives us a linear dependence relation linking the vectors ∇X, ∇W, and ∇B. Thus, if x and w are *stochastically independent*, then the vectors of the marginal effects of the action on the three probabilities are *linearly dependent*. The partitioned matrix has rank (at most) 2. One of the three bonuses is redundant (it can be constructed out of a suitable combination of the other two), and the two independent bonuses that are available cannot control the agent's three-dimensional action fully.

It may seem paradoxical that the additional indicator w that can be verified by the arbitrator is more valuable when it is not stochastically independent of the publicly verifiable x. The apparent paradox is resolved by recognizing that it is precisely the absence of independence that provides extra information from the event where both x and w equal 1. This creates an extra dimension or degree of freedom that can be used to improve the structure of the bonuses.

3

Relation-Based Contract Enforcement

3.1 Issues and Empirical Research

The purpose of institutions and mechanisms of economic governance is to induce individuals to take cooperative or honest actions that achieve and sustain mutually beneficial outcomes in their economic interactions, countering the temptation of each individual to take opportunistic or cheating actions that promote his interest at the expense of the aggregate good. Similar issues arise in other fields, most prominently in evolutionary biology. Dugatkin (1999, pp. 17–27) gives a four-fold classification of the approaches to cooperation: (1) kin and family selection; (2) direct reciprocity; (3) selfish teamwork; and (4) group altruism.

The first of these is inherently biological. Each individual is genetically programmed to follow a specific behavioral strategy (phenotype), and natural selection favors the fitter genes, namely those that get higher reproductive payoff from the interactions over resources, mates, etc. But that does not imply individually selfish behavior. If a phenotype will engage in self-sacrifice to save n others when it shares a fraction f of the relevant genes with each of them, and $f\,n > 1$, then this strategy will work to the net benefit of the shared genes.

The other three of Dugatkin's pathways have more immediate economic relevance. Selfish teamwork arises in assurance games, where it is in the interest of each person to take the jointly desirable action if, but only if, the others do likewise. Such games have multiple equilibria, one where all take the jointly desirable action and another where none do. Then the players need a way to select the better of the two equilibria. For this, they must create common knowledge, or jointly held expectation, of the necessary actions, that is, they must make it a focal point. This is much easier than resolving a prisoner's dilemma, where each person wants to take the selfish or deviating action even if all others are taking the jointly desirable or compliant action.

Direct reciprocity is the case most conducive to resolving prisoners' dilemmas. In it, the same two (or more) players repeatedly play the dilemma game. Evidence from case studies in economics, politics, sociology, anthropology, and biology, and game-theoretic analysis, have given us a good understanding of the mechanisms for accomplishing good outcomes, and the conditions under which they succeed. A very elementary version of the theory was sketched in Section 1.7. More advanced theory was pioneered by Abreu (1986) and Abreu, Pearce, and Stacchetti (1990), and a textbook exposition is in Osborne and Rubinstein (1994). Important case studies include those of Ostrom (1990) on provision of public goods and management of common property resources (CPRs) in many groups and societies across many countries.

All successful mechanisms, in theory as well as in practice, work by creating a future cost to the individual of taking an action that brings him an immediate personal benefit. The nature and the size of the cost can vary widely across different situations; the common requirement is that the future cost should outweigh the immediate benefit in the individual's own calculation based on his own preferences, whether for material things, social standing, internal guilt, or whatever.

Theory and case studies agree on several of the desiderata for successful resolution of prisoners' dilemmas by direct reciprocity. First and foremost, the players should have sufficient regard for the future. If the payoffs are monetary, this requires a low interest rate at which the future is discounted. If the payoffs are subjective, it requires the players to be more patient. But an even more potent force that reduces the importance of the future in the players' minds is uncertainty about continuation of the relationship. Therefore successful resolution of multi-person dilemmas, like the ones in most case studies, requires a stable group: members should not be able to exit after deviating from the cooperative action, and newcomers who are not part of the agreement should not be able to enter. Second, any deviation should be detected quickly and accurately, and in multi-person dilemmas, the news of deviation by one member should be transmitted quickly and accurately to all. Then the prescribed punishment can be meted out to the miscreant equally quickly and accurately. The speed is important: otherwise the punishment would become more distant in time and get discounted more heavily in a potential miscreant's calculation. The accuracy is also important: if punishment may be unleashed in error even if one has not deviated, then the deterrent effect is lessened. Third, in multi-person dilemmas, participation in the collective action of punishing a miscreant is sometimes individually costly; this turns the punishment process into another prisoner's dilemma game requiring its own resolution.

Ostrom (1990, pp. 183–186) summarizes how these requirements are implemented in practice:

> in the smaller-scale CPRs [where] individuals repeatedly communicate
> and interact with one another in a localized physical setting, ... [they]
> learn whom to trust, ... [and] develop shared norms and patterns of
> reciprocity.

The general method is to

> make contingent commitments to follow rules that (1) define a set of appropriators who are authorized to use a CPR, (2) relate to the specific attributes of the CPR and the community, (3) are designed, at least in part, by local appropriators, (4) are monitored by individuals accountable to local appropriators, and (5) are sanctioned using graduated punishments.

Item (1) in this list pertains to the need for a stable group, and items (2)–(4) pertain to the speed and accuracy of detection of any cheating and spread of the information around the group. The emphasis on the importance of local knowledge and information networks is noteworthy.

Theory and case studies are agreed on most of these points, with an important exception. In the theory of repeated games, punishments are usually drastic and long lasting, like the grim-trigger strategies in Section 1.7. The argument is that the harshest feasible punishments best deter deviating actions, and therefore sustain an equilibrium with the most cooperative outcome. In reality, however, graduated punishments fare better. This is item (5) in Ostrom's list, and it is supported by the findings of other case studies like Ellickson (1991, pp. 53, 57). The intuition is that one player may inflict occasional harm on others through inattention or miscalculation rather than deliberate deviation. Then a friendly notification, and an opportunity to make restitution, will remedy the situation without triggering the collapse of mutually beneficial future compliance with the tacit agreement. Only if the deviation persists should it be interpreted as deliberate and lead to harsher punishments. While some models of repeated games with imperfect monitoring, for example Fudenberg and Maskin (1986), can be interpreted as suggesting graduated punishments, to my knowledge there is no explicit treatment of this in the theoretical literature. Some of this literature is also restricted in its practical applicability, because it focuses on the limiting case where the players are extremely patient (the so-called folk theorem).

Given the advantages of direct reciprocity when it comes to sustaining cooperation, we should expect that traders will try to sustain good bilateral relationships, and that is indeed the case. For example, Hendley and Murrell (2003) surveyed firms in the transition economy of Romania, and gave weighted scores to the importance these respondents attached to various mechanisms that support their transactions. Almost 56% of the weight was on bilateral mechanisms ("personal relationships and trust", and "relying on each other's own incentives").

However, in many economic situations, each member of a group plays the dilemma game against different others at different times. For example, a seller may meet different buyers at different times, and any one buyer of a durable good does not meet the same seller at all frequently. Thus almost half of the weight in the Hendley–Murrell survey went to non-bilateral mechanisms, and in turn half of that was on the kinds of non-state mechanisms that are the focus of this book ("third-party social or business relationships" and "using private dispute-resolution services"). Thus Lawlessness and Economics addresses a substantial issue in transition economies and less-developed countries.

Greif (1993, 1994) studies groups of traders, each of whom needs to consign goods to others to sell on his behalf, and needs different partners at different times. Outside the context of trade, Ensminger (1992, Chapter 4) studies relationships between cattle owners and their herders. While these relationships are reasonably long lived, herders leave to marry or for other work. Therefore each owner will employ several herders over his lifetime. The cattle must travel to grazing grounds far from home. To supervise the hired herders and ensure they take good care of the cattle and do not steal, the owners try to maintain at least one close relative in the cattle camp (Ensminger 1992, p. 116). But they also develop complex patronage or even paternalistic relationship with non-relatives (Ensminger 1992, pp. 117, 121), and include a large back-loaded part in the herder's compensation. Of course the owner may then want to renege on this payment; his compliance is ensured by his reputation consideration since he will want to hire other herders in the future (Ensminger 1992, pp. 119–121). Also, if the owner misbehaves, the social norms among the Orma allow the employee herders to retaliate, including shirking and even selling his cattle (Ensminger 1992, pp. 119, 120). Notice how the governance system uses a mixture of methods to achieve cooperation: rewards and punishments in cases of direct reciprocity, and social norms in group interactions. Ellickson (1991) studies a group of farmers in northern California; the cattle of one might encroach upon the land of another and cause damage, and different pairs may be involved in such a situation at different times. Again, attempts are made to resolve disputes bilaterally first; if that fails, the aggrieved party can spread negative gossip about the miscreant and invoke social sanctions.

Johnson, McMillan, and Woodruff (2002) present empirical work based on survey data of firms from several former socialist economies in eastern Europe, and other similar findings from Vietnam. They used questionnaires and interviews to gather information about

(1) characteristics of the firm—activity, size, competition, membership of trade association;

(2) relationships with main customers—prior information, duration, frequency, switching cost, payment arrangements and trade credit, disputes and their resolution, spread of information about disputes; and

(3) the firms' belief in the efficiency and fairness of the state courts.

A brief summary of their findings is as follows.

(1) Even in countries where courts are believed to function well, relational contracting based on repeated interactions is used extensively. (Actually, the "shadow of the law" idea explored in Chapter 2 says this is true of all countries including the United States.)

(2) Prior information is important in assessing risk and offering credit in a new relationship.

(3) Trust builds up quickly in bilateral relationships in response to good experiences.

(4) Relational contracting works better if customers' switching costs are high. (The intuition derived from one-shot or short-term games says that high switching costs should make the hold-up problem more serious, but in long-term ongoing relationships, worsening the outside option can lead to a better equilibrium of the game.)

(5) If it is believed that courts work well, new customers or ones with low switching costs are more likely to be offered credit.

(6) However, effectiveness of courts is irrelevant to the functioning of established relationships.

The last point was discussed at the end of Section 2.3. Many of the others await theoretical modeling.

In the rest of this chapter I will focus on the theoretical problems of sustaining cooperative outcomes in groups where pairs of traders have little direct reciprocity. In such situations, if Player A deviates for an immediate gain in his dilemma game with Player B, the probability of his meeting B in the future is likely to be too low for direct reciprocity to be effective. This adds some further necessary conditions for the achievement of a cooperative in all games played by pairs in the group. A's current cheating can give rise to a future cost for him only through his interactions with other people C, D, ..., in the group. For this, (1) the information that A cheated B has to be conveyed to C, D, ..., and (2) these others have to find it in their personal interest to take the actions that have the effect of punishing A for his having cheated B. An interesting example of the importance of information and enforcement of multilateral sanctions comes from Guinnane (1994), who attributes to these factors the success of agricultural credit cooperatives in nineteenth century Germany and the failure to transplant them to Ireland in the early twentieth century.

Of the two conditions, the second can be problematic because the only way to inflict the cost on A may be for others to forgo their mutually beneficial interactions with him. In other words, punishment may be a collective-action problem, which is another multi-person prisoner's dilemma. In theory, this can be resolved by stipulating equilibrium strategies where compliance means not only taking the mutually beneficial actions in the first place, but also taking the appropriate punishment actions in response to anyone's deviation. In other words, failure to participate in a punishment is itself a deviation. In reality, such solutions are buttressed by people's instincts to punish, even at a personal cost, others who cheat on an explicit or implicit social contract. Fehr and Gächter (2000) present evidence of such behavior. We can understand it conceptually in terms of Dugatkin's (1999, pp. 22, 23 and Chapter 4) fourth pathway, namely group altruism. Groups that successfully instill such preferences in their members, for example by socialization and education, will achieve good outcomes and succeed in their competition with other groups who do not attempt similar socialization or education of their members. More generally, this can explain many instances found by behavioral economists where individual behavior differs from that predicted by economic theories based on purely selfish preferences (Camerer 2003, especially Sections 2.1 and 2.7). Going even farther, Wright (2000) argues that the ability to achieve jointly desirable outcomes in non-zero-sum games is the key to evolutionary success in humans.

Fulfillment of the first of the two conditions, namely the transmission of information, depends on the size of the group, the network of contacts among them, and the technology of communication. These issues constitute the major theme of the rest of this chapter.

The additional problems posed by the lack of direct bilateral reciprocity can be avoided if pairs within the group who experience a successful initial meeting can arrange to continue meeting each other. Ghosh and Ray (1996) develop a model of such cooperation without information flows. They consider a heterogeneous population where some people are so impatient that they will cheat in any play of the dilemma game, whereas others are sufficiently patient to sustain a cooperative outcome in a repeated relationship with another patient player. The type of a partner cannot be identified in advance. Ghosh and Ray investigate the possibility of an equilibrium where a patient player will choose the compliant action when playing a new partner, and if this reveals the partner to be patient, the pair will continue their bilateral interaction. The value of doing so is greater the larger is the fraction of impatient players in the population, because that worsens the expected payoff from the alternative available to each of the patient players in the pair, namely trying to form a new relationship with another random player. We expect that in any group such possibilities of direct reciprocity will be exploited to the extent possible. But there are limits to this: death, retirement, or relocation may break up existing partnerships, and change or expansion of business may require the formation of new ones. Therefore it is important to study the issues of cooperation in groups where pairs meet at random without direct reciprocity, and examine whether and how the information networks can work to achieve a cooperative outcome.

Theoretical work on this was initiated by Kandori (1992), and further developed by Ellison (1994). They analyze a process of contagion, where a player who is the victim of an episode of cheating "loses trust" and starts to cheat in his own future interactions. Someone contemplating the first deviation from a cooperative situation must then recognize the possibility that this spread of cheating will infect his own future partners. I will consider an explicit process of communication where the victim spreads the information to others.

Communication flows better in networks that are connected by ties of business (Bernstein 1992, 2001), ethnicity (Rauch 2001), and so on. Another important factor is the size of the group. Intuition suggests that communication networks will weaken as the size of the group increases. Both formal theoretical modeling and case studies support this. Ostrom (1990, pp. 188, 189) finds that a small size is an important condition for successful resolution of collective-action dilemmas.[1] Large groups can overcome the disadvantage, but this requires special arrangements such as the construction of hierarchies of smaller groups. Bernstein (1992) describes a similar hierarchy of bourses of diamond traders.

3.2 Relation-Based and Rule-Based Governance

If information flow in a group is sufficiently good, a cooperative outcome may emerge automatically as an equilibrium of the repeated game of random pairwise matchings. Otherwise, the group has to seek other institutions of governance, and these may include more formal court-like organizations. Ensminger (1992, Chapter 6) describes this process among the Orma tribe in Kenya. A system of consensus-based rule by councils of local elders is giving way to one where a chief is appointed by the national government, acts more like a civil servant, and uses the official instruments and powers of the state. This pertains to the settlement of social disputes, but presumably similar changes are occurring in the governance of economic transactions.

Greif (1994, 1997) offers especially interesting contrasting studies of two groups with different internal enforcement systems, and correspondingly different sustainable sizes. Maghribi traders, who relied on multilateral group governance, could not expand the scope of their operations. Genoese traders, who used a more bilateral system with formal governance, fared better as trading opportunities expanded. Greif's theoretical models are system specific, and we need a model that can encompass both if we are to understand the reasons for their different outcomes, how the

---

[1] This is a somewhat different game than that of pairwise matching from a large group, but the issues of information transmission are similar.

limits of the self-governing system are determined, and what happens at intermediate sizes of groups. That is the aim of the formal model I will construct in this chapter.

One might think that modern technology has improved information flows to perfection. Indeed, eBay has developed a good system where buyers give ratings to sellers and vice versa, and each transactor can check the average rating of the person with whom he is contemplating doing business. However, this too has its limits, and as eBay has expanded, it has found it necessary to institute more formal methods to prevent fraud (McMillan 2002, pp. 78, 79).

The above discussion suggests that a system based on voluntary information flows and self-enforcing equilibrium works for small or well-knit groups, whereas large groups need more formal institutions of information dissemination and enforcement. Li (2003) offers an explanation based on differences that arise in the costs of systems of the two types as the scale of the group is increased. Self-enforcing "relation-based" groups face rising marginal costs: members added at the margin are almost by definition less well connected, making it harder to communicate information with them and to ensure their participation in any punishments. Formal or "rule-based" governance has high fixed costs of setting up the legal system and the information mechanism (disclosure rules and auditing procedures), but once these costs have been incurred, the marginal costs of dealing with strangers are low, and may even decrease. Therefore the total costs of the relation-based system will be smaller at small sizes, and those of the rule-based system will be smaller at large sizes. This makes intuitive sense, but for a deeper understanding one must make more precise the way in which diminishing returns or rising marginal costs set in as a relation-based system grows larger. This is also necessary to understand what happens at intermediate sizes.

Relation-based governance works well in small groups that are connected by extended family relationships, neighborhood structures, and ethno-linguistic ties, because such links facilitate repeated interactions and good communication. This idea is similar to the sociologists' concept of embeddedness (Granovetter 1985). Economists recognize the importance of family and social networks in less-developed economies, but often regard them as being unimportant in modern advanced economies, and therefore ignore them in that context. Granovetter argued that the differences are much less sharp than is commonly thought, and criticized the New Institutional Economics from this perspective. The persistence of relational arrangements under the shadow of the law in advanced economies is now well recognized, and Chapter 2 provides some models of it. However, the analysis of this chapter shows that relation-based governance does indeed lose its relative efficacy as the scale of economic transacting grows. This supports the usual economic distinction as a matter of degree, if not as a sharp dichotomy between less-developed and advanced economies.

3.3 Limits of Relation-Based Governance

A model that can pose and answer the question of how diminishing returns set in and limit the size of a self-governing community needs several features. First, there must be a concept of size, which can then be varied to examine the consequences of so doing. Next, there must be a concept of closeness or distance between people in the community, to capture the intuition that people in a larger community will on average be less close to others. Finally, there must be some potential economic benefit of having a larger community; otherwise the whole issue of whether successful economic governance is possible in a large community would be moot.

To fulfill these requirements, I construct a model where the traders are a continuum distributed along a circle. The units are so chosen that the density of traders per unit arc length is 1. Interactions between any pair of traders must travel a route along the shorter of the two arcs of the circle connecting them. Let $2S$ denote the circumference of the circle; then for any one trader, the most distant other trader, namely the diagonally opposite one, is located a distance S away. Thus S measures the size of the community.

The circle stands for the spectrum of any relevant socioeconomic differences, not only or necessarily geographical ones. Thus the differences among traders could be in any one of several dimensions. Some example are resource endowment, including different types of land, labor, physical or human capital; different technologies; differences of geography and climate; and ties or differences of kinship, ethnicity, language, culture, or religion. The circle is of course a specific way to model these, but the general intuition for the results that emerge from the model is robust, and I will comment on this when discussing the main results.

Meetings, Communication, and Trade

Each trader is randomly matched with another in two separate time periods, the first representing the present and the second the future. The future creates the possibility of punishment that can sustain honesty in the present. The matches are independent across time. This creates the need for an information-transmission mechanism whereby others in the community may find out about the cheating of any one of them. In reality, traders will try to sustain bilateral relations so as to be able to sustain honesty by direct reciprocity. But there are also many economic situations where repeated bilateral interactions are rare, and in others there is the risk of bilateral relationships being severed because one of the partners has to move, or retires, or dies. Therefore theory should examine situations where the person you trade with in the future is not the same as the one you contemplate cheating now, and independent matches are the simplest way to model this.

The random matchings have a local bias. One is more likely to meet a closer neighbor than a more distant one. Specifically, I assume that for any one trader in each period, the probability of meeting another trader decreases exponentially with the distance x between them. Let α be the rate of decay of this probability with distance. Then the actual probability is equal to

$$\frac{e^{-\alpha x}}{2\,[\,1 - e^{-\alpha S}\,]\,/\,\alpha}.$$

The denominator is just a normalizing factor to ensure that the probabilities of matches at all distances between 0 and S on either side of any one trader sum to 1.

The parameter α captures the matching technology. The smaller is α, the less localized the technology. In the limit as α tends to 0, the distribution of matches tends to uniformity over the whole circle. Localization is a realistic assumption, even in the Internet age. Any one trader may post information about himself on the web, but a match requires someone to check this site. A search engine will typically find thousands of potential sites, and people, being constrained by time, will select the ones they have some familiarity with, namely ones local to them. However, the assumption has a different restrictive aspect, namely that I am leaving such a process of search in the background and specifying the probabilities exogenously in a reduced form. This, and the negative exponential function, are needed for tractability, but it would be an interesting research challenge for the future to endogenize the search and matching process.

While one is less likely to meet more distant traders, the potential gain from dealing with them is larger. Specifically, I assume that the gains from trade increase exponentially with distance, and θ is the rate of this increase. The parameter θ can be thought of as reflecting the idea of comparative advantage in trade theory. Consider some examples related to the distance concepts listed above. If the space is socioeconomic, with traders located according to the ratio of land to labor they possess, then a landowner will benefit more from meeting someone who primarily owns the complementary input, labor, than from meeting another landowner. If the distance reflects differences in technology or knowledge, an electrical engineer will stand to gain more from meeting another engineer with a complementary technology, for example a mechanical or chemical engineer, than from meeting another electrician. Geographical and climatic differences enable people to grow different crops and trade to benefit from variety in consumption. In some other respects, for example local public goods or goods for which tastes are culture specific, interaction may be more beneficial the more similar the partners are; this is like sociocultural items in that list. Such trades will unambiguously best be carried out using automatic self-governance in small communities of similars. But governance of global

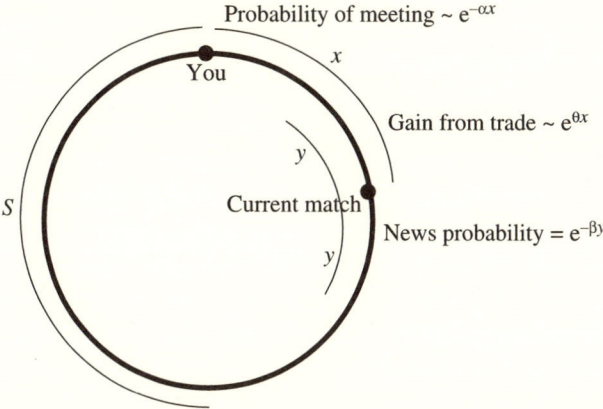

Figure 3.1. Locations, matches, and information transmission.

trade is regarded as an important concern in the real world; therefore there must be significant transactions whose potential benefits rise with expansion of the scope of trade. My focus is on those transactions. Again, the exponential form is special, but the qualitative results are unaffected by this choice.

Finally, there is localization of information. If a trader cheats his first-period match, then the probability that a third person located at a distance y from the victim of this cheating finds out in time for action in a possible second-period match is exponential with a rate of decay β, that is, $e^{-\beta y}$. The parameter β is a feature of the communication technology. The choice of negative exponentials is special, but natural. If one thinks of a chain of contact and communication with a probability p that the victim will inform his immediate neighbor, and that neighbor will inform his next neighbor, and so on, then a geometric or negative exponential form will result.

As with matching, information technology reduces the magnitude of the problem (lowers β) but does not eliminate it. Indeed, the problem of information transmission may have been replaced by that of information overload. A recent Google search for "cheat or cheating" produced about 2 110 000 results. The searcher has to narrow this down, and is likely to do so on the basis of nearness to him in an appropriate (geographic, economic, or social) sense. Thus the assumption of localization of information continues to make sense even in the Internet age.

Figure 3.1 illustrates the various concepts. What are the plausible relative magnitudes of the three parameters α, β, and θ? First, $\theta > 0$ is important for the existence of gains from expanding the scope of trade. Next, we need $\alpha > \theta$ for convergence of expected values when S is large. To simplify some later notation, I define $\lambda = \alpha - \theta > 0$. Finally, if the technologies of transportation and communication are intrinsically linked, then α and β will have similar values and will shift together.

At one time, meeting and communication were literally the same thing. Even in the Internet age, face-to-face meeting and communication remain important, and the World Wide Web itself is a common medium for matching and communication activities, so we should expect β and α to have similar values. This is not maintained as an assumption; I will use it to guide our thinking about alternative logically possible cases of results. In specific contexts, econometric analyses similar to those of Conley and Udry (2001) on technology transmission could be used to estimate these parameters.

In each period, when two traders are matched, they decide whether to trade in the light of what they know about each other. Each always knows the other's location (and therefore the distance x between them); in addition, each may have heard about any past cheating by the other. I assume that the players are otherwise symmetric and their game is a prisoner's dilemma, so its payoff matrix is $e^{\theta x}$ times a basic matrix like Table 1.2 in Section 1.7.

Equilibrium

The set-up should suggest an immediate intuition about the resulting equilibrium. If a trader cheats his current partner, he gets an immediate gain as usual in the prisoner's dilemma. The potential cost is that his future partners may hear of this, in which case they will refuse to play with him. The option of not playing is what helps sustain cooperation even though the horizon is only two periods long; the idea was explained in Section 1.7.

While the idea is simple, to translate it into the formal set-up of game theory requires some further technical work. Some of it is in the mathematical appendix (Section 3.6); further details including numerical solutions can be found in Dixit (2003b). This section gives only some basic intuitions and simple formulas.

The localization of information and communication leads to a corresponding localization of honesty: equilibria of the game are characterized by a distance X, which I call the extent of honesty, such that in the first period of trading, a matched pair will behave honestly if, and only if, they are closer to each other than X. The intuition is that cheating becomes more attractive the more distant the partner. Consider the various effects of cheating a current partner who is farther away from you. First, the immediate gain is larger because payoffs increase with distance. Next, the current partner's location does not affect the distribution of distances of people you may meet the next period. However, it does affect the probability that these future matches will have heard of your cheating. By the localization of matches and information, if you cheat someone farther away from you, the news is less likely to reach potential future partners closer to you, and they are the ones you are more likely to meet in the future. Therefore the likelihood of losing those trades, and therefore the expected future cost of cheating, is smaller when the current partner is farther away. A countervailing effect is that the news is more likely to reach some traders who are farther from you, and trades with them are more valuable. But the probability of meeting them decays faster than the value of the trade increases. The overall result is that the net benefit from cheating increases with the distance between you and your current partner. Therefore the structure of equilibria, where people behave honestly with others within a certain distance of themselves, is quite intuitive.

Note the nature of the localization of honesty. It is not the case that the world splits into a number of disjoint communities, such that each of them can sustain honest dealing between any pair of its own members but honesty is infeasible if two traders from two different communities meet. Rather, we have overlapping neighborhoods of honesty. Consider an example where the extent of honesty is three villages. Suppose B lives two villages away from A, and C lives two villages away from B in the same direction, so C lives four villages away from A. Then a meeting between A and B will result in honest trade, as will a meeting between B and C, but not a meeting between A and C.

As usual in such games, there can be multiple equilibria, each characterized by its own X and sustained by its own expectations—if everyone believes that honesty is possible only over a small neighborhood, then they will expect matches outside this small neighborhood to cheat and will therefore cheat themselves. But I will give the self-enforcing system its best shot by focusing on the largest X that can be an equilibrium. Call this the "extent of honesty," and to make explicit its dependence on the size of the circle S, write it as a function $X(S)$. Of course the extent of honesty depends not only on S, but also on all the other parameters that went into the specification of the model—the meeting and communication parameters α and β, and the rate of gain from trade expansion, θ. Some of these are considered later. But perhaps the most interesting question is: when is it possible to have honesty over the full circle, that is, $X(S) = S$? Let us begin by calculating the gains from such honesty.

Gain from Expanding the Scope of Honest Trade

Social benefits arise when honest trade is sustained in period-1 matches. Leaving aside the multiplicative factor for the excess payoff from mutual honesty over mutual cheating in the prisoner's dilemma, the size of this gain is given by the probability that a trader is matched with another within the extent of honesty, that is

$$V(X, S) = \frac{\alpha}{2\,(1 - e^{-\alpha S})}\, 2 \int_0^X e^{-\alpha z}\, e^{\theta z}\, dz$$

$$= \frac{\alpha}{\alpha - \theta}\, \frac{1 - e^{-(\alpha - \theta) X}}{1 - e^{-\alpha S}}.$$

This is increasing in X for any fixed S, and decreasing in S for any fixed X.

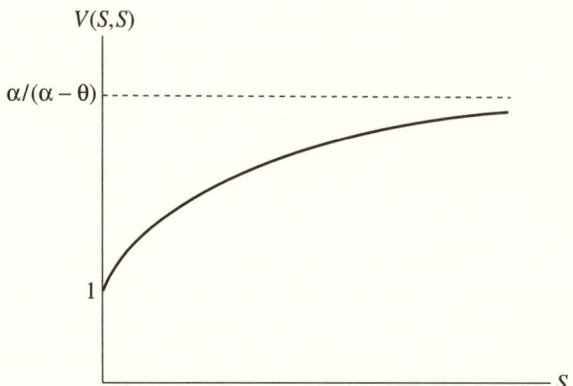

Figure 3.2.   Benefits of sustaining honesty over larger circles.

In particular, the benefit from sustaining honest trading over the whole community in all first-period trades is given by

$$V(S, S) = \frac{\alpha}{\alpha - \theta} \frac{1 - e^{-(\alpha-\theta) S}}{1 - e^{-\alpha S}}. \tag{3.1}$$

Figure 3.2 shows this function. Note that $\theta > 0$ is important for it to be increasing, and $\alpha > \theta$ for convergence as S increases.

The Limits of Honest Trade

The localization of matches and information suggests that honesty over the full circle ($X(S) = S$) should be possible for small S but not for large S. That is indeed true: there is an S^* (which in turn depends on the other parameters α, β, and θ) such that honesty over the full circle is possible for $S < S^*$ but not when $S > S^*$.

The results of the model thus far have been sensible but unsurprising given the localization assumptions that were built into its structure. But next comes what is perhaps the most interesting and non-obvious finding from this model: for plausible parameter values, as S increases beyond S^*, the extent of honesty $X(S)$ decreases.

The intuition for this is seen from Figure 3.3. The circle on the left is of critical size S^*. Therefore a trader located at O, when meeting another at P, is indifferent between honesty and cheating. The circle on the right is somewhat larger: $OP_1 = OP_2 = S^*$, with added people between. If O meets P_1 and cheats, the probability that P_2 finds out is now less than 1; whereas it was equal to 1 before. So the cost of cheating has decreased. The larger is β, the bigger this effect, because then the news-transmission probability decays faster. But if O cheats P_1, he risks that any period-2 meetings he may get with the new traders located between P_1 and P_2 may become unproductive if they have heard of his cheating P_1. This effect is bigger the larger is θ (because

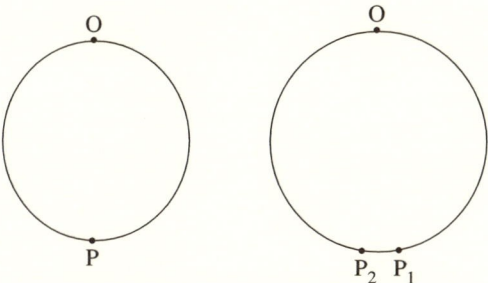

Figure 3.3. Effects of increase in S beyond S^*.

then the potential gains from these meetings are bigger) and/or the smaller is β (because then the probability of news transmission to these traders is higher).

The balance of the two effects depends on β and θ. If β is large relative to θ, the first effect will be stronger and $X(S)$ will decrease as S increases beyond S^*. Numerical calculations (Dixit 2003b) show that the former effect dominates for the plausible ranges of the parameters, so $X(S)$ decreasing is the plausible case. Specifically, $\beta > \theta$ is an overly sufficient condition for $X(S)$ to be decreasing. And we see from the discussion of the parameters as they were introduced that $\beta \approx \alpha > \theta$ is the plausible case.

What happens when S gets very large? The answer again depends on β. If this is not too large, then the declining $X(S)$ asymptotes to a positive level X^*, which can be called the extent of honesty in a large world. But if β exceeds a critical level that depends on the other parameters, then $X(S)$ hits zero for a finite S, so honesty can collapse totally in a large world.

To sum up, Figure 3.4 shows a typical $X(S)$ for the plausible case where the function is decreasing beyond S^* and asymptotes to a positive level.

The decline of honesty as the size of the world grows beyond the limit of global self-governance was explained intuitively using Figure 3.3. This makes it appear crucially dependent on the assumption that the traders are located along a circle. However, the general idea behind the picture is much more robust. All we need is that people have a limited capacity for processing information, with the result that, faced with the information overload available in this Internet age, they choose to look at what is coming from local sources that are known to them. Take any other structure of spatial location, for example a disc in two dimensions or a sphere in three dimensions, and consider a trader, call him A, located at a boundary of this. All of his available contacts are somewhere inside the disc or the sphere, and are starting links in a chain of communication that leads to another trader B. Now let the space expand, so A becomes interior to the new bigger disc or sphere, and his contacts get redistributed. Some of the older contacts will become weaker or wither away, and be replaced by new contacts with new neighbors in the added regions of

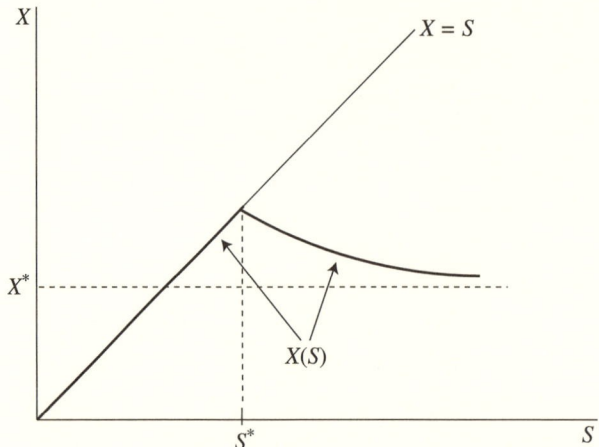

Figure 3.4.   Best equilibrium X as a function of S.

the space. Some of these new contacts may become part of a new chain that reenters the old part of the space and leads to the same old B. But these new paths travel through the added outer regions of the space. They must therefore be on average longer than the old ones, and therefore information will travel less well from A to B than it did before. In other words, any two traders in the original trading world will become less well connected as the world expands. This will lead to the same kinds of results as the circle.

Next, how do these critical magnitudes S^* and X^* depend on the parameters α, β, and θ? Intuitively, a decrease in β, by reducing the localization of communication, should increase the extent of honesty. The effects of the other parameters are less clear. The mathematical details are in the appendix (Section 3.6).

Perhaps unsurprisingly, numerical calculations show that the equilibrium depends most sensitively on the information-localization parameter β, in the sense that lowering β has a larger effect on the size S^* of the largest honestly self-governing community than an equal decrease in the other parameters. This conforms to the empirical observations of Ostrom (1990) and others about the importance of communication in groups and networks.

External Enforcement

In this section I compare the self-enforcing governance analyzed so far, and the alternative discussed by Li (2003), namely formal or official rule-based governance. Suppose that at a cost c per unit of arc length along the circle, any cheating can be detected and the information made available to future traders. This should be thought of as an auditing or monitoring system, which future traders can consult to find out their potential partners' histories. This could be a credit-history agency

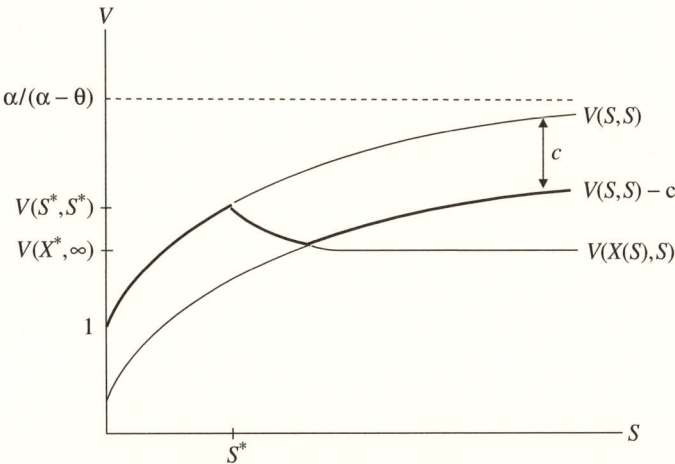

Figure 3.5. Optimal enforcement modes in different-size worlds.

or a trade association set up by the group of traders, or a state legal system. To give this alternative its best chance (just as I gave the self-governance system its best chance by focusing on the maximal possible X, namely $X(S)$), I will assume that it is implemented benevolently to maximize the representative trader's payoff. I will assume that the detection system covers the whole circle, and that its costs are recovered from the traders by levying a lump sum charge c on each of them. (Remember that the mass of traders per unit arc length has been normalized to 1.) Under this system, when the semi-circumference of the circle is S, the payoff for each trader will be $V(S, S) - c$, where the function V is defined by (3.1).[2]

How does such a system of external enforcement compare with the self-enforcement system studied in the previous sections? To make the comparison, let us first find the payoff under self-enforcement as a function of S. When $S \leqslant S^*$, self-governance is possible over the full circle, yielding payoff $V(S, S)$ to each trader. When S increases beyond S^*, in our plausible case the maximum feasible extent of honesty $X(S)$ decreases. Then the payoff $V(X(S), S)$ decreases since $V(X, S)$ is increasing in its first argument and decreasing in its second argument. Eventually the payoff falls to $V(X^*, \infty)$.

Figure 3.5 compares the two payoff functions. The figure shows the gross and net payoffs from external enforcement; these are the two parallel curves $V(S, S)$ and $V(S, S) - c$. It also shows a falling curve for self-enforcement beyond S^*, starting

---

[2]The system of rule-based governance in my model has no fixed cost and a constant cost per unit length; therefore it has constant returns, rather than increasing returns as suggested by Li (2003). If I allowed a fixed cost F, the average cost of the rule-based system would be $F/S + c$, and its net payoff would be $V(S, S) - F/S - c$. This would not affect the qualitative picture of Figure 3.5 or the results. Readers can similarly experiment with other assumptions about the cost of the rule-based system.

at $(S^*, V(S^*, S^*))$ and going to $(\infty, V(X^*, \infty))$. The thick curve in three separate segments is the payoff function that arises from choosing the better of the modes of enforcement for each S.

When $S \leqslant S^*$, self-enforcement is globally effective, and saves the detection cost c, so it is obviously superior to external governance. Beyond S^*, there is an interval where the payoff from self-enforcement falls below the gross payoff $V(S, S)$ from external enforcement but remains above the net payoff $V(S, S) - c$ of that system. Thus self-enforcement no longer works over the whole circle, but external enforcement is not yet cost-effective. So long as the condition

$$c < V(\infty, \infty) - V(X^*, \infty) = \frac{\alpha}{\alpha - \theta} - V(X^*, \infty)$$

is satisfied, the rising curve $V(S, S) - c$ for external enforcement and the falling curve $V(X(S), S)$ for self-enforcement eventually cross. Beyond that point, external governance is preferable. However, its eventual payoff $V(\infty, \infty) - c$ may or may not climb back up to $V(S^*, S^*)$, the best possible payoff under self-governance. It will do so if c is not too large, specifically, if

$$c < V(\infty, \infty) - V(S^*, S^*) = \frac{\alpha}{\alpha - \theta} - V(S^*, S^*).$$

If this is not the case, then it is preferable (if it is feasible) to split up a large world into smaller self-contained circles of size S^* each.

In other words, small communities can achieve full self-governance using their own information systems and do not need external governance. In very large communities, the benefits that are available from trade with distant partners can only be realized by instituting a system of external governance at a cost. Communities of an intermediate size fare worst: they are too large for self-governance but too small for external governance. When an expanding economy reaches the size where external governance becomes just cost-effective, "it is darkest just before the dawn" for it. However, even very large communities with external governance may or may not be better than the optimal-sized self-governing small communities.[3]

3.4   Related Theoretical Models

The motivation for the model of the previous section came from observations on the limits of self-governance. The general idea of explaining this using localization of contacts and information dissemination was clear and intuitive, but that left the freedom to choose several specifics of the model. I made and analyzed one such

---

[3]To put this more precisely, the function composed of the thicker segments in Figure 3.5 has two local maxima, one at S^* and the other at ∞, either of which may be the global optimum depending on the parameters. The function has a local minimum at the point where the payoff curves for the self-governance and external enforcement modes cross; its global minimum is at $S = 0$.

set of choices; others have made other choices. Here I summarize some of these models, and their similarities and differences to mine.

Kranton (1996) constructs a model in which individuals can choose between bilateral repeated interactions, which must be self-enforcing, and an anonymous market, which requires each trader to search for a partner, but does not have enforcement problems. The market is the outside opportunity that defines the incentive compatibility constraint for the former. If more people choose the market, it is thicker and offers better prospects for search. This tightens the incentive-compatibility constraint for bilateral relationships and therefore makes it harder to sustain self-enforcing cooperation in them. Conversely, if more people engage in reciprocal bilateral exchange, the market is thinner, bilateral exchange can be sustained more easily, and offers higher payoff. Either system can prevail in equilibrium even when it is socially less efficient.

The model of Bowles and Gintis (2000) is closer to mine. They consider disjoint networks, which are like islands in a sea of an anonymous market. The members of each network trade only among themselves. The larger is a network, the higher is the probability of finding a trading partner, but the worse is the signal about his past behavior. They find the equilibrium and optimal size of a network. They have a richer specification of search and information flow within a network. They allow no information flows between a network and the market, yet migration can take place into and out of a network. By contrast, I do not have disjoint networks but overlapping neighborhoods of honesty for each trader. Both trade and information can go across these neighborhoods. I can also examine the effect of changing the size of the world as a whole.

Calvert (1995a,b) models communication by stipulating an equilibrium in which each trader is required to report to all others the identity of his current partner and the outcome of their trade. Failure to report is itself a deviation from equilibrium and brings on the punishment. This is necessary because reporting is costly and victims would otherwise not supply this public good to the group. However, it vastly raises the cost of the mechanism, because in a well-functioning system, trades with good outcomes constitute the vast majority of all trades. Instead, I rely on the natural tendency of victims to complain to their neighbors, and theirs to pass on the gossip along the network. This is a probabilistic mechanism that decays with distance, but that is also realistic.

Fafchamps (2002) considers traders each of whom is connected to a subset of the others by a network of contacts, which allows information about the history of a trader to disseminate to others over time. His focus is on the dynamic process by which spontaneous order may emerge, not on comparing different systems of governance. Kali (2002) uses random graph theory to model clustering with self-governing local interaction versus a market with arms-length interaction. The distinction depends on a "complexity parameter" that measures the randomness of connections between pairs of nodes in the graph. His assumptions about the process of search are questionable, but the mathematical techniques he develops are promising.

3.5   Assessment and Prospects

To some extent, the formal model of Section 3.3 succeeds very well. It improves our understanding of how information transmission becomes less good as the size of the group expands. It gives us the limits of global self-governance in terms of parameters that capture the efficacy of the technologies of matching and communication. We see that in communities that are too large for full self-governance, there emerge neighborhoods that can sustain honesty in dealings among people sufficiently close to each other. And the model goes beyond what it was rigged to do—the results about intermediate sizes getting the worse of both governance modes, and the anti-globalization possibility, are new and not immediately intuitive.

The model invites some unusual and speculative applications. One such pertains to the problem of the decline of civil society in the United States and some other modern societies, which has been much discussed and lamented following Putnam (2000). The kinds of links that are supposed to have frayed or disappeared—churches, charities, local social and business associations like Rotary Clubs—serve many purposes. Among other things, they provide the contacts and information networks, and repositories of social norms and sanctions, which make it possible for individuals to build reputations, and for the society to achieve self-governance in economic transactions. The model suggests that as economies become larger and more globalized, such self-governance must eventually give way to formal rule-based governance. Then the communal networks lose some of their purpose, and their relative decline becomes understandable. If this is true, then at least from an economic perspective the decline of civil society may be less damaging. To quote Sobel (2002), "[t]he jobs of social capital are getting done in other ways." Of course, I recognize the complexity of the phenomenon, and would not regard this economic explanation as contributing more than a small and speculative part of its explanation.

More broadly, the model makes only a little headway into a rich and complex reality, leaving room for a great deal of further research. As usual, the issues ignored in the first theoretical pass at the problem are ones of multiple dimensions and dynamics. Many groups and networks perform multiple functions, of which search and matching are especially important. Rauch (2001) emphasizes this in the context of ethnic networks; other networks that facilitate such market making include bourses, exchanges, and industry associations (Bernstein 1992, p. 119). These functions can interact with the governance function studied here. For example, terminating a miscreant's membership in a group or network constitutes a harsher punishment if that reduces the efficacy of his search for trading partners. Therefore joint models of search and governance may yield some further insights and results.

Next, the model of this chapter obtains and compares equilibria for different sizes S of the community; thus the analysis of varying S is an exercise in comparative statics, not dynamics. But in practice, the size S increases in real time, and the parameters α and β decrease as the technologies of matching and communication improve. Dynamics brings in numerous other considerations—history dependence, expectations, and so on. It introduces a process of reputation-building, and strategies such as front-loaded or back-loaded payments to improve compliance. Bilateral relationships may be embedded in group interactions, and strategies may emerge to help sustain one using punishments available in the other. In Section 3.1 I mentioned some empirical and case studies bearing on these matters; theoretical exploration of these issues is largely open.

In the rest of this section I will focus on just one aspect of dynamics. Growth, and expansion of the scope of trade, will bring a shift from relation-based to rule-based governance, but this will be a slow transition. The two systems will coexist and interact, creating other problems. Here is a brief discussion of some of these issues, intended to serve as a source of ideas for future theoretical research.

Some Implications about Relation-Based Systems

Businesses in a relation-based system will expand at those margins where diminishing returns set in most slowly. This will mean preserving the closeness of the relation, even at the cost of undertaking a new activity that is not economically so close—not such a good complement in production or consumption. In other words, in such a system we will see diversified conglomerates whose component parts have nothing in common except common ownership by a closely knit extended family or similar network. One does indeed see such hodgepodge family empires in many less-developed countries, for example India and Turkey. The South Korean *chaebol*, and the Japanese *zaibatsu* and their successor *keiretsu*, are also cases in point. Even in advanced industrial countries with rule-based governance, there are incentives to build diversified conglomerates—tax systems with double taxation of dividends make it costly to take profits out of the corporate sector and therefore artificially lower the cost of reinvesting retained earnings, and agency problems allow top management to indulge in its taste for running large empires. But in smaller and less-developed countries where relation-based governance prevails, the incentives to expand into seemingly unrelated activities are that much stronger.

Another way to express this is to say that a relation-based system has a larger benefit of internal finance from the supply side. This benefit is usually looked at from the demand side—the needs of a firm's finance for investment are met at lower cost from retained earnings than from external borrowing. But here the point is that the return to retained earnings is higher if reinvested within the firm than is possible from investments in external markets.

Where borrowing and lending between different firms and their owners occurs, it will tend to be within some identifiable group defined by links that enable enforcement of implicit contracts based on reputation. This suggests that the "crony capitalism" that is observed in many less-developed countries (and condemned by outsiders) may have its place within their governance structure. Of course you deal with, and lend to, cronies. Non-cronies may defraud you and run away with your money; having no relation with them, you would have no recourse. Rubin (1994, p. 15) points out that similar "crony socialism" existed under the central planning systems in socialist economies, and continued in the transition period.

But this compartmentalization of capital markets has a cost; it constrains the movement of capital to its most productive uses in response to changing conditions. Therefore it comprises another source of diminishing returns for the relation-based system. Transition to a rule-based system would allow more efficient reallocation of capital to take advantage of productive opportunities outside the group.

Finally, although a relation-based system has low *fixed* costs, it can have large *sunk* costs—the reputational capital that makes time-separated transactions credible has to be built up, and is valuable. The combination of large sunk costs, and the small size of the economy where relation-based governance usually prevails, can create high entry barriers. Therefore one should expect to see high concentrations, or even monopolies, in such systems. That is indeed observed, not only in finance and production, but also in trade (see Ensminger 1992, p. 27).

Obstacles to Transition

As an economy expands or as its trade with other countries grows, a point will come when the present value of the social benefits of shifting toward a more rule-based governance will exceed the costs of the required investment. But the switch need not occur at the optimal point. There are many reasons why the political and economic realities will delay the shift.

First and foremost, the fixed costs of rule-based governance are a public investment; therefore society must solve a collective-action problem to put such a system in place. This is not automatic; there are the usual problems of free riding, underestimation of the benefits to future generations in today's political process, and the veto power held by those who stand to lose from the change.

Even when the public investment for a rule-based system has been made, people used to the relation-based system who want to switch must make some private investments to learn the rules and their operation. Their benefit from the switch will depend on how many others make the switch. This positive feedback externality can lead to too few switchers, or even a lock-in that keeps the old system in use.

In turn, the expectation of this can reduce the social benefits of the changeover and therefore delay or deter the initial public investment.

The benefits of the new system may be unequally distributed, and some participants may even lose. The reputational capital in the relation-based system is an asset that would become worthless in a pure rule-based system, so incumbents stand to lose from the change and will therefore resist it by political means. The currently successful businesspeople and financiers, who are almost by definition the heaviest users of the existing relation-based system, are also usually active participants in the political process, and adept at marshaling their special interests in an organized way. They can also stall and frustrate a government's attempts at reform.

The system of rules and their enforcement itself must at first establish a reputation for integrity and efficacy. This takes a long time and strict supervision even given much good will. The questionnaire work of Johnson, McMillan, and Woodruff (2002) shows the great difficulties experienced by the governments of most transition economies in their attempts at such reputation-building.[4] In many countries, the attempts of the top levels of the government at making and enforcing reliable governance systems can be ruined by some middle-level officials who attempt to make quick profit from their newfound power. There are evident problems of this kind in most transition economies. Also, we saw in Section 2.3 that in the phase when the system of rules is imperfect but improving, it can offer better outside payoffs to the participants in the prevailing relation-based system. By thus increasing their incentives to cheat their current partners, it can worsen the outcomes of the relation-based system.

These issues may go some way toward explaining Rodrik's (2003, p. 17) finding that

> [t]he policies required to initiate a transition from low-income equilibrium to a state of rapid growth may be qualitatively different from those required to reignite growth for a middle-income country. At low levels of income, with reasonable institutions and reasonable policies, it may be easy to achieve high growth up to semi-industrialization. But the institutional requirements of reigniting growth in a middle-income country can be significantly more demanding.

In terms of the model of this chapter and the discussion of dynamics above, the difference can be understood as follows. Growth starting from a low level can be achieved using relation-based governance in small communities of traders with good relationships and information networks, so long as the state does not actually

---

[4]In a different context, see Berger (1997) for an account of the process, involving some accidents, by which the German Bundesbank acquired its reputation for independence and for its anti-inflation monetary policy.

inhibit such developments with its policies. McMillan and Woodruff's (1999) study of non-state governance in Vietnam illustrates this. But to go beyond the middle-income level requires greater integration into a large economy, where relation-based governance is inadequate. The necessary shift toward rule-based governance is more demanding because it must overcome the additional problems of collective action, vested interests and so on.

How might such investment in the framework of rules get made? An example suggests that private action may provide the lead that spurs collective public action. In 1898, when Elbert Gary and J. Pierpont Morgan started Federal Steel, they "took the then unusual step of issuing quarterly reports" because "both men believed that corporations issuing publicly traded securities had to account for their financial performance" (Strouse 2000, p. 398). At first there was no public process such as external audits to guarantee the truthfulness of these accounts; presumably Morgan's own reputation and integrity, acquired in the prevailing relation-based system of finance, gave them credibility. But the public gradually found that inadequate, perhaps because others entering the arena of raising finance from the general public did not have the same reputation. A few years later, then president Theodore Roosevelt said that he would not "accept the publication of what some particular company chooses to publish as a favor, instead of demanding what we think ought to be published from all companies as a right" (Strouse 2000, p. 439). And still later, Morgan said that "business in the twentieth century would have to be conducted with glass pockets" (Strouse 2000, p. 600). This episode also serves to emphasize a point I made in the discussion of Section 2.5, namely the endogeneity of verifiability, and the value of making more information publicly verifiable. Cooter (1994, p. 216) gives other examples, historical and recent, of the process by which arrangements of governance in private voluntary associations are later adopted and enforced by the apparatus of state law.

Factors Undermining the Relation-Based System

Forces operate on the other side to undermine a relation-based system when it comes into contact with other rule-based systems. If capital-owners in the relation-based system become able to invest abroad under a rule-based system and earn the going return there, that will raise the outside opportunities of the participants in each ongoing repeated game of relation-based finance, and thereby unravel its tacit cooperation equilibrium. This may be happening in East Asia now. Similarly, as improvements in transportation technology or lowering of trade barriers with other countries, or liberalization of regulation within or across countries, bring a relation-based production system into contact with other economies and other markets, its firms will discover better opportunities outside their previous relationships; this can undermine the previous repeated game equilibrium.

If or when a relation-based economy needs to import capital, whether financial or direct investment, it will find it difficult to do so. Unless foreigners are stupid or gradually develop relationships with host-country businesses, they will be reluctant to lend. Conversely, firms in a relation-based system may be reluctant to borrow from lenders who are not part of their relation network, for fear that the strangers may withdraw their capital suddenly. So a relation-based economy may fail to grow if it needs foreign capital, unless it changes over successfully to a rule-based system where anyone can invest with the confidence that the only uncertainties will be those arising from natural economic shocks, not those of borrowers' strategic default or fraud or lenders' capital flight.

Of course the difficulties of bringing together two such different systems of financial transactions are not insurmountable. Intermediaries can develop relations on both sides, and profit by providing these services for a fee. The Rothschilds did this in Europe with great success for over a century, literally by having relations on both or all sides (see Ferguson 1998, 1999).[5] In the second half of the nineteenth century, the United States was a major capital importer. This was facilitated by the Morgans—Junius S. operating in London and J. Pierpont in New York,—who established a relation-based chain of trust between borrowers in the United States and lenders in the United Kingdom and Europe (see Strouse 2000). In modern times, Hong Kong served a similar role, dealing with lenders—Western ones on a basis of rules and overseas Chinese ones on the basis of relations—and with borrowers—investing firms in mainland China on a basis of relations (Li and Lian 1999, Section 3.2).

Interfaces and Mixed Systems

Li (2003, footnote 5) recognizes that "[r]elation-based governance and rule-based governance represent a theoretical dichotomy. In reality, most governance systems contain elements of the two extreme forms." Even in the United States today, which is as close to having a rule-based governance as any country at any time, we see continued use of relation-based governance at many points. In fact external legal enforcement of a contract when a breach occurs is often the last resort rather than the first. Its more important role is as a backstop or a threat point that underlies the renegotiation of the deal between the parties (see Williamson (1985, pp. 164–166, 168) and the discussion in Sections 2.1 and 2.2). And international trade and capital flows require interaction of different governance systems—a rule-based and

---

[5]Recalling the different information structure of the two modes, it is interesting to note that the Rothschilds did not use double-entry bookkeeping, the essential tool of public reporting and verification, for many years, relying instead on individual partners' knowledge of their own profits and trust among them (see Ferguson 1998, pp. 103, 104).

a relation-based system, or two relation-based systems with different preexisting relationships.

What can we expect to see at such interfaces? Most important are the frictions and instabilities that arise when people or firms or banks coming from different systems, and having different expectations about behavior, transact with each other. Li (2003) emphasizes this aspect. The clash of expectations can lead to speculative booms and busts; in his account of financial bubbles through history, Chancellor (1999, p. 325) finds that "[e]conomies in the process of liberalization appear to be especially susceptible to outbreaks of speculation." Next come asymmetries, some of which favor the relation-based system. People used to dealing in such a system will find it easier to initiate some transactions in a rule-based system than vice versa. This may be one reason—in addition to any formal trade barriers— why Japan, South Korea, and Taiwan have been more successful in exporting to the United States and the United Kingdom than vice versa. Anyone can come and tap into US distribution channels, get trade credit, or engage in advertising and other promotional activities. In relation-based economies these activities are mostly carried out by firms that have long-standing relationships with others in the country, and who will not easily deal with outsiders for fear of spoiling these relationships. To penetrate these markets, an outsider must work patiently to build up his own relationships, or invest in building up his own network of distribution, etc., before he can expect success. Outsiders who come from other relation-based systems do not have ready access to existing networks of relations either, but they better understand the importance of such relation-building investments. Therefore they are likely to have more success; for example, European exporters to East Asia have generally enjoyed modest success, better than the Americans. This also helps explain why the US government and lobbyists for exporting industries in the United States are so keen to get the East Asian countries to adopt a more open system or rules.

The asymmetry may be even more pronounced for capital flows. Savers from a relation-based system can buy assets in a rule-based system with more confidence than vice versa. This has implications for capital flows in both directions. An investor from a rule-based system who lends to someone in a relation-based system without developing the necessary relationship in advance is asking to be robbed. A saver from a relation-based system can invest in a rule-based system without such fear. Paradoxically, this may undermine the relation-based system by giving its participants a good outside opportunity (see Section 2.3). Li (2003) discusses these aspects in greater detail in the East Asian context.

Another asymmetry favors the rule-based system. Compare two systems that initially operate separately from each other. If a new technology of a given technical superiority becomes available, a relation-based system will be slower to adopt it than a rule-based system. The reason is as follows. An incumbent, given his sunk stake in the old technology, has less to gain from switching to the new. But if competitors can enter easily, then they are going to destroy the value of the incumbent's stake anyway, so he might as well do it himself and at least exploit some first-mover advantage to get the quasi-rent on the new technology. However, as was argued above, a relation-based system is likely to have smaller scale and large sunk investments in relationships; therefore it is likely to have higher natural entry barriers than a rule-based system. Therefore the incumbents in a relation-based system are less threatened by competitors' entry, and more likely to indulge in their desire to delay switching. Now bring together in trade two such systems, one rule based and the other relation based. The former, being used to the mode of slow adoption of new technologies, will be at a handicap unless it can reform quickly. Incumbents in the relation-based system will of course realize this, and will exert political influence to delay or limit the opening up, or at least to secure protection for themselves.

Other Systems and System Design

Relation-based and rule-based systems are conceptual pure categories that mix in different ways in practice. In some situations, the diminishing returns of a relation-based system can be countered without going to a fully centralized rule-based alternative. One such system has a hierarchical structure, with small relation-based self-governing communities, and one or more tiers of more formalized channels of information linking them together. Bernstein (1992, p. 144) describes such arrangements between diamond-trading bourses in different cities. This may be especially helpful to middle-sized communities which would otherwise, according to the model of Section 3.3, fare poorly in comparison with smaller self-governing communities or larger ones that have successfully made the transition to full rule-based governance. Dixit (2003c) constructs a model of such a two-tier system, and finds that it can mitigate the diminishing returns of self-governance. It retains the local information advantages of a small community, merely adding a formal network of information transmission among the much smaller number, namely a group of supervisors, one from each local network. Another system that can bridge the gap between relation-based governance in small-scale communities and rule-based governance in large ones is the community responsibility system studied by Greif (2003). This system prevailed in Europe in the pre-modern period. It exploited the fact that in those days the communal identities of people were relatively easily identifiable to outsiders because of differences in language, dress, food, and so on, whereas individuals could be tracked well within a community. Then the system worked by holding a community jointly liable for default by any member of it, leaving the community to track down the individual miscreant and recover the sums from him. This is a different kind of two-tier system, each community being the lower tier and the collectivity of communities the upper tier.

Less-developed countries and transition economies confront the most important policy questions related to the themes of this chapter, namely what kind of institutions they should adopt. The correct answer is likely to be a mixture in most cases, and the details of the mixture will depend on the specifics of the country, its history, and its economic prospects. Theoretical understanding of the merits and the drawbacks of conceptually pure systems is essential for good design of the right mixture, as is evidence on the performance of similar systems in other countries and at other times. But these must be supplemented by a lot of local knowledge and experimentation. Rubin (1994) argues that transition economies should develop their legal systems in this way, starting with private arrangements, especially arbitration, and building on the knowledge gained in their operation. Rodrik (2000, pp. 10–15) offers some thoughtful observations on all these matters.

3.6   Mathematical Appendix

Here I describe the more formal details of the model, and give proofs for the results that were explained intuitively in Section 3.3.

The Trading World

The traders are a continuum, uniformly distributed along a circle of circumference $2S$. The mass of traders per unit length of arc is normalized to 1. I will speak of a trader located at a point instead of the density at a point; I hope that the reduction in pedantry more than compensates for the slight loss of rigor. The distance between two traders is measured as the shorter of the two arc lengths between them, clockwise and counterclockwise.

Matches

There are two periods. The first period is the one where honesty or cheating are the crucial issue; the appropriate rewards or punishment come in the second period, which may as usual stand for the reduced form of a longer future. The payoffs are expressed in present values so no further discounting is necessary. In each period, traders are randomly matched in pairs. The matches are assumed to have the following properties.

(M1) Independence. The actual match in period 1 does not affect the probabilities of matches in period 2.

(M2) Localization of matches. In each period, each trader meets exactly one partner. For each trader, the probability of meeting another located at distance x is equal to

$$\frac{e^{-\alpha x}}{2\,[\,1 - e^{-\alpha S}\,]\,/\,\alpha}\,.$$

(M3) Desirability of trade expansion. The payoffs from a match at distance x are proportional to $e^{\theta x}$. (The complete payoff matrix will be specified shortly.)

(M4) Localization of information. If a trader in a match cheats the other, the probability that a third person, located at distance y from the victim of the cheating, receives news of this cheating is $e^{-\beta y}$.

The intuition and motivation for these assumptions were discussed in the text. But two technical comments are added here.

(1) I am assuming that news travels from the victim to any third person along the shorter arc of the circle connecting them. If news travels in both directions, then the probability of it reaching someone distant y from the victim is

$$1 - (1 - e^{-\beta y})(1 - e^{-\beta(2S-y)}).$$

For any fixed y, as S goes to infinity, this goes to $e^{-\beta y}$, the same as my unidirectional probability. Therefore my results for large S are entirely unaffected by my assumption. For smaller S, two-way flow would increase the probability of spread of news and therefore reduce the incentive to cheat, but the qualitative results remain unaffected.

(2) We have a degree of freedom to choose the unit in which distance is measured. In fact what matters is not physical (or socioeconomic) distance as such, but the probabilities $e^{-\alpha S}$ and $e^{-\beta S}$ and the size of the gain $e^{\theta S}$. If the unit of distance is halved, S is doubled but the parameters α, β, and θ are all halved, leaving αS, βS, and θS unchanged. An implication is that all the crucial magnitudes, for example the maximum size of the world compatible with global honest self-governance, are homogeneous of degree -1 jointly in the three parameters α, β, and θ.

Player Types, Information, Strategies, Payoffs

The traders come in two behavioral types of players, called Normal or N-type and Machiavellian or M-type; the latter should be thought of as especially skillful cheaters. Both types are uniformly distributed along the circle. Their proportions in the population are $(1 - \epsilon)$ for the N-types and ϵ for the M-types. The number ϵ is assumed to be small. The type of each player is not directly observable to others, but they may condition the probabilities of a person's type based on any observables. It will be seen that the role of the few Machiavellian traders is to pin down expectations out of equilibrium and to prevent a cheater from attempting to escape punishment by claiming that the cheating was just an error.

In each period, independent and identically distributed (IID) random matchings are made, as specified in (M1) and (M2) above, to determine trading pairs. Each

Table 3.1. Payoff matrix for meeting of two N-types in period t.

		Trader N2	
		Comply	Deviate
Trader N1	Comply	C_t, C_t	L_t, W_t
	Deviate	W_t, L_t	D_t, D_t

player in a pair knows the other's distance x, and with the information mechanism specified in (M4) may know the other's past history of cheating if any. The stage game of each matched pair proceeds as follows.

(G1) Each decides whether to play. These choices are simultaneous. The outside opportunity for each is normalized to 0. If both choose to play, the outcomes depend on their actions and types as specified next. Thus the game is a two-sided dilemma with option not to play, as in Section 1.7, Table 1.3, but it is analyzed a little differently here to suit the particular context. As there, the honest and cheating actions are formally labeled Comply and Deviate, respectively.

(G2-n) When two N-types meet—this accounts for most of the matches—in period t, the game has a payoff matrix $\exp[\theta\, x]$ times the symmetric but time-dependent form of the prisoner's dilemma matrix of Table 1.2, namely Table 3.1.

(G2-m) If an N-type meets an M-type, the N-type gets L_t regardless of his own action, and the M-type gets a positive payoff. If two M-types meet, they each get positive payoffs.

The payoffs are assumed to satisfy the following inequalities.

(P1) $W_t > C_t > D_t > L_t$. This simply says that the stage game between two N-types is a prisoner's dilemma.

(P2) $(1 - \epsilon)\, D_t + \epsilon\, L_t > 0 > L_t$. This says that an N-type will choose to play, rather than take the outside opportunity, against a random opponent even if the latter is going to cheat, but not against a known M-type. The two together create an expected cost of cheating for an N-type: if you cheat in period 1, and your period-2 match gets to know of this, he will not play you, and you will get 0 instead of D_2. This device for achieving cooperation with finite repetitions is similar to that in Benoit and Krishna (1985). Note that the assumption places an upper bound on ϵ. (If ϵ is very small, (P2) is approximately $D_t > 0 > L_t$.)

(P3) $W_1 - C_1 < D_2$. This says that in a distanceless world, if cheating is detected and publicized with certainty, then there exists an equilibrium where all N-types choose Comply in period 1. (To be more precise, both sides of the inequality should be multiplied by $(1 - \epsilon)$.) The role of this assumption is to confine the question of honest behavior to the context of uncertain dissemination of information across distance that is the focus here. To simplify later algebra, define $k = (W_1 - C_1)/D_2$, then (P3) is equivalent to $k < 1$.

Equilibrium

The solution concept is Perfect Bayesian Equilibrium. This can be characterized by a number X, such that Normal types behave honestly in period 1 when meeting someone located at a distance X or less from themselves, and cheating otherwise. To be more precise, the equilibrium strategy for N-types is as follows.

(i) In period 1 choose to play, and choose the action Comply if the partner's location is X or less away from you, and Deviate if between X and S.

(ii) In period 2, if you have received information that your current match's period-1 match received L_1, then choose not to play (take the outside opportunity); else play and choose Deviate.

M-types always choose to play, and their strategies can be kept in the background of the whole analysis.

Think of this for now as specifying a "candidate" equilibrium and put it to the test. The only actions and beliefs at issue are those of the N-types. Most aspects of these are obvious.

(1) In period 1, when the partner's type is not known, choosing to play has positive expected payoff by (P2).

(2) In period 1, if the partner is located at distance between X and S, his strategy specifies that he should play Deviate. Then it is optimal for you to play Deviate also: it gives a better payoff at that time than Comply, and since the partner is not going to receive L_1, has no adverse consequences for you in period 2.

(3) In period 2, if you have no information about the partner's cheating in period 1, then choosing to play and cheating are clearly optimal.

(4) In period 2, if you have received information that your current partner's period-1 match got payoff L_1, then given the strategies in the candidate equilibrium, your Bayesian inference is that your current partner is an M-type. Therefore choosing not to play is optimal by (P2). This is the crucial role of the M-types in the model. Without them, there would be no cheating in equilibrium, and therefore the inferences drawn after a deviation could be arbitrary. A deviator could claim that it was just a mistake and ask the period-2 partner to play for the sake of the low, but positive, payoff D_2. Now the partner is deterred from acceding to such a request by his Bayesian calculation that the partner

is an M-type and therefore he will instead get the negative payoff L_2. To repeat, the N-types' behavior is driven by their fear of being confused with the M-types that are known to lurk in the population, but there should be few enough M-types that on average the N-types still want to play.

(5) It only remains to check whether, or more precisely, under what conditions, it is optimal to choose Comply in period 1 if the current match is located at distance X or less. This is done in the following lemma and proposition.

Lemma. *Suppose an N-type finds that his period-1 partner is distant X from him. If his belief is that this partner will play Deviate even if an N-type, then his best response is also to play Deviate. If his belief is that this partner, if an N-type, will play Comply, then his best response is also Comply if $F(X, S) \geqslant 0$, and Deviate if $F(X, S) < 0$, where the function $F(X, S)$ is defined by*

$$F(X, S) = \frac{\beta \, e^{-\lambda X} - \lambda \, e^{-\beta X}}{\beta^2 - \lambda^2} + e^{-(\beta+\lambda)S} \frac{(\lambda \, e^{\beta X} - \beta \, e^{\lambda X})}{\beta^2 - \lambda^2} - k \, e^{\theta X} \frac{1 - e^{-\alpha S}}{\alpha}.$$

$$(3.2)$$

Proof of the lemma. Focus on any one trader, called Oscar for identification and located at the point O on the circle shown in Figure 3.6. If Oscar believes that his period-1 partner will play Deviate if an N-type, then Oscar expects a better period-1 payoff by responding Deviate than by responding Comply. Also, by (P1) and (P2), even if Oscar plays Deviate, Oscar's partner, whether an N-type playing Deviate or an M-type, is not going to get the bad payoff L_1. So the action has no period-2 consequences for Oscar. Thus Deviate is the optimal response for Oscar in this situation.

If Oscar believes that his period-1 partner, located at distance X from him, will choose Comply if an N-type, then Oscar stands to gain an immediate

$$(1 - \epsilon) \, (W_1 - C_1) \, e^{\theta X}$$

by choosing Deviate instead of Comply. The expected cost of this to Oscar arises from the possibility that if his period-2 partner is an N-type, and has heard that Oscar cheated before, then he will refuse to play with Oscar. To calculate the expected cost, we must calculate the probabilities of the match and of the partner having heard of Oscar's cheating for each possible location z, multiply by the payoff loss $D_2 \, e^{\theta z}$, and integrate over z. The expression for the news probability is different in four different arcs of the circle, as shown in Figure 3.6.

In the arc between Oscar's location (O) and that of the period-1 partner he cheated (X), the distance between the general point Z_1 and X is $(X - Z_1)$. In the arc extending from X to the point S diametrically opposite O, the distance between the general point Z_2 and X is $Z_2 - X$. On the other side of O, up to the point $S - X$ diametrically

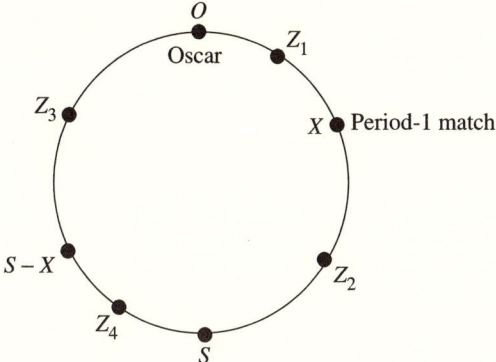

Figure 3.6. Calculation of the expected cost of cheating.

opposite X, the distance between the general point Z_3 and X is $(X + Z_3)$. Finally, between $S - X$ and S, the shorter arc connecting X and the general point Z_4 is along the side of the circle away from O, so the distance is $(2S - X - Z_4)$. Then the expression for the expected cost is

$$
\frac{(1 - \epsilon) D_2}{2 [1 - e^{-\alpha S}]/\alpha} \Bigg[\int_0^X e^{-\alpha Z_1} e^{-\beta(X - Z_1)} e^{\theta Z_1} \, dZ_1
$$
$$
+ \int_X^S e^{-\alpha Z_2} e^{-\beta(Z_2 - X)} e^{\theta Z_2} \, dZ_2
$$
$$
+ \int_0^{S-X} e^{-\alpha Z_3} e^{-\beta(X + Z_3)} e^{\theta Z_3} \, dZ_3
$$
$$
+ \int_{S-X}^S e^{-\alpha Z_4} e^{-\beta(2S - (X + Z_4))} e^{\theta Z_4} \, dZ_4 \Bigg].
$$

For Oscar's optimal response to be Comply, this expected cost should exceed the immediate gain. Using the definitions $k = (W_1 - H_1)/D_2$ and $\lambda = \alpha - \theta$, evaluating all the integrals, and simplifying, we get the condition in terms of the function $F(X, S)$ defined in (3.2).   □

A technical remark about the lemma: ϵ, the proportion of M-types in the population, does not affect the sign of $F(X, S)$, it only scales the payoffs by the common factor $(1 - \epsilon)$. Of course ϵ must be positive. Intuitively, we need a few M-types so the fear of being confused with one of them keeps the N-types honest. Technically, if $\epsilon = 0$, the equilibrium would not survive a Cho–Kreps type refinement.

Proposition 3.1. *For each S, there exists a unique $X(S)$ such that an equilibrium with strategies as defined above exists for any X satisfying $0 \leqslant X \leqslant X(S)$.*

The formal proof first verifies that F is a decreasing function of X holding S fixed. Then three cases arise.

(1) If S is such that $F(0, S) < 0$, then $F(X, S) < 0$ for all X and it is always optimal for an N-type to cheat in period 1, so the candidate equilibrium is not an actual equilibrium for any X, that is, $X(S) = 0$.

(2) If S is such that $F(S, S) > 0$, then the candidate equilibrium has self-fulfilling expectations of honest behavior for any X between 0 and S, so $X(S) = S$.

(3) If $F(0, S) > 0 > F(S, S)$, then by monotonicity there is a unique $X(S)$ in $(0, S)$ such that $F(X, S) \geqslant 0$ for $0 \leqslant X \leqslant X(S)$ and $F(X, S) < 0$ for $X(S) < X \leqslant S$. The candidate equilibrium is sustained by self-fulfilling expectations in the former range, but not in the latter range because there each trader finds it better to play Deviate even if he expects others to play Comply.

Proof of Proposition 3.1. Differentiating the expression in (3.2),

$$\frac{\partial F}{\partial X} = \frac{\beta \lambda}{\beta^2 - \lambda^2} \left[-(e^{-\lambda X} - e^{-\beta X}) + e^{-(\beta+\lambda)S} (e^{\beta X} - e^{\lambda X}) \right]$$
$$- k\theta e^{\theta X} \frac{1 - e^{-\alpha S}}{\alpha}$$
$$= -\beta \lambda \frac{e^{\beta X} - e^{\lambda X}}{\beta^2 - \lambda^2} \left[e^{-(\beta+\lambda)X} - e^{-(\beta+\lambda)S} \right] - k\theta e^{\theta X} \frac{1 - e^{-\alpha S}}{\alpha}$$
$$< 0 \quad \text{for } 0 < X < S.$$

$\square$

The Limits of Honest Trade

In the discussion following Proposition 3.1, the logical possibilities for the extent of trade $X(S)$ were seen to range from 0 all the way to S. How do the actual outcomes vary with S? The localization of matches and information suggests that honesty over the full circle ($X(S) = S$) should be possible for small S but not for large S. This is seen more formally from the following proposition.

Proposition 3.2. *There exists a unique positive S^* such that $X(S) = S$ for $0 \leqslant S \leqslant S^*$, and $X(S) < S$ for $S > S^*$.*

Proof of Proposition 3.2. This consists of examining for what values of S we have $F(S, S) \geqslant 0$.

When $X = S$, (3.2) simplifies to

$$F(S, S) = \frac{e^{-\lambda S} - e^{-\beta S}}{\beta - \lambda} - k e^{-\lambda S} \frac{e^{\alpha S} - 1}{\alpha}$$

$$= e^{-\lambda S} \left[\frac{1 - e^{-(\beta - \lambda) S}}{\beta - \lambda} - k \frac{e^{\alpha S} - 1}{\alpha} \right].$$

Define $\Phi(S)$ to be the expression in square brackets on the right-hand side. The sign of $F(S, S)$ is the same as the sign of $\Phi(S)$.

We have $\Phi(0) = 0$ and

$$\Phi'(S) = e^{-(\beta - \lambda) S} - k e^{\alpha S}$$

$$= e^{\alpha S} [e^{-(\beta + \theta) S} - k],$$

so $\Phi'(0) = 1 - k > 0$ by (P3). Therefore $\Phi(S) > 0$ for S sufficiently small.

Next I show that $\Phi(S)$ becomes negative for sufficiently large S. There are two cases to consider. If $\beta - \lambda > 0$, then as $S \to \infty$, the first term in the expression for $\Phi(S)$ goes to $1/(\beta - \lambda)$ and the second goes to ∞, so $\Phi(S)$ eventually becomes negative. If $\beta - \lambda < 0$, then some rearrangement of terms shows that

$$\Phi(S) = e^{\alpha S} \left[-\frac{e^{-\alpha S} - e^{-(\beta + \theta) S}}{\lambda - \beta} - k \frac{1 - e^{-\alpha S}}{\alpha} \right].$$

As S becomes large, the first term in the square brackets goes to zero, and the second goes to $-k/\alpha$, so again $\Phi(S)$ becomes negative eventually.

Finally, note that $\Phi'(S) > 0$ if and only if $e^{-(\beta + \theta) S} > k$, that is, $S < -\ln(k)/(\beta + \theta)$. (Since $k < 1$, $\ln(k) < 0$, so the right-hand side is positive.) So $\Phi'(S)$ changes sign only once, from positive to negative. Therefore $\Phi(S)$ changes direction only once, from increasing to decreasing.

Putting all this together, we see that $\Phi(0) = 0$, then $\Phi(S)$ become positive for small positive S, then it starts to decrease, and becomes negative as S goes to infinity. Therefore $\Phi(S)$ can cross zero once and only once, in its decreasing phase. This point defines the unique S^*. $\qquad\square$

Proposition 3.3. *As $S \to \infty$, $X(S)$ tends to a positive limit X^* if $k(\beta + \lambda) < \alpha$. Else $X(S)$ reaches zero for a finite S.*

Proof of Proposition 3.3. Letting S go to ∞ in (3.2),

$$F(X, \infty) = \frac{\beta e^{-\lambda X} - \lambda e^{-\beta X}}{\beta^2 - \lambda^2} - k e^{\theta X} \frac{1}{\alpha} = 0.$$

Then

$$F(0, \infty) = 1/(\beta + \lambda) - k/\alpha.$$

This is positive if and only if $k (\beta + \lambda) < \alpha$; then the X^* defined by $F(X^*, \infty) = 0$ is positive. Otherwise, by continuity of F, $F(0, S)$ becomes and stays negative beyond a finite S, so $X(S) = 0$ there. $\qquad\qquad\qquad\qquad\qquad\qquad\qquad\qquad\square$

Comparative Statics

Here I examine the dependence of S^*, the largest world size compatible with self-governance, and X^*, the extent of honesty in a very large world, on the parameters α, β, θ, and k. First, from the freedom to choose the unit in which distance is measured, the following proposition is obvious.

Proposition 3.4. *Each of S^* and X^* is homogeneous of degree -1 jointly in (α, β, θ) for any given k.*

Finally, I consider the effects on S^* and X^* of changing the parameters α, β, θ, and k one at a time. These effects are stated in the following two propositions.

Proposition 3.5. *S^* is a decreasing function of each of α, β, θ, and k.*

Proof of Proposition 3.5. From Proposition 3.2, S^* is defined as the unique positive S satisfying $\Phi(S) = 0$. We also saw in the proof of that proposition that at this point $\Phi(S)$ goes from positive to negative values, so $\Phi'(S^*) < 0$. Now take the definition of $\Phi(S)$ in the proof, and notice that it can be written as

$$\Phi(S) = \int_0^S e^{(\alpha - \beta - \theta) z}\, dz - k \int_0^S e^{\alpha z}\, dz = 0.$$

To do comparative statics with respect to any parameter, say k, differentiate totally:

$$\Phi'(S^*) \frac{\partial S^*}{\partial k} + \frac{\partial \Phi(S)}{\partial k}\bigg|_{S=S^*} = 0.$$

Since $\Phi'(S^*) < 0$, the sign of $\partial S^*/\partial k$ is the same as that of the partial derivative of $\Phi(S)$ with respect to k. And

$$\frac{\partial \Phi(S)}{\partial k} = -\int_0^S e^{\alpha z}\, dz < 0;$$

therefore $\partial S^*/\partial k < 0$. Similarly,

$$\frac{\partial \Phi(S)}{\partial \beta} = \frac{\partial \Phi(S)}{\partial \theta} = -\int_0^S z\, e^{(\alpha - \beta - \theta) z}\, dz < 0;$$

therefore $\partial S^*/\partial \beta = \partial S^*/\partial \theta < 0$.
    Finally,

$$\frac{\partial \Phi(S)}{\partial \alpha} = \int_0^S z\, e^{(\alpha - \beta - \theta) z}\, dz - k \int_0^S z\, e^{\alpha z}\, dz.$$

Each of the terms in the expression for $\Phi(S)$ is positive, and the two are equal at $S = S^*$, so dividing each of the terms in the expression for $\partial\Phi(S)/\partial\alpha$ by the corresponding term in the expression for $\Phi(S)$, we see that the sign of $\partial\Phi(S)/\partial\alpha$ at S^* is the same as the sign of

$$\frac{\int_0^S z\, e^{(\alpha-\beta-\theta)z}\, dz}{\int_0^S e^{(\alpha-\beta-\theta)z}\, dz} - \frac{\int_0^S z\, e^{\alpha z}\, dz}{\int_0^S e^{\alpha z}\, dz}.$$

Both ratios are weighted averages of z over $[0, S]$. The first has weights proportional to $e^{(\alpha-\beta-\theta)z}$, while the second has weights proportional to $e^{\alpha z}$. So the first gives relatively higher weights to smaller z, and is therefore smaller. Thus $\partial\Phi(S)/\partial\alpha$ is negative, and therefore $\partial S^*/\partial\alpha < 0$. $\qquad\square$

Proposition 3.6. *X^* is a decreasing function of each of β and k.*

Proof of Proposition 3.6. Using the workings in the proof of the lemma, we can write

$$F(X, \infty) = \frac{1}{2}\left[\int_0^X e^{-\alpha Z_1}\, e^{-\beta(X-Z_1)}\, e^{\theta Z_1}\, dZ_1 \right.$$

$$+ \int_X^\infty e^{-\alpha Z_2}\, e^{-\beta(Z_2-X)}\, e^{\theta Z_2}\, dZ_2$$

$$\left. + \int_0^\infty e^{-\alpha Z_3}\, e^{-\beta(X+Z_3)}\, e^{\theta Z_3}\, dZ_3 \right] - k \int_0^\infty e^{-\alpha Z}\, dZ.$$

Now X^* is defined by $F(X^*, \infty) = 0$. Differentiating totally with respect to k, we have

$$F_X(X^*, \infty)\, \frac{\partial X^*}{\partial k} + \left.\frac{\partial F(X, \infty)}{\partial k}\right|_{X=X^*} = 0.$$

We know from the proof of Proposition 3.1 that $F_X < 0$. Therefore the sign of $\partial X^*/\partial k$ is the same as the sign of the second term on the left-hand side, which is obviously negative.

An increase in β lowers the integrands everywhere in the expression for $F(X, \infty)$, so $\partial F(X^*, \infty)/\partial\beta < 0$ and therefore $\partial X^*/\partial\beta < 0$. $\qquad\square$

The effects of changing α and θ on X^* are ambiguous in sign.

4

Profit-Motivated Contract Enforcement

4.1 Issues and Empirical Research

Chapter 3 compared two modes of contract enforcement:

(1) self-governance, based on community information networks and ostracization or other forms of sanctions; and

(2) formal state governance, based on a framework of laws and of auditing and monitoring mechanisms.

The first was limited by the matching and communication technologies; in large worlds it may fail altogether, or fail to realize the full economic benefits of comparative advantage. The second depended on the community's ability to solve the collective-action problems of investing in the infrastructure of laws and monitoring, and to overcome the power of vested interests with sunk capital in the status quo. What if self-governance is infeasible, either because the community is too large or the information network and the system social norms and sanctions are too weak, and formal state law is unavailable, either because the state is too weak or lacks resources, or because it regards the activities in question as themselves illegal?

In this situation, members of the community are unable to consummate transactions that would bring them economic gains. This is their economic problem. But every economic problem is an economic opportunity. Someone who can solve the problem, turning the potential gains into actual ones, may be able to charge a fee for this service. In our context, if the government does not provide contract enforcement using its general revenues, then a private person may be able to do so for a profit. In this chapter I examine this case of private profit-motivated contract enforcement. Private protection of property rights is the subject of the next chapter.

To recapitulate the general point made in Section 3.1, theoretical and empirical literatures alike identify two difficult problems that confront large populations trying to resolve prisoners' dilemmas: collecting and conveying information about previous cheating; and erecting a credible structure of punishments to deter cheating in current and future periods. The principle that "economic problems are also economic opportunities" applies to both of these.

Anyone can, at a cost, collect information about individual traders' histories of cheating, and sell this information to other prospective traders in the future. Trade associations often collect and provide such information to their members; Bernstein (1992, 2001) gives good examples of this. Three different forms of such associations can be distinguished. The first kind, exemplified by relatively small groups of specialized commodity traders (Bernstein 2001), are mainly concerned with trades among pairs of its own members, and provide information about members' past actions in their trades with other members. The second and third kinds are concerned with interactions between a member on one side and a non-member (general public) on the other side. Of these, the second kind collect information about cheating by one of the general public and provide it to their members; credit-approval services maintained by Visa and Mastercard are an instance of this. The third kind, usually known as Better Business Bureaus, keep track of their members' behavior and make this information available to the public. This enables their members credibly to create and maintain reputations. The diamond traders' club in Bernstein (1992), which governs transactions between its members and other dealers who may or may not be members, seems to be a mixture of these types.

In some situations, third parties charge a fee to provide information to one side of a transaction about the history of the other side; agencies that rate the creditworthiness of people or firms, or services that monitor the quality of goods and services provided by firms, are well-known examples. Such a for-profit intermediary must solve two other problems: he must discourage free riding, by making the information unavailable or useless to non-payers; and he must credibly promise not to misuse the information, for example for extortion or double crossing. But this is simplified by the fact that the intermediary's relationships with all customers are bilateral and non-anonymous: while two traders may meet each other only infrequently, each of them can meet the intermediary every period. In other words, the difficult problem of resolving prisoners' dilemmas in random pairwise matchings from a large population is converted into the somewhat easier problem of resolving prisoners' dilemmas of direct bilateral reciprocity between each member of the population and the intermediary. This is conceptually similar to solving the problem of double coincidence of wants by introducing money. The issuer of money gets seignorage; the information intermediary charges a fee for his services.

A suitably qualified intermediary can also provide an enforcement service, that is, inflict punishments on behalf of customers. Milgrom, North, and Weingast (1990) have a well-known study of private judges enforcing "the law merchant" (LM) in medieval France, who performed both functions. First, such a judge or intermediary kept records on the behavior of traders in the markets over which he offered his services. Second, he adjudicated disputes brought before him by one of the traders. Milgrom et al. model this in a game with the following steps.

(a) In each period, each player is matched with a partner whom he is unlikely to have met before and is unlikely to meet again.

(b) Each player in such a pair can, by paying a fee, query the LM about his current partner's history of behavior in previous matches.

(c) Each such pair then plays a one-time prisoner's dilemma game.

(d) If either of the players in this game cheats, the other can, by paying another fee, complain to the LM, but only if the victim had queried the LM about the partner's history in step (b) above.

(e) If such a complaint is lodged, the LM investigates at a cost and, if appropriate, awards the plaintiff a judgment (monetary restitution) against the defendant.

(f) A losing defendant decides whether to pay the judgment. An unpaid judgment becomes another act of cheating, and is recorded as such by the LM.

Under appropriate conditions on the various parameters, and for a suitably calculated structure of fees, this system has an equilibrium outcome where everyone (including the LM) behaves honestly. The intuition is that the LM's record-keeping solves the information problem that would exist in a large population of traders with infrequent bilateral matches, and then punishment strategies of repeated games can work. Thus the LM serves as a complement to, not a substitute for, the usual reputation mechanism.

Milgrom et al. argue that the LM institution also contributed to the formulation of a uniform set of standards for commercial transactions across large areas of Europe, and therefore played a part in the evolution of modern commercial laws.

The most memorable example of private intermediation in the literature comes from Diego Gambetta's (1993) renowned study of the Sicilian Mafia. He begins his book (Gambetta 1993, p. 15) by recounting what a cattle-breeder told him.

> When the butcher comes to me to buy an animal, he knows that I want to cheat him [by giving him a low-quality animal]. But I know that he wants to cheat me [by reneging on payment]. Thus we need Peppe [that is, a third party] to make us agree. And we both pay Peppe a percentage of the deal.

Gambetta goes on to say (1993, p. 16) that in this context

> Peppe was mainly selling information, ... for this service ... he received a 2 percent commission. When in addition he acted as a guarantor of quality and payment, the percentage increased.

Some things about Gambetta's generic Mafioso Don Peppe are worth emphasis; they will form the basis for the formal model of this chapter. Peppe provides his services to the people on both sides of the transaction. They use his services voluntarily. The services are of two kinds, ex ante information about the other party's history of behavior, and ex post punishments meted out in response to any cheating. The fees for the latter (enforcement) service are higher than those for the former (information) service. The parties to any transaction may not have any direct bilateral reciprocal interaction with each other, but each of them has such interaction with Peppe.[1]

Organized crime performs functions of economic governance in other countries, and has done so throughout history. It usually operates at times or in niches where the state is absent. Bandiera (2003) traces the origins of the Mafia's enforcement role to nineteenth century in Sicily after the abolition of feudalism. Publicly provided security was inefficient and banditry widespread; landowners began to hire guards of former feudal lords and some of the tougher bandits to protect their property. In Japan in August–September 1945, when the government had collapsed after defeat in World War II but the occupying US forces had not yet restored order, the Yakuza played a major role in getting markets restarted (Whiting 1999, pp. 10, 11; Dower 1999, pp. 140–148). Similar activities are found in Russia and other transition economies (Varese 2001).

Of course, mafias engage in many activities, and Peppe's intermediation may now comprise only a small part of these, but it remains a good example for my purpose. Indeed, Gambetta (1993, pp. 19, 85) argues that protection should be regarded as the Mafia's main business; if it engages in some activities that may need its own protection services, this is just "downstream vertical integration." Perhaps one can regard the Mafia as an organization that specializes in providing protection, while individual mafiosi may be entrepreneurs engaged in the activities that need the protection. The Mafia may also engage in extortion, or creating the need for protection of property by itself creating a threat to the property; these are strategies that need to be examined as a part of the equilibrium of the game.

Peppe in his information role resembles a credit-rating agency or even a restaurant guide, except that he acts for both sides of the deal. In the guarantor or enforcer role, he resembles the official legal system, but has different information acquisition methods and different methods of punishment, and is motivated by private profit rather than by social welfare. In this chapter I will construct a formal model of Peppe's information and enforcement.

Among its results, the model explains why Peppe's commission for enforcement is higher than that for information. You may think this a trivial question, and think of obvious answers: enforcement activity is riskier to provide; the state's criminal

---

[1] However, Peppe deals with the traders individually. He does not gather the whole group of traders together and make them a multilateral, all-or-nothing offer that achieves an optimum as in the Coase Theorem. The efficiency of Peppe's intermediation is an open question, and will be studied below.

Table 4.1. The prisoner's dilemma for each pair and period.

		Player 2	
		Comply	Deviate
Player 1 {	Comply	C, C	L, W
	Deviate	W, L	D, D

law (if it is functioning) may intervene; the miscreant whom Peppe is trying to punish may prove tougher than Peppe; and so on. All these arguments say that the cost of providing enforcement is higher than that of providing governance by information alone; they are supply-side reasons. But Gambetta (1993, pp. 68–71) emphasizes that Peppe usually acts as a monopolist in enforcement over an allocated territory, defined by geography or the type of activity being protected (although conflicts over monopoly rights or over territories may break out among Mafiosi or their families). A monopolist charges a price above cost, based on the customer's willingness to pay. Therefore we must look for demand-side reasons, namely explain why Peppe's customers are willing to pay more for the enforcement service than for the information service. The model does that.

For expository simplicity and to minimize the mathematics, in the main text of the chapter I consider only a very special model that leaves out many important features. In the mathematical appendix to this chapter (Section 4.6), I generalize the model to include some of these features and examine their effect on the results. Even then, the exposition in this chapter leaves out many considerations; some of these are treated in Dixit (2003a).

4.2 The Structure of the Model

The traders in the model constitute a large population. Each period, pairs from this population are matched at random (IID) to play a prisoner's dilemma game. Thus everyone meets someone else every period, but there is almost no bilateral repeated interaction. As explained in Chapter 3 (p. 64), this is a conceptual simplification, the purpose of which is to isolate out for theoretical study the issues that remain after the parties' attempts to maintain a good direct relationship have been taken as far as possible.

The payoff matrix of the prisoner's dilemma game is the same as that of Table 1.2, except that for expository simplicity in the text I assume that the two players are symmetrically situated, making the subscripts on the payoffs unnecessary. The resulting payoff matrix is shown in Table 4.1. In informal discussions, the actions Comply and Deviate will often be referred to as honesty and cheating, respectively.

The game is played only if both players choose to do so. Each can instead unilaterally decide to take an outside option whose payoff is normalized at 0. But to avoid a proliferation of taxonomy I assume that even mutual cheating will be better than the outside option, leaving the readers to consider other cases. Thus the payoffs satisfy the chain of inequalities

$$W > C > D > 0 > L.$$

In this simple version I ignore all possibility of information transmission among the players themselves. Therefore left to themselves the players will always choose to play and choose Deviate, yielding the payoff D to each player in each period.

Next introduce an intermediary who seeks to make a profit by helping the players achieve better outcomes. Following the observations of Gambetta (1993, pp. 68–71), I assume that at any one time the intermediary has a monopoly over the services he provides to this population of traders. However, there can be initial or ongoing competition for this monopoly; in other words, it is a contestable monopoly. Note that there is no outside enforcement to ensure the intermediary's honesty; that has to be studied as a part of the game of bilateral repeated interaction between the intermediary and each trader.

The possibility of good outcomes from equilibria of such games depends crucially on the rate at which future payoffs are discounted. The discounting can reflect the market rate of interest that a player could earn if he receives payment earlier, or it can be a subjective measure of a player's impatience, depending on the context. But discounting can also arise because of the uncertainty of continuation of the relationship. Traders may have to leave the market for reasons outside their control (and to keep the analysis simple I will assume that they are then replaced by newcomers). The intermediary faces competition from others for his monopoly position; therefore he has an uncertain lifetime, either in the limited sense of being ousted from this market or even in a literal sense. To allow all these aspects in the model, suppose that δ is the pure discount factor (1 unit of payoff next period is equivalent to δ units this period), λ is the probability that each trader survives from one period to the next, and λ_0 is the probability that the intermediary survives from one period to the next. Then the effective rate of interest r at which a one-period future is discounted is given by

$$\frac{1}{1+r} = \delta \, \lambda \, \lambda_0. \tag{4.1}$$

The lower is any of the three discount factors on the right-hand side, the higher is the implied overall discount rate r.

I consider two types of services separately. One consists of keeping track of any history of individual traders' deviation and selling this information for a fee. I call a person (or organization) providing this service an information intermediary, or Info for short. The other service is to deter cheating by the trader with whom a customer is currently matched, by threatening to inflict some dire punishment in response to such behavior. I call a person providing this service an enforcement intermediary, or Enfo for short. The next section considers Info's intermediation, and the one after that, Enfo's.

4.3 Information Intermediaries

Let I denote Info's cost of servicing each customer in each period. I assume that if a customer of Info gets cheated, Info finds this out without incurring any further cost. This may be because he provides his service by accompanying his customer (physically or metaphorically) to the trade. This broadly accords with Gambetta's (1993, p. 36) description of what Peppe does in his information role. Credit-rating agencies, too, are likely to be told by their customer firms or lenders if a buyer or borrower defaults. A customer who has just been cheated probably actually gets a little satisfaction from complaining, but even if he incurs a small cost by complaining, a contract like that in Milgrom, North, and Weingast (1990) will enable Info to induce the customer to report the other party's current cheating. I will subsume this in the cost I. In addition, Info can detect at a further cost any occurrences where someone who is not his customer gets cheated. But we will see later that such costly detection is not optimal for Info.

At the start of each period, Info chooses his fee F and invites traders to become his customers. More precisely, the contract that Info offers to each trader has the following form.

> Pay me F now. When your match is revealed, I will tell you what I know of that player's history. If he has a history of cheating, or if he is not my customer, you should play Deviate; this will not count against you in the future. Otherwise you should play Comply.

Each trader decides whether to accept this offer. Then the pairings are revealed. Info tells his customers their partner's history of behavior, but Info's truthfulness is not automatically guaranteed. Each trader can also observe whether his current partner is Info's customer. Based on this information, each decides whether to play this period's game; in the case I am considering the answer is yes. Info may double cross a customer by conspiring, for a separate fee, with the person on the other side of the deal and mislead the customer into choosing Comply while the other plays Deviate. And Info may extort money from a trader with a clean history by threatening to assert that he has cheated in the past. After all the pairwise games for this period are played, Info keeps a record of any cheating of his customers, and decides whether to carry out at an extra cost any additional detection activities.

Info merely tells a customer either "I know your match has cheated in the past" or "As far as I know, your match has not cheated in the past." If Info says the latter and the other trader cheats this time, the customer has no recourse and Info will not inflict any punishment on the cheater. (Enforcement intermediaries are the subject of the next section.) The customer equally has no recourse if Info lies about the other party's history (and extracts an additional fee from the other party for allowing him to cheat in this way); we have to find conditions under which the equilibrium is proof against such double crossing by Info. Similarly, we have to check whether Info has any incentive to extract extortion payments by threatening falsely to assert a history of cheating by someone who in reality has a clean record. Since customers' contracts with Info cannot be externally enforced, Info cannot credibly enter into long-run contracts with large up-front fees to control customers' cheating. Therefore I do not consider such contracts.

I will look for an equilibrium of the following kind. (a) Everyone is Info's customer. (b) Info reveals his information truthfully and does not engage in any extortion or double crossing. (c) The customers follow the strategies suggested by Info. Other equilibria are possible, but this one is most successful in solving the problem at hand, so it is the natural one to select for this exposition. To test for such an equilibrium, we must examine the incentives of all players to deviate from it unilaterally. The no-deviation conditions impose constraints on Info's fee. I now consider the various deviations one at a time.

When everyone else is following the strategies stipulated above, any individual customer of Info has the net payoff $C - F$. If he had chosen not to become a customer, Info would have authorized his partner to play Deviate. Knowing this, the individual would himself play Deviate, for the payoff D. Therefore we have one equilibrium condition $C - F \geqslant D$, or

$$F \leqslant C - D. \tag{4.2}$$

The inequality is weak because the definition of Nash equilibrium only requires that a unilateral deviation should not get the deviating player a strictly higher payoff. The same remark will apply to the inequalities that follow.

What if someone becomes Info's customer but cheats? This gets him an immediate extra payoff $(W - C)$. But thereafter Info conveys this information to all his future partners (under the stipulated strategies they are all Info's customers). The reduction in payoff from the game is $(C - D)$. But knowing this, he should not pay to become Info's customer in the future, so his loss is mitigated to $(C - D) - F$. Equilibrium requires that the interest flow per period on the immediate gain, $r\,(W - C)$, should not exceed the subsequent per-period loss. This can also be expressed as a bound on Info's fee:

$$F \leqslant (C - D) - r\,(W - C). \tag{4.3}$$

If (4.3) holds, so does (4.2); therefore the latter is redundant.

The conditions (4.2) and (4.3) can be interpreted in another way. For any one customer, $(C - D)$ is the payoff difference in a period between being Info's customer and not being so. That must be an upper bound on the fee Info can charge. But if he charged that much, the customer would get zero surplus or rent from his relationship with Info. He can get an immediate $(W - C)$ by playing Deviate, with no future consequences because the future rents are all zero. This is a clear incentive to cheat. To prevent that, Info must give the customer a rent each period, at least equal to the interest on this one-time gain. That is just what (4.3) says.

Next consider the condition that rules out Info's extortion. If Info falsely asserts that a customer has a history of cheating, that player loses $(C - D)$ (a non-customer expects D anyway and so has nothing further to lose). Therefore this is the maximum Info can extort from any one player in any one period. This is a standard one-sided prisoner's dilemma of the kind discussed in Section 1.7 (Figure 1.1). Info has a bilateral relationship with each trader. In each period, the trader decides whether to become Info's customer. If yes, then Info decides whether to extort an extra payment. In a one-shot game, it is ex post optimal for Info to extort, and therefore in the subgame-perfect equilibrium the trader would not become his customer. In the repeated game, an equilibrium where the trader becomes Info's customer and Info does not engage in extortion can be sustained by the grim-trigger strategy of reversion to the one-shot equilibrium of the game between Info and this trader, namely the situation described in the previous sentence, where the trader does not become Info's customer. Then Info stands to lose his profit $F - I$ for each subsequent period. Therefore the equilibrium condition is that the interest on the one-time gain from extortion should not exceed the subsequent loss per period, that is,

$$F - I \geqslant r\,(C - D)\,. \tag{4.4}$$

Finally, consider the condition to rule out Info's double crossing. Info can double cross a customer by conspiring with the trader on the other side, allowing him to play Deviate and promising not to hold this against him in the future. (The question of credibility of this promise hinges on the same game as, and is therefore covered by, the analysis of Info's extortion strategy above.) The trader on the other side gets an extra $(W - C)$ from doing so, and this is the maximum that Info can extract from him for giving him this opportunity to cheat the current partner. What about Info's future losses? These depend on how the victim of the double cross interprets it. He knows that his partner cheated, but this could be because the partner deviated from his equilibrium strategy directly, or because Info deviated from his, in conspiracy with the partner. Since neither of these things should have happened on the equilibrium path of the game, the theory does not help us choose from these two possibilities. Write q for the probability that the victim interprets the deviation as Info's double-crossing. In this event, the grim-trigger strategy for the victim is not to trust Info again, causing Info a loss of his profit $(F - I)$ in each future period. Therefore the condition to rule out Info's double crossing is

$$q\,(F-I) \geqslant r\,(W-C)\,. \tag{4.5}$$

The procedure of stipulating an exogenous probability is admittedly ad hoc. In the mathematical appendix to this chapter (Section 4.6) I consider a more general and more satisfactory model where the population has a proportion of behavior types or short-run players who always choose Deviate. Then some cheating occurs along the equilibrium path, and the probability q can be endogenized.

When all traders are Info's customers, the question of investigating at extra cost any instances where a non-customer gets cheated becomes irrelevant. However, such investigation is not optimal in any case. If Info is engaged in such detection, then a trader should choose Comply even when his current partner is not Info's customer, because he knows that Info will detect and report this cheating to future customers—Info cannot credibly commit not to do so. Knowing this in turn, even a non-customer of Info expects his current match to choose Comply. Thus he gains nothing by paying Info, and can remain a free rider. Info can prevent this free-riding by not doing any extra detection. That also saves the direct cost of such detection; therefore it is clearly optimal for Info.

Finally, for Info to undertake this activity profitably, we need $F \geqslant I$, but that is ensured by (4.5) and therefore need not be considered separately.

We can put all the conditions into one chain of inequalities:

$$(C-D)-r\,(W-C) \geqslant F \geqslant I + r\,\max[\,(C-D),\,(W-C)/q\,]\,. \tag{4.6}$$

If the payoffs C, D, and W, the interest rate r, and the probability q are such that the expression on the left end of this chain of inequalities is at least as large as the one on the right end, then an F can be found that satisfies the whole chain and permits an equilibrium of the kind stipulated. If the left-end expression is strictly larger than the right-end one, there is a range of permissible values of F. To maximize his profit, Info will set his fee F_I at the top of this range. (The subscript "I" stands for Info.) If q can be chosen, it is in everyone's ex ante interest to set it high enough to permit an equilibrium.

The larger is r, the smaller is the left-end expression and the larger is the right-end one, making the inequalities harder to satisfy. And from (4.1) we see that r is larger when any one of δ, λ, and λ_0 are smaller. Of particular interest is the effect of λ_0. If the competition for Info's monopoly becomes more intense, his expected lifetime decreases, that is, λ_0 decreases.

Consider this competition in slightly greater detail. Write K_I for the up-front sunk investment to enter the contest to become an Info, P_I for the probability of success, and Π_I for the per-period profit while enjoying the monopoly as the incumbent

Info. Then the dynamic zero-profit condition of equilibrium in the ex ante contest (assuming risk neutrality) is

$$K_{\mathrm{I}} = \frac{P_{\mathrm{I}} \, \Pi_{\mathrm{I}}}{1 - \delta \, \lambda_0} \, . \tag{4.7}$$

We can think of this equation as endogenizing any one of the magnitudes. We can also bring in other considerations. The per-period profit Π_{I} might be endogenized by introducing ongoing expenditures on advertisement or fighting competitors. The probability of success could be endogenous depending on the size and abilities of the pool of potential Infos. The sunk investment K_{I} could be endogenous, for example advertising or acquiring a reputation for toughness, like an entry fee in a no-refund contest.[2] Most interesting is the possibility that an incumbent Info may have to engage in continuing contest with challengers trying to take his place; this would endogenize his survival probability λ_0.

If, other things being equal, $\Pi_{\mathrm{I}}/K_{\mathrm{I}}$ increases, then λ_0 must fall to restore (4.7). A more profitable Info monopoly leads to more cutthroat competition for it, and that reduces the life expectancy of any incumbent. This in turn makes it harder to satisfy the conditions (4.6) of equilibrium. An Info with a short life expectancy is more tempted to engage in extortion or double crossing. Also (4.3) shows that a lower λ_0 and therefore higher r implies a lower F_1—a more transient Info has to give his customers more surplus to keep them playing Comply. Then the fee may not cover Info's cost. For all these reasons, it may be impossible to sustain private intermediation precisely in those situations where the benefit of effective intermediation is large and therefore such opportunities are very profitable. There may have been an element of this in Russia during the last decade.

4.4   Enforcement Intermediaries

The activities and the resulting relationships and outcomes with an enforcement intermediary have some similarities to those of an information intermediary, but the two differ in some respects. Enfo accompanies each customer to the trade, whether physically or metaphorically, and finds out whether he was cheated. The cost of this is likely to be quite similar to the cost I of Info's corresponding activities. However, Enfo does not merely keep a record of cheating; he inflicts immediate punishment on the trader who cheated his customer. Actually inflicting such a punishment carries an extra cost. If the punishment is drastic enough, and Enfo's threat of inflicting it is credible, then it deters cheating. Therefore Enfo does not have to carry out his threat and bear the cost of the action. In the model I assume this to be the case. But the credibility has to be based on an acquired reputation, which requires a substantial up-front investment; Gambetta (1993, pp. 43–46) discusses the nature and the cost

---

[2]Hirshleifer and Riley (1992, Chapter 10) analyze such contests.

of this reputation. Thus Enfo's investment cost of entry K_E is likely to exceed Info's K_I by a substantial magnitude.

The structure of the game with Enfo is quite similar to that with Info. The only difference is that Enfo's contract says: "Pay me F now. In return, if your current match cheats you, I will inflict the dire punishment on him." Once again I look for an equilibrium where everyone is Enfo's customer and everyone including Enfo behaves honestly. The no-deviation conditions are different from those for Info's intermediation in several ways. First, Enfo does not report to his customers the history of their current partner's behavior, so he has no opportunity to extort money from anyone by threatening to misrepresent this history.

Next consider the possibility of a trader's deviations. As a customer of Enfo's and playing Comply (the equilibrium specification), he gets net payoff $C - F$. If he were to decline Enfo's offer to become a customer, Enfo would give his current partner (who is Enfo's customer in the stipulated equilibrium) the authorization to cheat with impunity. The deviant non-customer had better not himself cheat, because that would subject him to Enfo's terrible punishment. Thus in the dilemma game the non-customer would get the loser's payoff L. He would have done better not to play the game at all and get 0. In other words, a non-customer's payoff is 0. The condition to rule out a deviation is therefore $C - F \geqslant 0$ or

$$F \leqslant C . \tag{4.8}$$

What about becoming a customer but playing Deviate? This gets a payoff $W - F$ from the dilemma game, but it subjects the cheater to Enfo's punishment, because the other player is Enfo's customer in the specified equilibrium. I am assuming that the punishment is sufficiently drastic to lower the payoff below that from playing Comply. Therefore no new condition arises here.

The condition to rule out Enfo's double crossing is the same as Info's, namely (4.5). Therefore the full chain of inequalities is

$$C \geqslant F \geqslant I + r (W - C)/q . \tag{4.9}$$

If the payoffs C, W, the interest rate r, and the probability q permit such an F to be found, Enfo will set his fee F_E at the top of the feasible range, namely $F_E = C$.

Compare (4.9) with the corresponding condition for Info (4.6). The left-end expression in Enfo's chain of inequalities is greater than that for Info, while the right-end expression for Enfo is smaller than that for Info. Thus the range of feasible values of the fee is larger for Enfo than for Info. In other words, sometimes when an equilibrium with Info's intermediation is not feasible, one with Enfo's intermediation may be feasible.

When both kinds of intermediation are feasible, the comparison shows that Enfo's fee exceeds Info's fee:

$$F_E = C > (C - D) - r (W - H) = F_I .$$

The inequality shows two sources of the difference. First, in the game of any one period, the difference of payoffs between customer and non-customer traders is larger with Enfo than with Info. Customers get C with both, but Info's non-customers can cheat and get D, whereas Enfo's customers must drop out of the game and get 0.[3] Second, Enfo threatens to inflict an immediate punishment; he does not rely on any repeated games with cheaters and does not have to share any rent with them.

This is the point mentioned near the end of Section 4.1. Gambetta (1993, p. 16) notes that enforcement intermediaries charge a higher rate of commission than purely information intermediaries. Since each is a monopolist, at least temporarily and in his territory, we have to look for explanations from the demand side. That is exactly what we have here. Customers' willingness to pay Enfo is higher than that with Info, because their immediate payoff difference from being customers is higher, and because they cannot require Enfo to share any rent with them.

This may suggest that any would-be intermediary would prefer to be an Enfo than an Info. However, that leaves out consideration of the up-front cost. Since K_E is likely to be much higher than K_I. Even though the profit flow for an Enfo is higher than that for an Info, the rate of return to the initial investment may not be. And even if it were, the initial competition for entry, and the ongoing struggle to maintain one's monopoly against newcomers, can decrease Enfo's life expectancy to a point some may regard as unacceptable.

Next let us compare each of the intermediation modes with an ideal social optimum. The social gain from mutual honesty (choice of Comply) as opposed to mutual cheating (choice of Deviate) is $C - D$.[4] Info's fee is less than this. In other words, Info cannot capture the full social benefit his intermediation makes possible. Therefore information intermediation may be undersupplied relative to the social optimum. Enfo's fee, on the other hand, exceeds the social gain made possible by his intermediation. After paying Enfo, the traders may be left with less than the payoff they would have obtained without any intermediation at all! This is an equilibrium with a lock-in. Once an equilibrium with Enfo gets established, each individual has only the choice between being a customer and opting out of the game. No individual can bring about a switch to the equilibrium that has higher payoff; that requires collective action. As Gambetta (1993, pp. 197, 198) points out, the Mafia often enters by invitation, but "protectors, once enlisted, invariably overstay their welcome."

---

[3]I am assuming $D > 0$. If that were not the case, then in the case of Info's intermediation, pairs who saw that one of them was a non-customer would decline to play the game. Thus this source of difference would vanish, but it would not turn and go in favor of Info.

[4]Again, this is so given the assumption that $D > 0$; otherwise it would be simply C.

Finally, consider a variant of enforcement where Enfo can punish only those cheaters who are themselves his customers. Thus in effect Enfo punishes a cheater only if both sides to the transaction are his customers. This may be because he does not know how to find non-customers later. With this enforcement technology, both sides of the transaction will get payoff C if both are Enfo's customers. But if one person is not a customer, he is immune from Enfo's punishment and therefore expected to cheat. Knowing this, the other will cheat as well, and the payoffs will be D for each. Therefore in an equilibrium where everyone is Enfo's customer, each trader will be willing to pay a fee up to $C - D$ for Enfo's services. It may seem strange that the traders are willing to pay for the privilege of being subject to Enfo's punishment. The explanation is that it enables them to make a credible commitment to honesty and thereby get an honest response from their matches on the other side who are also customers. Schelling (1960, p. 43) made this point in connection with the official legal system.

> Among the legal privileges of corporations ... are the right to sue and
> the "right" to be sued. Who wants to be sued! But the right to be sued
> is the power to make a promise ... a prerequisite to doing business.

With the private Enfo, this has to be a part of a mutually reinforcing system—this right is valuable to you in deals with others who have also signed up as Enfo's customers and will therefore credibly reciprocate your honesty. Gambetta (1993, p. 20) also recognizes the importance of "purchasing protection against oneself," and Dasgupta (1988) offers a formal analysis. The phenomenon is also similar to Williamson's (1985, Chapters 7 and 8) idea of "giving hostages" to guarantee one's own good behavior.

4.5 Assessment and Prospects

The model captures several features of for-profit intermediation, and yields some results that are observed in reality. The finding that the traders may be trapped into an undesirable equilibrium under an enforcer is a good example, as is the result that the mafioso intermediary's commission is higher when he provides enforcement services than when he provides information only. The model goes further in giving us a better understanding for such results. Specifically, the "demand-side" explanation of the difference in commissions is noteworthy in this respect. The model also finds that violence is more likely when the mafioso provides enforcement services (Gambetta 1993, p. 18) and in the competition among rival mafiosi.

However, other forms of intermediation are not dealt with in the model. These include one-sided intermediation, for example credit-rating agencies, and situations where intermediaries are hired by a group with a contract designed by the group to maximize its welfare rather than the profit of the intermediary. Finally, many intermediaries perform search and matching functions; these can be linked with information and enforcement activities. As usual, a rich menu for theoretical research is still available.

In the mathematical appendix that follows, I take some small steps to generalize and enrich the very simple model of the two preceding sections. Three dimensions of generalization are introduced there.

(i) Asymmetry. In most economic transactions, the players on the two sides are different in many respects. Buyers on one side and sellers on the other is the most usual distinction. The magnitude of the temptation to cheat, and the future consequences of such cheating, differ greatly for the two. For example, firms that produce durable consumer goods are usually in the market for a long time, and their reputation for good or poor quality can be spread by the media, but their consumers may be in the market only infrequently, and may be tempted to renege on payment unless the firms have a good network for exchanging information.

(ii) Public information. The model of the text ignored any avenues of information dissemination other than the services provided by the intermediary. In practice some public information about traders' behavior is available, and it is of interest to examine the interaction between such information and the intermediary's service.

(iii) Behavior types. In the model of the text, all traders were identical and rational maximizers. Then in the equilibrium there was no cheating. Many applied models of repeated games have the same structure, but it is neither a good representation of reality, nor is it theoretically satisfactory. In reality there are some innately honest people, and some who are either innately dishonest or so short-lived that future consequences of cheating are not relevant for them. Theoretically, we saw above how the interpretation of deviation from equilibrium strategies becomes problematic when the deviant strategies are never played by anyone on the equilibrium path of the game. In the generalization I introduce behavior types in such a way that there is some cheating in equilibrium.

4.6 Mathematical Appendix

Asymmetric PD Stage Game

There are two sides, 1 and 2 (e.g. buyer and seller), with numerous individuals on each side. Everyone plays every period with another randomly matched player, but there are no repeat pairings so no direct reciprocity. Table 4.2 shows the payoff matrix of the prisoner's dilemma game that is played by any one such pair. In the informal discussion that follows, the actions Comply and Deviate are often referred to as honesty and cheating, respectively.

Table 4.2. Asymmetric prisoner's dilemma for each pair and period.

		Side 2	
		Comply	Deviate
Side 1	Comply	C_1, C_2	L_1, W_2
	Deviate	W_1, L_2	D_1, D_2

Each player has an outside opportunity normalized to zero. To reduce the taxonomy in this exposition, I assume

$$W_i > C_i > D_i > 0 > L_i \quad \text{for } i = 1, 2.$$

Behavior Types

I assume that the players on each side come in three types.

(1) Honest/Obedient: these constitute fractions α_i of the populations. They play Comply unless Deviate is authorized in a sense to be explained below.

(2) Dishonest: these form fractions β_i of the populations. They live only one period; and always play Deviate.

(3) Opportunist: they form the remaining fractions $\gamma_i = 1 - \alpha_i - \beta_i$ of the populations, and are standard rational calculators of their self-interest.

The presumption is that most of the population is Opportunist, that is, α_i and β_i are small and γ_i is close to 1. The innate behavioral traits are rationalized by supposing that the Honest types live for ever, the Dishonests live only one period. I also assume that the Opportunists have probability of survival λ_i from any one period to the next. The players who die in any one period are replaced in the following period by like-type newborns.

I first consider how such a situation will work without an intermediary.

Self-Governance

Information

I assume that if ever a trader makes an unauthorized choice of Deviate, there is a probability π_i that he will be discovered and publicly labeled a cheater for the rest of his life, as if he is branded "Bad" on the forehead. I look for tacit coordination, sustained by grim strategies that are triggered when one's partner is observed to have a Bad label.

Candidate Equilibrium

I consider stochastically stationary subgame-perfect equilibria sustained by grim-trigger strategies. The equilibrium strategies are specified as follows.

- Everyone plays Deviate if faced with an opponent who has a public Bad label, and players with a public Bad label themselves play Deviate. This is a Nash equilibrium of the stage game and therefore satisfies the requirement of subgame perfectness.

- When faced with an opponent who does not have a Bad label:

  (i) Honest types play Comply;

  (ii) Dishonest types play Deviate;

  (iii) there are two possibilities for the behavior of Side-i Opportunists without a Bad label (hereafter called "unlabeled Opportunists" for brevity, irrespective of whether they never cheated or got away with cheating):

    Ci—play Comply unless the other party has a Bad label;

    Di—play Deviate regardless of the label of the other party.[5]

Whether the Side-1 player's best response to the possible choices C_2 and D_2 of the Side-2 player is C_1 or D_1, and whether the Side-2 player's best response to the possible choices C_1 and D_1 of the Side-1 player is C_2 or D_2, depends on, among other things, π_1 and π_2. Then there can be four different types of stationary equilibria in pure strategies: (C1,C2), (D1,D2), (C1,D2), and (D1,C2). I now develop a classification of the possible stationary equilibria as functions of (π_1, π_2).

Introduce the following notation: ϕ_i^a is the probability that a randomly picked Side i player will play Comply, ϕ_i^b the probability that he will play Deviate but does not have a Bad label, and $\phi_i^c = 1 - \phi_i^a - \phi_i^b$ the probability that he has a Bad label. Of course, in equilibrium these probabilities are endogenous, and required to be correct (equal to the population proportions taking the respective action).

When Side-i Opportunists play Ci,

$$\phi_i^a = \alpha_i + \gamma_i , \qquad \phi_i^b = \beta_i , \qquad \phi_i^c = 0 . \qquad (4.10)$$

The calculation when Side-i Opportunists play Di needs care because people with Bad labels may die and their successors are born without a Bad label. But a simple calculation yields

$$\phi_i^a = \alpha_i , \qquad \phi_i^b = \beta_i + \gamma_i (1 - p_i) , \qquad \phi_i^c = \gamma_i p_i , \qquad (4.11)$$

where the p_i are the ergodic proportions of Opportunists who have Bad labels. These can be found in terms of the basic parameters of the problem. Since I do not need the precise solutions, I merely refer interested readers to Dixit (2003a).

---

[5] To avoid confusion, note that when used as a label of an Opportunist's action and the corresponding stationary state, the letter C or D is roman and the number 1 or 2 is not a subscript, and when used as the symbol for a payoff in the stage game, the letter C or D is in math italics and the number 1 or 2 is a subscript.

Opportunists' Choices

Let V_i denote the payoff in expected present value terms for a Side-i Opportunist with a Good label. This satisfies the dynamic programming recurrence relation (shown for Side 1, that for Side 2 being exactly analogous):

$$V_1 = \max \left\{ \phi_2^a C_1 + \phi_2^b L_1 + \phi_2^c D_1 + \delta \lambda_1 V_1, \right.$$
$$\phi_2^a W_1 + \phi_2^b D_1 + \phi_2^c D_1 + \delta \lambda_1 V_1$$
$$\left. - \delta \lambda_1 (\phi_2^a + \phi_2^b) \pi_1 \left[V_1 - \frac{D_1}{1 - \delta \lambda_1} \right] \right\}.$$

The first line results when the Side-1 Opportunist plays C1 (plays Comply when the other player is unlabeled and Deviate when the other has a Bad label). The second and third lines show the payoff when he deviates to D1. In each case the current payoff is the expected value from meeting various types on the other side with various probabilities in the stage game. The continuation payoff from the deviation includes the expected future cost, which is shown on the third line. This occurs only if the match does not have a Bad label (probability $\phi_2^a + \phi_2^b$) and in that event the probability that the Side-1 cheater acquires a Bad label is π_1. If this happens, his punishment phase starts next period (effective discounting $\delta \lambda_1$) and the payoff loss equals the difference between the optimum V_1 and the expected value $D_1/(1 - \delta \lambda_1)$ of the mutual cheating payoff for the rest of his life.

This, together with the values of ϕ_2^a, etc., in the various cases of Ci and Di, enables us to calculate the critical boundaries of the public information probability π_1, and similar boundaries for π_2, which determine the optimal responses of one side to the actions of the other. For the sake of brevity I omit the algebraic details—they can be found in Dixit (2003a)—and merely give a heuristic explanation.

The answer turns out to depend on whether $D_1 - L_1 > W_1 - C_1$ or the other way round. In the former case, the Side 1 Opportunist's one-time benefit from playing Deviate is higher if the other side is also playing Deviate than if it is playing Comply, that is, the prisoner's dilemma is more acute in its "defensive" aspect than in its "offensive" aspect. I call this the Defensive case, and the opposite the Offensive case. For the sake of brevity I confine the discussion here to the Defensive case; the other is treated in the working-paper version of Dixit (2003a). Of course it is possible to have the Defensive case for one side and the Offensive case for the other side.[6]

In the Defensive case for Side 1, the one-time benefits of cheating are larger for a Side-1 Opportunist when Side 2 is D2 than when it is C2. Therefore a higher

---

[6]This distinction in the prisoner's dilemma game seems interesting, but to my knowledge it has not been noted in previous literature.

probability of getting a Bad label is needed to deter a Side-1 Opportunist's cheating. Therefore the critical value of π_1 that makes a Side-1 Opportunist indifferent between C1 and D1 is higher when Side-2 Opportunists are playing D2 than when they are playing C2. (The opposite applies if the Offensive case prevails on Side 1.) It can also be shown that if Side-2 Opportunists play D2, the critical boundary is a downward-sloping function $\pi_1(\pi_2)$ in the Side-1-Defensive case. (It can be upward-sloping in the Side-1-Offensive case if the offensive benefit of cheating is sufficiently larger than the defensive benefit.)

All this was for a Side-1 Opportunist; similar analysis for a Side-2 Opportunist follows by interchanging the labels 1 and 2.

Taxonomy of Stationary Equilibria

Now we can put together all these calculations to classify stationary equilibria. Figure 4.1 shows the full set of logical possibilities when the Defensive case prevails on both sides. The sides of the box are the ranges of π_1 and π_2, from 0 to 1 in each case. The vertical line is the critical value of π_1 for Side-1 Opportunists' indifference between C1 and D1 as responses to C2, and the downward-sloping curve to its right is the critical function $\pi_1(\pi_2)$ of Side-1 Opportunists' indifference between C1 and D1 in response to D2. These two lines divide the box into three regions.[7] In the leftmost region, D1 is the Side-1 Opportunists' best response whether Side-2 Opportunists play C2 or D2; in the rightmost region, C1 is their best response regardless of whether Side-2 Opportunists play C2 or D2; in the middle, Side-1 Opportunists' best response matches the behavior of Side-2 Opportunists.[8] Similarly, the horizontal critical boundaries of π_2 divide the box into three regions for the best responses of Side-2 Opportunists.

Combining the three-way classifications in the two dimensions gives nine kinds of possible stationary equilibria. In the four corner regions, Opportunists on each side have uniformly best responses and we get corresponding stationary states. In the northeast corner the outcome is (C1,C2) and in the southwest corner it is (D1,D2). These are the intuitive outcomes: (C_1, C_2) should occur when both detection probabilities are very high, and (D_1, D_2) when both probabilities are very low. In the northwest and southeast corners, only one side fears detection sufficiently to act honestly even when the other side is cheating. This may be true in some instances. For example, consumers' credit-card fraud may be easily detected (high π_1) so they

---

[7]The regions are given similar sizes solely for convenience in graphing and labeling; for actual parameter values the left region is likely to be much larger. If the gain from cheating is large enough, or the survival probability is low enough, then the critical values of π_1 may exceed 1, that is, even the certainty of getting a Bad label may not suffice to deter cheating. Then the right and perhaps even the middle region may be missing.

[8]In the Offensive case, in the middle third, the best response of Side-1 Opportunists will be to take the opposite action to that of Side-2 Opportunists.

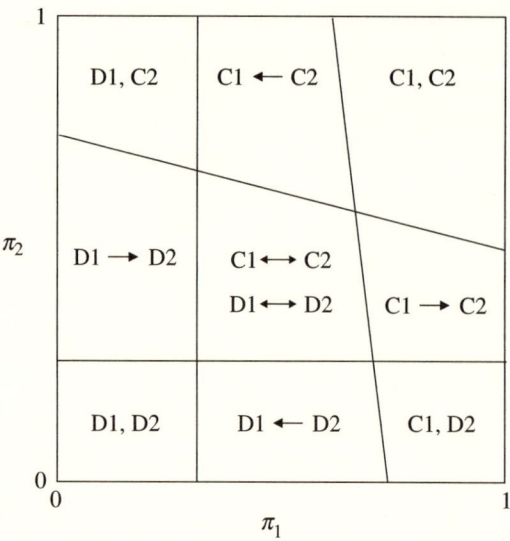

Figure 4.1. Possibilities with self-governance in the Defensive case.

behave honestly in the matter of payment, but if restaurants are short-lived (low λ_2), they may cheat on quality. In the middle regions on each of the four sides of the box, each side's Opportunists' best response matches the action of the other side's Opportunists; the labels and arrows in these regions show the choices and the direction of causation. On the left side, for example, Side-1 Opportunists' best response is D1, and this leads Side-2 Opportunists to choose D2—cheating spreads like an infection. Similarly, in the middle region along the top edge, honesty spreads by infection. Finally, in the central region of the box, there are multiple stationary states (C1,C2) and (D1,D2), with either honesty or cheating on one side sustained by like behavior on the other.[9] The (C1,C2) outcome is Pareto preferred, and may get selected by a focal-point mechanism, but a lock-in to the (D1,D2) state remains possible.

In the three regions to the southwest, the outcome is (D1,D2), which can benefit from two-sided intermediation (considered here). In the central region, (C1,C2) is possible, but an intermediary can try to make a "regulated injection of distrust" (Gambetta 1993, p. 25) in this situation so as to secure the (D1,D2) outcome and then provide his service for profit. For plausible parameter values these four regions requiring two-sided intermediation cover most of the square (Dixit 2003a, p. 458);

---

[9] In the Offensive case, the multiple stationary equilibria in the middle region are (C1,D2) and (D1,C2). In mixed cases where one side has the Offensive case and the other the Defensive case, the middle region has stationary states with mixed strategies.

therefore I will focus on this case. In the regions with (C1,C2) and (C1,D2) outcomes, one-sided intermediation suffices.

Information Intermediary (Info)

As was noted just above, the likeliest outcome in conditions of weak public information transmission is that the prisoner's dilemma cannot be resolved by self-governance. Now consider information intermediation in this situation. The structure of the game between Info and the traders on the two sides was mostly described in the text, as was the nature of the equilibrium being sought; these matters need not be repeated here. The introduction of behavior types requires one new point. If in a particular match it turns out that only one side is Info's customer, then it is in Info's interest to let his customer play Deviate and not count this as an instance of cheating for future reference. I will assume that in such a situation, customers of the Honest type will follow Info's instructions and play Deviate. This is the "authorized cheating" that was mentioned when defining Honest types above.

Recall that I am looking for conditions that yield an equilibrium where everyone is Info's customer and everyone except the innately Dishonest types behaves honestly. I calculate each player's incentive to deviate from his equilibrium strategies when everyone else is following theirs. Such calculation is not relevant for the Honest and Dishonest behavior types; that leaves the Opportunists and Info.

Opportunist's Strategies

Consider a Side-1 Opportunist. He takes as given the strategies of the other players.

Info.

(i) Will let his Side-2 customers cheat a Side-1 non-customer; in fact he will instruct and authorize his Side-2 Honest customers to do so.

(ii) Will record any instance where a customer gets cheated, and report the cheater's history to future customers, and allow or instruct them to play Deviate against the previous cheater, even though the cheater may offer to sign up as a customer later.

Side-2 Honests. Will choose Comply unless authorized by Info to play Deviate.

Side-2 Dishonests. Will play Deviate no matter what.

Side-2 Opportunists. Will play Comply against Info's customers with no known history of cheating; they will play Deviate against those customers for whom Info reports a history of cheating, and against all non-customers.

Let V_1 denote the present value payoff to a Side-1 Opportunist with a clean history. He can take any of four actions this period.

(i) He can become Info's customer by paying F_1, and choose Comply. Then the one-shot game will give him a payoff $(\alpha_2 + \gamma_2) C_1 + \beta_2 L_1$, and the continuation value V_1 starting next period.

(ii) He can become a customer by paying F_1, but play Deviate. The one-period payoff is higher, $(\alpha_2 + \gamma_2) W_1 + \beta_2 D_1$; let $\hat{V}_1$ be the continuation value starting next period.

(iii) He can stay a non-customer but choose Comply anyway. All of his Side-2 matches will play Deviate, so he will get a current-period payoff L_1, but his record will stay clean and the continuation payoff will be V_1.

(iv) He can stay a non-customer and play Deviate. This will get him a current-period payoff D_1, and the continuation payoff $\hat{V}_1$. His effective discount factor taking into account the probability of his own survival probability is $\delta \lambda_1$. (Info's survival probability enters separately.)

Therefore his dynamic programming problem is

$$V_1 = \max \{ (\alpha_2 + \gamma_2) C_1 + \beta_2 L_1 - F_1 + \delta \lambda_1 V_1$$

$$(\alpha_2 + \gamma_2) W_1 + \beta_2 D_1 - F_1 + \delta \lambda_1 \hat{V}_1 ,$$

$$L_1 + \delta \lambda V_1 , \ C_1 + \delta \lambda_1 \hat{V}_1 \} .$$

It is easy to see that the third action cannot be optimal. But much algebraic manipulation is needed to find the conditions for the first action to be optimal. I omit most of it, except for the equation defining $\hat{V}_1$, which shows how Info's survival probability enters the picture.

The continuation value $\hat{V}_1$ after a choice of Deviate can be decomposed as follows. With probability π_1 this will earn a public Bad label, and all future matches will play Deviate, so this player will also play Deviate and get D_1 every period; the present value is $D_1/(1 - \delta \lambda_1)$. With probability $(1 - \pi_1)$ there will be no public bad label, but since all players on Side 2 are Info's customers in the stationary state we are testing, Info will find out. If Info survives until the next period (probability λ_0), he will instruct all his Side-2 customers to play Deviate. Then the Side-1 customer will get the one-shot payoff D_1 and the continuation value $\hat{V}_1$ again. With probability $(1 - \lambda_0)$, Info will not survive, when the Side-1 Opportunist can make a fresh start, which has value V_1. Thus

$$\hat{V}_1 = \pi_1 \frac{D_1}{1 - \delta \lambda_1} + (1 - \pi_1) \lambda_0 [D_1 + \delta \lambda_1 \hat{V}_1] + (1 - \pi_1)(1 - \lambda_0) V_1 .$$

Omitting some long and tedious algebraic manipulation, the condition for the Side-1 Opportunist to become Info's customer and choose Comply is

$$F_1 \leqslant [(\alpha_2 + \gamma_2) C_1 + \beta_2 L_1 - D_1]$$

$$- r_1 [(\alpha_2 + \gamma_2) (W_1 - C_1) + \beta_2 (D_1 - L_1)] , \quad (4.12)$$

where

$$r_1 = \frac{(1/\delta\lambda_1) - \lambda_0\,(1 - \pi_1)}{(\pi_1/1 - \delta\lambda_1) + \lambda_0\,(1 - \pi_1)} \, . \tag{4.13}$$

The condition (4.12) is a generalization of the condition (4.3) in the text. The first line on the right-hand side is the Side-1 Opportunist's one-period payoff difference between being Info's customer and not; the second line is the rent Info must leave him to offset his temptation to cheat while a customer. The implicit interest rate for the Side-1 Opportunist is r_1, as defined by (4.13), which in turn is a generalization of (4.1) in the text.

As any of δ, λ_1, λ_0 increase, r_1 decreases, and the upper bound on F_1 increases. The same effects arise when π_1 is higher; thus better public information helps Info. This may seem paradoxical, but the explanation is that better public information lowers the payoff to a non-customer, and therefore increases the willingness of the Opportunist to pay Info. But this is a local result; if public information becomes too good, that is, π_1 and π_2 become too large, then the outcome of self-governance may become (C1,C2), making Info redundant. Thus the Infos of this world may want to make public information a little better but not too much so. This mixed result contrasts with Gambetta's (1993, pp. 24–28) unqualified argument that Peppe benefits from creating endogenous distrust in the population.

Info's Strategies

As in the text, Info does not carry out costly detection of cheating when the victim is not his customer, because that also helps him solve a free-rider problem. The analysis of Info's extortion is similar to that in the text, so I omit it. The behavior types create some new issues for the analysis of Info's double crossing. When there are Dishonest types in the population (that is, when $\beta_i > 0$, no matter how small), a customer who gets cheated cannot be sure that Info double crossed him; it could be just the bad luck of having been matched with one of the Dishonests. Thus the game between Info and an Opportunist customer has imperfect monitoring. The Side-1 Opportunist customer gets the low payoff L_1 with probability 1 if Info double crosses, and with the smaller probability β_2 otherwise.

In this game, the best possible equilibrium can be sustained by the following strategy (see Dixit 2003a for further discussion). If a Side-1 Opportunist customer gets the L_1 payoff, then a punishment phase is triggered with probability q_1 using a public randomization device (such as a coin toss whose outcome both the trader and the Info observe together), and lasts so long as this trader lives. In the punishment phase the trader becomes a non-customer and plays Deviate. In equilibrium this is triggered with probability $\beta_2\,q_1$ each period even though Info has not double crossed; therefore for efficiency q_1 should be kept as low as is compatible with incentive constraints.

An added complication arises if Info is finite-lived ($\lambda_0 < 1$), because all customers in this punishment phase are released from it when their Info dies, which makes the population proportions non-stationary. Therefore in this section I confine the analysis to the case of an immortal Info ($\lambda_0 = 1$).

Even with the stationary structure and a special simple punishment, the analysis gets intricate, because now in the stationary state there are some Opportunists in the punishment phase who play Deviate. Their proportion x within their type in the stochastically stationary state can be calculated as follows. In equilibrium play, a proportion $(1 - x)$ of Side-1 Opportunists are not in the punishment phase, and therefore not playing Deviate. Any one of these meets a Side-2 Dishonest with probability β_2. In that event, with probability $\lambda_1 q_1$ the punishment phase will be triggered—he will survive and become a non-customer next period. A proportion x are in the punishment phase, and each of them will stay in it the following period with probability λ_1. (With probability $1 - \lambda_1$ he will die, and his replacement will start afresh in the customer phase.) Therefore

$$x = (1 - x)\, \beta_2 \, \lambda_1 \, q_1 + x \, \lambda_1 \, .$$

Solving for x, the population proportions of Side-1 Opportunist customers and non-customers, denoted by κ_1 and ν_1 (with $\kappa_1 + \nu_1 = \gamma_1$), are

$$\kappa_1 = (1 - x)\, \gamma_1 = \frac{1 - \lambda_1}{1 - \lambda_1 + \beta_2 \, \lambda_1 \, q_1} \, \gamma_1 \, ,$$

$$\nu_1 = x\gamma_1 = \frac{\beta_2 \, \lambda_1 \, q_1}{1 - \lambda_1 + \beta_2 \, \lambda_1 \, q_1} \, \gamma_1 \, .$$

Now we can obtain the condition for Info not to double cross a customer on Side 1. If he does so, the match on Side 2 gains an extra $W_2 - C_2$, and this is the maximum Info can extract from him. The probability that the Side 1 customer is an Opportunist is $\kappa_1 / (1 - \nu_1) = \kappa_1 / (\alpha_1 + \beta_1 + \kappa_1)$. In that event, with probability q_1 the punishment phase will kick in, and last while the trader lives. There Info will lose his profit $F_1 - I_1$ every period. The expected present value of this is calculated using the effective discount factor $\delta\lambda_1$. Therefore the no-double-crossing condition is

$$W_2 - C_2 \leqslant \frac{q_1 \, \kappa_1}{1 - \nu_1} \, \frac{\delta\lambda_1}{1 - \delta\lambda_1} \, (F_1 - I_1) \, ,$$

or

$$F_1 \geqslant I_1 + \frac{1 - \nu_1}{\kappa_1} \, \frac{1 - \delta\lambda_1}{\delta\lambda_1} \, \frac{W_2 - C_2}{q_1} \, . \tag{4.14}$$

This generalizes the no-double-crossing condition (4.5) in the text.

We must also recalculate the Side-1 Opportunist customer's decision, now that some Side-2 Opportunists will be in a punishment phase. The result of the long and

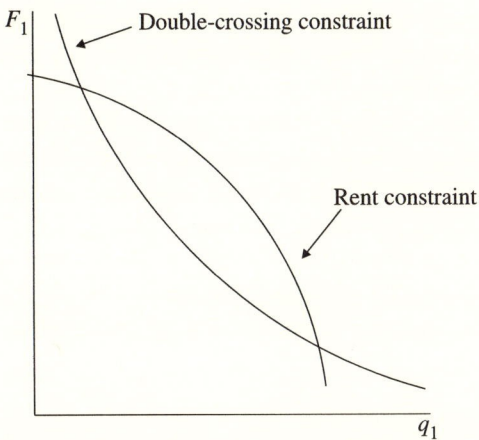

Figure 4.2. Conditions to rule out trader's cheating and Info's double crossing.

tedious calculation is

$$F_1 \leqslant [(\alpha_2 + \kappa_2)\, C_1 + v_2\, D_1 + \beta_2\, L_1 - D_1]$$
$$- r_1\, [(\alpha_2 + \kappa_2)\, (W_1 - C_1) + \beta_2\, (D_1 - L_1)], \quad (4.15)$$

where the implicit discount rate r_1 is given by

$$r_1 = \frac{1 - \delta\,\lambda_1\,(1 - q_1\,\beta_2)}{\delta\,\lambda_1\,(1 - q_1\,\beta_2)}. \quad (4.16)$$

These generalize the equations (4.12) and (4.13) above.

As usual, the condition says that the one-time gain should not exceed the capitalized expected value of the subsequent stream of losses during the punishment. If the punishment phase to control Info's double crossing did not have to be triggered with positive probability along the equilibrium path, that is, if $\beta_2 = 0$ or $q_1 = 0$, then the discount rate would be just the familiar $r_1 = 1/(\delta\,\lambda_1) - 1$. But because of the additional need to control Info's double crossing, the effective discount rate is larger, and is given by (4.16). Another way to interpret the result is that in this situation of imperfect information, the punishment is triggered probabilistically even when Info has remained faithful. This lowers the customer's payoff from staying honest. To retain his incentive, Info has to give him more rent.

To control the Side-1 Opportunist's cheating, we need F_1 and q_1 to satisfy (4.15), which places an upper bound on Info's fee. To control Info's double crossing, we need F_1 and q_1 to satisfy (4.14), which places a lower bound on Info's fee. Figure 4.2 shows the two constraints and the lens-shaped region where both are satisfied. Of course the intersection may be empty for some ranges of the other parameters; then Info's governance becomes infeasible. When the region is non-empty, Info will choose the (q_1, F_1) combination at the northwest corner, minimizing the probability with which the punishment needs to be triggered along the equilibrium path, and simultaneously maximizing his fee.

The presence of behavior types introduces another new consideration. Info cannot directly observe the type—Honest, Opportunist, or Dishonest—of any individual, in particular of any newborns. If Info finds out about an act of unauthorized cheating, and then sees that person around at a later date, he can infer that the person must be an Opportunist. But the Opportunists have the smallest willingness to pay, so Info cannot use this revelation for price discrimination.

Why do Opportunists have the smallest willingness to pay Info? The condition (4.12) shows that

$$\text{Opportunists' willingness to pay} < (\alpha_2 + \gamma_2) C_1 + \beta_2 L_1 - D_1 .$$

(Here I have simply left out the rent term that was subtracted in the condition.) What about the willingness of the other two behavior types? They do not do any intertemporal optimization, so their willingness to pay Info is just the one-period payoff difference. An Honest type who is a customer will do just as well as an Opportunist (who plays Comply in our equilibrium). An honest type who is not a customer will play Comply (cheating is not an authorized action or punishment phase in this situation). But then he is sure to get payoff L_1, which is negative, so he would do better to take the outside option. I will allow Honest traders this much rational calculation—as non-customers, knowing that if they played, their nature would force them to choose Comply, they stay out. Therefore

$$\text{Honests' willingness to pay} = (\alpha_2 + \gamma_2) C_1 + \beta_2 L_1 .$$

A Dishonest type cheats even when a customer and therefore gets a higher payoff, so

$$\text{Dishonests' willingness to pay} = (\alpha_2 + \gamma_2) W_1 + \beta_2 D_1 - D_1 .$$

To sum up, Dishonests do better than Opportunists when they are Info's customers (because they cheat), and Honests do worse than Opportunists when they are not Info's customers (because then they have to drop out of the game altogether to avoid being cheated); thus for both of the other types the one-period payoff difference exceeds that for Opportunists.

But armed with this knowledge, Info could try a strategy of price discrimination to identify the high-paying honest types. If Info deviates to charge a fee higher than the Opportunists' willingness to pay, the remaining customers who go on to survive to the next period will be identified as Honest types. Info can then charge them their full willingness to pay. For the candidate stationary equilibrium to prevail, the present value of Info's subsequent extra gains by charging higher prices to the revealed

Honest customers should not exceed his forgone one-period profit from Opportunist customers. Since I am assuming that most of the population is Opportunist, this is the likely scenario.

Analysis of equilibrium with free entry, and the modeling of Enfo, are not sufficiently enriched by the new considerations introduced in the appendix; therefore I do not consider these matters here.

5

Private Protection of Property Rights

5.1 Issues and Empirical Research

Economic theorists have always recognized the importance of secure property rights in creating the right incentives to produce and to invest. North and Weingast (1989) emphasize its role in the rise of Western European economies. Students of less-developed countries (De Soto 2000; Rodrik 2000, pp. 6, 7) and transition economies (McMillan 2002) reinforce this lesson. They also show how insecure property rights remain in many countries. The threats to property rights come from two broad classes of predators. Other individuals may encroach on one's property, may extort money by making threats of damaging the property, or may steal the property outright; a weak state may be unable to deter or prevent such actions. Hirshleifer (2001, especially Chapters 3, 5, and 6) builds on this theme. Even worse, the state itself or its agents may engage in extortion of private property to further their own objectives, whether they be wasteful public monuments and displays, aggression against other states, or simple personal consumption. Olson (1993), Grossman (2002), and Shleifer and Vishny (1998, especially Chapters 1, 2, and 5) are among the many who have emphasized this aspect. Faced with such threats, individuals will be deterred from production and investment, but will also attempt to take some countermeasures to preserve their property.[1] In this chapter I consider some of these issues. As usual, this section contains an overview of some conceptual and empirical literature; subsequent sections develop some theoretical models to capture and pursue in depth some specific points and issues.

I begin with a statement of some general ideas about property rights; this summary is based on Barzel (1989), who in turn builds on previous work by Alchian (1965), Demsetz (1967), and others.

---

[1] Barzel (2002, especially Chapters 2, 7, and 8) gives a broad general discussion of the prior stage of state formation, where individuals can try to install safeguards against extortionate use of the state's coercive power.

Property rights over assets consist of

(a) control—decisions about how to use them;

(b) entitlement to income produced by them;

(c) alienation—selling one or both of the control or income rights, fully or partially, to someone else.

All of these are subject to formal or informal constraints. Control rights can be leased or sold under contracts, but where contracts are incomplete, the unspecified or residual rights remain with the owner. Income rights are often shared with other stakeholders under various social norms, terms or covenants in a higher-level contract, general laws, etc.; some control right may also be similarly shared. And sales are also subject to similar constraints, such as covenants restricting what homeowners can and cannot do to the exteriors of their homes, to fences and yards, and so on.

Legal property rights are not absolute. They are to some extent subject to private modification by mutual consent for mutual benefit. More generally, security of property rights depends on (a) government protection, (b) private protection, and (c) other people's attempts to capture some of the rights. All these are costly in different ways; therefore rights are generally not complete. "When transacting is costly, all contract forms are costly" (Barzel 1989, p. 31), so choice of governance form is at best a constrained optimum.

Most assets and commodities have multiple dimensions. It may be optimal to divide the property rights to different attributes of a commodity between different owners (Barzel 1989, p. 4). Different dimensions of assets and contracts interact: they may be mutually substitutes or complements. This can be utilized to achieve better outcomes from seemingly incomplete contracts. For example, in a short-term rental contract, the landlord is usually responsible for maintenance and improvement, whereas in long-term contracts, the tenant is. This goes with their natural incentives; therefore it can even be left unspecified (Barzel 1989, p. 35). When the rights and responsibilities governing real aspects of behavior have been efficiently specified, the financial aspects of the contract can adjust to satisfy the participation constraints and division of surplus.

Even a given attribute may have shared ownership, or if ownership is not specified or enforced because of incompleteness, it may be placed in the public domain. Actions of individuals in a shared ownership can be constrained for their mutual benefit. Income from an asset or attribute may be affected by the actions of others; transaction costs may preclude attainment of the optimum indicated by the Coase Theorem (Barzel 1989, pp. 4, 5, 86). As transaction technology (information, enforcement, etc.) changes, the nature and governance mode of property rights also evolves. Disputes arise when some previously unexercised rights become worth exercising, so an owner who had previously left them in the public domain now wants to reclaim them (Barzel 1989, pp. 65, 68).

Liebcap (1989) studies how property rights come to be delineated and enforced in the first place. His general idea (Liebcap 1989, Chapter 1) is that property rights are needed to reduce or eliminate efficiency losses due to common pool problems. But the process is political, with distributional conflicts. Bargaining may not lead to an efficient outcome, or may do so only with long delay. The analytical framework (Liebcap 1989, Chapter 2) argues that efficient adaptation of rights to new circumstances is more difficult if

(1) aggregate gains are small;

(2) the number of participants is large;

(3) interests are heterogeneous;

(4) the sizes of participants' gains or losses are private information;

(5) the efficient regime will involve greater concentration of wealth, so there will be more losers.

The outcome of the political conflict between the winners and losers may be determined by who is better able to organize for political action; this is usually the smaller group with more concentrated benefits or costs. These observations support the results of the theory of repeated games discussed in Section 1.7, and with the idea of Olson (1965) concerning collective action.

In the rest of his book, Liebcap develops some case studies.

(1) Mineral rights in California in the mid nineteenth century. The aggregate gains from avoiding a free-for-all among prospectors were huge, so the need for delineation of property rights was quickly recognized. Camps formed their own "governments" and "laws." Many of the resulting arrangements were then officially accepted, even though they did not conform to the Federal or State laws and practices. The homogeneity and lack of ex ante private information among the prospectors helped achieve agreement.

(2) Federal land policies in late nineteenth century in western US areas. Here the process of delineation of property rights was slowed by the conflicting interests of ranchers, timber companies, and homesteaders in matters of the size of land allocations, rules concerning fences, access to water, and so on.

(3) Fisheries. These raise some serious conflicts that delay or prevent agreement.

(a) More efficient incumbents are against uniform quotas and against tradeable quotas because they are hurt if low-efficiency incumbents can sell their quotas to better operators.

(b) Fish migrate, so property rights to an area may not solve externality problems. Also, efficiency-promoting arrangements may serve as a cloak for cartelization.

(4) Oil fields in Texas. Several drillers usually have the right to tap into a single pool of underground oil, so their free-rider problem needs to be solved by arrangements to treat the pool as a single entity and internalize the externality. The need for such arrangements, called "unitization," was widely recognized but the efficient arrangements were delayed or not made either in private arrangements or government-imposed rules. Asymmetric information at the time of the negotiation may have been the key difficulty.

For fisheries as well as oil, historically determined laws such as "rule of capture" also inhibited efficiency-enhancing adaptations.

Note that Liebcap is talking about rights to assets that exist in nature, such as land, forests, and mineral deposits, whereas much of Barzel's emphasis is on rights to assets that have to be produced, such as buildings and machines. The latter brings in the added issues of incentives to engage in this production and the efficiency of this productive activity. Even more complex issues arise in the context of other kinds of property, such as intellectual property and commercial brand names. These issues have to do with balancing private incentives to produce new assets of this kind and the social incentives efficiently to use the assets once they exist.

Ellickson's (1989) study of property rights in the eighteenth and nineteenth century whaling industry supports and extends many of these ideas by considering the information aspects of the enforcement of property rights. Many boats may participate in the killing of one whale, either simultaneously or sequentially. Or one boat may kill a whale and take it in tow only to lose it, and then another boat may find it. When disputes arise in such situations, their resolution depends on the verifiability of information. Therefore it makes sense to define property rights in the first place so as to be consistent with the verifiability of information regarding any violations of these rights. Ellickson finds that the definition of fishermen's property rights over whale carcasses did indeed differ across whale types and regions, and evolved over time, in just this way. This can be thought of as another aspect of the complexity inherent in the concept of property rights.

However, optimal evolution of property rights and their enforcement should not be taken for granted. Given this multiplicity of dimensions of property rights, the formal and informal, explicit and implicit allocations of rights among various claimants, the transaction costs of enforcing rights, and the conflicts that confront any attempts to change any rights, it is not surprising that reform is often stalled or makes matters worse. Ensminger (1997) presents an example involving interaction between state and non-state governance. Traditional property rights to land in Africa are a complex system—titles are granted to individual families by clan chiefs, and sales are subject to their approval and also that of heirs (all sons usually have expectations of equal division) (Ensminger 1997, pp. 169, 171). Many family stakeholders have usufruct rights (Ensminger 1997, p. 187). When the Kenyan government attempted to impose a system of formal land titles, this ran into conflict with the traditional arrangements. The expected capital market did not develop because lenders knew that foreclosure was infeasible in the face of opposition from family and community, so the land could not be used as collateral (Ensminger 1997, p. 188). Attempts to consolidate scattered holdings for scale economy reasons did not work because there was a good economic reason (diversification of risks) for the scattering (Ensminger 1997, p. 184). Many formally registered titles are now being allowed to lapse and revert to older arrangements, and the laws are being changed to resemble traditional forms more closely (Ensminger 1997, p. 189). Platteau (2000) similarly emphasizes the importance of developing public institutions for property right protection that build on, and work synergistically with, the historical and cultural endowment of norms and practices in a society.

If a government cannot or does not provide adequate protection for property rights, individuals and groups will attempt to provide private protection. They may do this using their own individual or collective efforts, or hire professional guards. The latter approach carries the risk that the guards become predators or extortionists; this problem exists with some governments too. The outcome of such games may be more or less efficient depending on the specifics of the situation—the technologies of protection and predation, the information, the skills in alternative occupations, the time-horizon of the participants, and so on. However, some form of private protection will usually be better than none at all.

Many instances of the different methods of protection can be observed in reality. Even in modern states with well-functioning governments, private protection supplements or replaces official policing: firms have private security guards, and homeowners have neighborhood-watch organizations and gated communities with private guards. In countries where the rule of law does not run very well, private protection becomes even more important; Gambetta (1993) gives a classic description and analysis of the origins and functions of the Sicilian Mafia, and Varese (2001) describes and discusses organized private protection in Russia in the 1990s.

Theorists have also studied alternative methods of private protection: the owner spending his own time and effort on protection, hiring specialized protectors who may be individuals or organizations like the Mafia, and so on. In these games, predators choose their targets knowing the form of protection that prevails in equilibrium, and the guards choose their strategies of pricing, entry, collusion, etc. This creates many complex interactions. Hirshleifer (2001, Chapter 6) considers the optimal allocation of a property-owner's effort between producing output using one's own property on one hand, and fighting over one's own or another's property or the output produced using such property on the other hand. He characterizes the equilibrium of the interaction between two such owners. I develop such a model in Section 5.2. Anderson and Bandiera (2002) add the possibility of hiring specialized protectors; I summarize and discuss their work in Section 5.3. Grossman (1995) considers the interaction of a private mafia and the government in providing enforcement of property rights, but his government is also a profit maximizer, so the basic effect of the mafia is to increase competition in the protection industry.

The effect of predation—whether by private bandits or by a kleptocratic government and its agents—on the incentives to produce and invest, and therefore on overall economic performance, depends crucially on the time-horizon of the predator. Olson (1993) emphasized this dichotomy and gave the two extreme types the memorable names of "roving bandits" and "stationary bandits." A roving bandit has a short time-horizon, perhaps because he faces strong competition from others who want to take his place. Such a bandit will grab as much as he can as fast as he can, destroying all incentives for his victims. A stationary bandit expects to prey on the same victims for a long time. He will find it in his own long-term interests to establish and maintain the reputation that he leaves individuals some of the fruits of their investments or efforts. The resulting incentives will generate more output and growth, and therefore more for the predator to take in the future. His optimal strategy will balance at the margin the gains from short-run grabbing and long-run cultivation and harvesting.

Can an economy under a stationary bandit be efficient? It is in the bandit's own interest to control his victim population so as to maximize economic efficiency; this will maximize his own take, after he has given the victims just the amount needed to keep them alive and to stop them revolting against his rule. Olson (1993) assumes that the bandit can only choose proportional taxation, and it is well known that such a tax inflicts an unavoidable distortion or dead-weight loss on the economy. But a smarter bandit might try a less-distorting instrument, for example lump-sum taxation or more general nonlinear taxation. The feasibility of such mechanisms depends on the information available to the bandit. The theory of mechanism design under incomplete information is well established in microeconomics; in Section 5.4 I will adapt it to study the efficiency of an economy under a stationary bandit.

Even though an economy ruled by a stationary bandit may fall considerably short of full efficiency, it will perform much better than that under a roving bandit. Supporting evidence can be found in the case studies of Pritchett (2003, p. 148).

> Under a regime that has reasonable institutional stability and is not
> completely dysfunctional, a rapidly increasing level of GDP per capita
> is possible up to semi-industrialization. ... [A]t their best, these types

of regimes, while they tolerate high levels of corruption, also demand some performance such that corruption does not become absolutely disorganized.

Disorganization becomes likely if a number of bandits compete with each other for the resources available for extraction, because this adds a common-resource-pool problem to the short-horizon problem (Shleifer and Vishny 1998, Chapter 5).

5.2 Production and Protection under Anarchy

The word "anarchy" is often used in the sense of complete chaos or disorganization, but Hirshleifer (2001, Chapter 6) argues for a more subtle distinction. He uses the word "amorphy" for the chaotic scramble for resources that are not owned or protected by anyone, or in other words, for cases of failure to solve common-resource-pool problems. By contrast, anarchy is interference competition; people attempt to sequester resources (assert property rights) and to defend these resources (provide private protection) from others' attempts at predation or theft. The equilibrium of an anarchic game of aggression and defense can exhibit spontaneous order. In this section I construct a simple model to give the readers a flavor of Hirshleifer's analysis.

The simple economy of the model has just two participants, each of whom initially controls one unit of resources, which may be his own labor time, or some other productive asset, or some combination of these. Each can allocate the resource at his command among one of three uses: production, defense of his output against the other's aggression, and aggression against the other's output. Let X_i, Y_i, and Z_i denote the respective allocations by player i for $i = 1, 2$. The resource constraint is

$$X_i + Y_i + Z_i \leqslant 1 .$$

The resource allocated to production yields output $(X_i)^\alpha$, where the parameter α is between 0 and 1, and indicates how quickly diminishing returns arise in production—the smaller is α, the faster do marginal returns to the resource diminish.

If an amount Y of defensive resources is pitted against an amount Z of aggressive resources, the probability that the initial owner of the output keeps it—or equivalently in the model, the fraction he keeps—is assumed to be given by

$$Y^\beta / (Y^\beta + \theta Z^\beta) . \tag{5.1}$$

The parameter θ measures the efficacy of the offense relative to that of the defense. The parameter β is between 0 and 1, and indicates how quickly diminishing returns arise in fighting activities. Both θ and β are properties of the technology of fighting; they may differ from one society to another, or change over time, as this technology changes.

When each of the two players is engaged simultaneously in production, defense of his own output, and predation against the other's output, the payoff to the first player is

$$\Pi_1 = (X_1)^\alpha \frac{(Y_1)^\beta}{(Y_1)^\beta + \theta \,(Z_2)^\beta} + (X_2)^\alpha \frac{\theta \,(Z_1)^\beta}{(Y_2)^\beta + \theta \,(Z_1)^\beta}.$$

The expression for Player 2's payoff is analogous.

The Nash equilibrium of this game can be found after a little algebra, which I relegate to the mathematical appendix to this chapter (Section 5.6.1). Specifically, I consider a symmetric outcome where the two players choose identical allocations in equilibrium.[2] The result is

$$X_1 = X_2 = \frac{\alpha \,(1+\theta)}{\alpha \,(1+\theta) + 2\,\beta\,\theta},$$

$$Y_1 = Y_2 = Z_1 = Z_2 = \frac{\beta\,\theta}{\alpha \,(1+\theta) + 2\,\beta\,\theta}.$$

The first point to note is the economic inefficiency of the equilibrium. The ideal would be for neither player to spend anything on aggression against the other's resources. Then neither need spend anything on defense of his resources, and both can devote their entire resources to production. With $X_1 = X_2 = 1$, each would enjoy an output equal to 1. But that is not a Nash equilibrium, because the game is a prisoner's dilemma. If one is defenseless, then the other can steal his entire output by spending just a little of his resources on predation. Anticipating this, each responds with some defensive expenditure, and the process escalates. In the resulting equilibrium, the resources spent on defense by one player equal those spent on offense by the other. This is a consequence of the special forms of the various functions in the model, but the general ideas are robust: each has a temptation to engage in some aggression, and each needs defensive expenditures to counter the other's aggression.

The formulas also show how the allocations will change if any of the technological parameters change. The productive use of resources (as measured by X) increases if (1) α increases, that is, diminishing returns set in more slowly in production, (2) β decreases, that is, diminishing returns set in faster in fighting, and (3) θ decreases, that is, the technology of fighting favors defense over offense. All of this is quite intuitive.

The model can be generalized in several ways. The players' abilities in production and fighting can be asymmetric. The functions for the probabilities or proportions of success in fighting can have other forms. The dynamics of responses and the stability of equilibrium should be analyzed. Hirshleifer (2001) explores many of

---

[2]If β exceeds 1, asymmetric corner solutions can arise. Hirshleifer (2001, Chapter 6) examines these.

these extensions, but a rich menu for research is still available. As before in this book, my purpose has been to give the readers a flavor of the theoretical reasoning, in the hope that they will pursue the ideas further in the literature and in their own research.

5.3 For-Profit Private Protection

In this section I outline a model of the interaction between predation and private protection. I closely follow Anderson and Bandiera (2002), who in turn build on some ideas and techniques from Grossman (1995) and others. The first subsection lays out the structure of the model, including a brief comment on the assumptions. Then the individual choices and the equilibrium are characterized. A general discussion of the achievements and the shortcomings of the model follows; as usual, the shortcomings constitute opportunities for research.

The Structure of the Model

The properties to be protected are assumed to be located along a circle of unit circumference. At any point of the circle, there is a continuum of such properties, indexed by a parameter α that ranges from 0 to 1. The value of property α is denoted by $V(\alpha)$, and these are arranged by decreasing value; that is, $V'(\alpha) < 0$ for all $\alpha \in (0, 1)$. Thus properties with index between 0 and α have value greater than $V(\alpha)$, and those with index between α and 1 have values less than $V(\alpha)$.

There are n specialized protectors, each covering a fraction $(1/n)$ of the circle. The n will be determined endogenously, either by free entry or by a collusive choice.

There are B bandits, and they will spread out uniformly so that (B/n) are in the territory of each protector. B is endogenous, determined by free entry given an exogenous outside opportunity.

An endogenous fraction λ of bandits go after property that is under specialized protection, and $(1 - \lambda)$ go after self-protected property.

Thus the model assumes that protectors and bandits come from distinct groups with separate entry conditions, and the property owners are a fixed distinct third group. In reality, we see some occupational choice between production, predation, and guarding. For example, in Sicily, Gambetta (1993, pp. 16, 17) says that people did make a choice between becoming traders or protectors, and Bandiera (2002) finds that the tougher bandits were selectively hired as guards. Allowing such mobility and choice would be an interesting extension of the model.

The Probabilities of Protection

Denote the probabilities of safe enjoyment of property (non-predation) by

$$\beta \text{ if self-protection} , \qquad \pi \text{ if hired specialized protection} .$$

For each of these probabilities, the odds are assumed to be proportional to the numbers of people engaged in the competing activities of protection and predation, with an exogenously given parameter θ that captures the relative advantage of predatory effort over protection effort. Thus, under self-protection,

$$\beta = \frac{(1-\alpha)/n}{(1-\alpha)/n + \theta\, B\, (1-\lambda)/n}, \tag{5.2}$$

and under hired specialized protection,

$$\pi = \frac{R\,\alpha}{R\,\alpha + \theta\, B\, \lambda/n}. \tag{5.3}$$

Note that there are B/n bandits and one protector (not $1/n$) per segment. These equations are like (5.1) with two differences: here β is set equal to 1, and a new parameter R is introduced. R measures the protector's reputation for toughness; the model assumes this is exogenous, but an extension can endogenize it.

The probabilities β and π depend on B and n, which are themselves endogenous results of individuals' decisions. But the model assumes that everyone acts as a "probability-taker." This is reasonable for individual property owners and bandits, but less reasonable for an organized mafia acting collusively, so it will be partially relaxed in that context.

Each Specialized Protector's Pricing Strategy

The protector in each of the n segments of the circle is assumed to set his own pricing policy. The model assumes that he cannot observe the α of any individual property, therefore he must set a uniform price common to all. In a dynamic model, protectors may gradually find out the values of individual properties and use this knowledge to charge discriminatory prices. Even in a static model, if there is another dimension of choice, for example the quality of protection, then specialized protectors can offer a nonlinear price–quality schedule that achieves some discrimination based on the property-owners' self-selection.

If the price is p, then owners of properties $[0, \alpha]$ will buy protection, where

$$(\pi - \beta)\, V(\alpha) = p. \tag{5.4}$$

Thus the owners of higher-valued properties buy protection, while owners of lower-valued properties self-protect. This seems reasonable, but other assumptions could give a different result. For example, suppose a fixed amount r of resources is needed for self-protection. Then those α with $V(\alpha) < r$ cannot self-protect. Since fixed costs of specialized protection can be spread over a number of owners, that mode may be feasible while catering to owners of low-end properties.

Given the assumptions, the profit of the protector on each segment of the circle will be

$$\frac{\alpha}{n} \, (\pi - \beta) \, V(\alpha) - f \, ,$$

where f is the fixed cost. (This is assumed to be constant but in reality it may be a function of n, and the shape of that function can affect the average-cost curve and therefore the nature of the equilibrium.) The first-order condition for maximization is simply

$$V(\alpha) + \alpha \, V'(\alpha) = 0 \, , \tag{5.5}$$

which fixes the equilibrium α^* independently of any parameters other than those included in the function V. Specifically, α^* does not depend on π or β. Remember that the protector is assumed to take π and β as given parameters. Their dependence on α in (5.2) and (5.3) appears at the equilibrium stage where all these equations are solved together. Then the π and β assumed by the protector satisfy the requirement of rational expectations.

To understand (5.5), think of (5.4) as an inverse-demand curve, defining the price p as a function of the quantity α. Changes in the parameters π and β shift this inverse-demand curve vertically by a constant multiplicative factor. Standard price theory tells us that such a shift merely changes a monopolist's profit-maximizing price by the same factor, leaving the quantity unchanged.

A simple functional form will illustrate this:

$$\text{if } V(\alpha) = V_0 - \alpha \, (V_0 - V_1), \quad \text{then } \alpha^* = V_0 \, / \, [2(V_0 - V_1)] \, .$$

Bandits' Choices

Consider someone who has already decided to become a bandit. He does not know the α of any specific property, but can observe the form of protection being used. He will divide his attention between properties with specialized protection ($\alpha < \alpha^*$) and those with self-protection ($\alpha > \alpha^*$) to equalize his expected take from the two:

$$(1 - \pi) \int_0^{\alpha^*} V(\alpha) \, d\alpha = (1 - \beta) \int_{\alpha^*}^1 V(\alpha) \, d\alpha \, . \tag{5.6}$$

Next consider the population of would-be bandits. Their total mass is made equal to 1 by choice of units. They are uniformly distributed with respect to their outside opportunities over the interval $[0, w]$, where w is exogenous. Then the marginal Bth bandit's outside opportunity, $B \, w$, must equal his income from banditry (deriving from attacks on either self-protected or professionally guarded properties; the two are equalized by (5.6)). That is,

$$B \, w = (1 - \pi) \int_0^{\alpha^*} V(\alpha) \, d\alpha = (1 - \beta) \int_{\alpha^*}^1 V(\alpha) \, d\alpha \, . \tag{5.7}$$

This contains two equations linking the variables B, β, and π; note that α^* was already determined by (5.5).

Equilibrium with Free Entry of Specialized Protectors

This is determined by a zero-profit condition:

$$\frac{\alpha}{n}\,(\pi - \beta)\,V(\alpha) = f\,. \tag{5.8}$$

Then the five equations contained in (5.2), (5.3), (5.7), and (5.8) determine the five variables $(B, \lambda, \pi, \beta, n)$.

Equilibrium with a Collusive Mafia

The Mafia chooses n to maximize total profit:

$$\alpha\,[\,\pi(n) - \beta(n)\,]\,V(\alpha) - f\,n\,.$$

Here it is assumed that the Mafia recognizes the dependence of β and π on n shown in (5.2) and (5.3), but still takes B and λ as given, that is, the Mafia and the bandits play a simultaneous-move game resulting in a Nash equilibrium. It is not clear whether this is reasonable; Anderson and Bandiera (2002) also consider the possibility that the Mafia subsidizes some activities of bandits. For this, the Mafia must be a leader or first mover with respect to the bandits, and their game cannot be Nash. It is also assumed that the Mafia does not try to set the pricing policy of any of its n protectors; they argue that this behavior is realistic.

This maximization (captured by its first-order condition) replaces the zero-profit condition that applied under free entry, and together with (5.2), (5.3), and the two equations in (5.6), determines the equilibrium $(B, \lambda, \pi, \beta, n)$.

The equations do not have closed-form solutions either in the free-entry case or with a monopolist mafia. Numerical methods can be employed, but we can obtain useful comparisons without solving either case explicitly.

Comparison of Free Entry and Collusion

The Mafia collusively chooses a smaller n than that in the free-entry equilibrium. The intuition for this is the usual one whereby a monopolist restricts entry (or output) to increase the price. But how is entry prevented? Coercion backed by threats of violence would be the obvious answer in the context, but are there any non-violent methods? Anderson and Bandiera (2002) suggest that the fixed (sunk) cost for individuals is higher than that for an organized mafia (normalized on equal reputation). Then the mafia may use an excess-capacity strategy (mafiosi hangers-on), and the threat of using this capacity in a price war makes it unprofitable for any outsider to enter.

Predation

When there is no outside enforcement, the protector's honesty is not guaranteed. That must be explained within the model by considerations of repeated interactions. That is, the protector's fee must be large enough that he prefers the ongoing flow of these payments to the large one-time benefit he may gain by stealing the property he is supposed to protect. Modeling similar to that in Chapter 4 can handle this, but most models of private protection, including that of Anderson and Bandiera (2002), leave this aspect implicit. They do consider the possibility that an organized mafia may profit by subsidizing bandits for attacking unprotected (or self-protected) property, so as to increase the market for its own product.

Dependence on w

Numerical solutions of the model show that the organized mafia's maximized profit in equilibrium has an inverse U shape as a function of w, the bandits' outside opportunity. This is interpreted as a difference across societies with different levels of development. If w is small, banditry is attractive relative to the outside opportunities. Then there are many bandits, and in turn many protectors emerge, making it difficult to coordinate them. Conversely, if w is large, there are few bandits, and the potential revenues that can be earned by providing a coordinated protection service are small. So organized mafias are most likely to emerge during the middle stages of development.

Here the assumption that property owners, potential protectors, and bandits are three distinct groups may be important. In a model of occupational choice, the bandits' outside opportunity would be endogenous, and linked to the incomes available in production or protection. A more general model of this kind presents an interesting research opportunity.

Social Optimum

When one person buys specialized private protection, some bandits shift from protected to unprotected (or self-protected) property. This is a negative externality inflicted on the lower-value-property owners in the equilibrium. A government concerned with social welfare will internalize this externality, and may in addition apply a higher weight to the welfare of the poorer owners. However, the rich may then prefer private protection. This may lead to cream-skimming, and the political economy of the situation may even defeat any attempts to institute a formal legal system of protection.

Relation to Case Studies

Now we can assess the model in relation to the facts and concepts of the subject. The model scores highly in two important respects.

First, it captures a negative externality observed in reality (Gambetta 1993, p. 27). When some people buy protection, the predators' attention shifts to the rest, who then need protection more. The model takes us further by showing that the owners of smaller or lower-value properties are the ones who suffer more from this externality; that seems to fit with casual observations.

Second, the model directly tackles one of Barzel's (1989, pp. 2, 31) central points. Security of property rights depends on (a) government protection, (b) private protection, (c) the efforts made by other people to capture one's property. All these are costly in different ways; therefore rights are generally not complete. When transacting is costly, all contract forms are costly, so choice of governance form is a constrained optimum (at best). The model shows how the balance between these forces depends on the underlying parameters.

Finally, the model improves our understanding of the "protection industry" depicted by Gambetta (1993). It examines alternative ways in which the industry may be organized—a monopoly, or a collection of local monopolies limited by free entry—and the outcomes of the alternative forms. In turn, this can be a useful input to the design of public policies against the undesirable features of private protection.

However, the model conceals, or ignores altogether, some other matters that are also important in reality. First, it assumes that producers, protectors, and predators come from entirely different populations with entirely different outside opportunities. In reality there is considerable mobility and choice across these occupations; therefore analysis of occupational choice under anarchy has considerable interest. Second, it assumes that the protectors will not themselves become predators; the necessary repeated relationships are kept implicit, but they may interact in important ways with the included features. Finally, the model ignores many other subtleties that arise in defining and enforcing property rights. For example, Barzel's (1989) analysis shows the importance of multiple dimensions and heterogeneous interests; Liebcap's (1989) study emphasizes the political process of adaptation of property rights to changing circumstances. Ensminger's (1997) study of traditional systems of defining and enforcing property rights also brings out the multidimension, multi-stakeholder nature of the problem, and warns us that attempts to impose modern systems of formal laws on such societies can cause more harm than good. Many and rich possibilities remain open for theoretical analyses of these issues.

5.4   A Predatory State and Its Citizens

In the two preceding sections the threat to property rights was assumed to come from other private individuals. But in many countries, the supposed protectors of property rights, namely the government and its agents, are themselves the predators; Olson (1993), Shleifer and Vishny (1998, especially Chapter 1), and many others have emphasized this problem. If the state predators are short-lived "roving bandits," the incentives to produce and invest may be destroyed completely. But longer-lived "stationary bandits" will recognize that they stand to gain over the long run by committing themselves not to steal too much at any one time. In this section I develop some elementary consequences of this idea.

If people perceive a threat to their property rights, whether from the government or from any other source, one of their responses will be to conceal their assets to the extent possible. They will hide tangible property. They will deny the existence of intangible property; for example, highly productive individuals will pretend to have low productivity because they know that if the truth is revealed, the government will simply force them to work harder. Another response will be to shirk in their efforts if they know that the government will take away most or even all of the output. The government, in turn, can spend resources to monitor and audit the people's activities and abilities in its attempt to extract more from them.[3] But the cost of achieving perfect revelation by direct supervision or observation is likely to be prohibitive. Therefore the government will find it desirable to supplement direct auditing or monitoring policies with others that offer the people material incentives to expend effort and to reveal their assets and skills.

Stated thus, the interaction between a predatory government and its public is simply another instance of the general problem of mechanism design that has been studied extensively in economic theory over the last three decades (see Mas Colell, Whinston, and Green 1995, Chapter 23). Mechanism-design problems have a principal who must hire an agent to perform some task. The agent has some advance private information, which could be about his own preferences or skills. Aspects of the agent's actions and the outcomes may be unverifiable. And the principal has to ensure that the agent gets at least as much payoff from the interaction as he can get from his opportunities elsewhere. The principal offers a contract to the agent, aiming to maximize his own expected payoff subject to the constraints of the agent's incentives and participation. In conventional theory, when the government is the principal, its objective is assumed to be social welfare, and constraints include the need to raise some resources required for public expenditures. But when the government is predatory, its objective is to maximize its own take from the economy, and the constraints include lower bounds on the consumption or utility it must provide the workers to keep them alive, or perhaps to prevent them from staging a revolt against the government. But the mathematics of the two problems is very similar. I illustrate this below. Specifically, I exploit the analogy between a benevolent government's problem of designing an optimal income tax schedule and a kleptocratic

---

[3] McMillan (2002, pp. 94–101) describes how such interactions played out in China starting in the late 1970s, and how farmers' investment and efforts could be sustained despite the lack of formal property rights and despite the sporadic interference by the government and its agents.

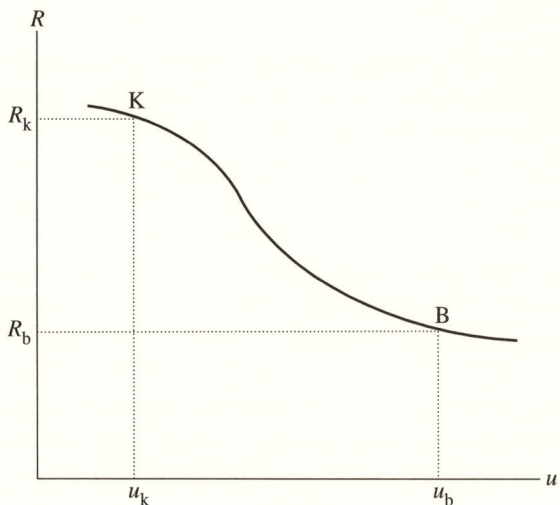

Figure 5.1.   Taxation by benevolent and kleptocratic governments.

government's problem of designing an optimal system of extortion, to reinterpret many standard results of the former and apply them to the latter.

The intuitive argument is shown in Figure 5.1. Given the constraints on the information available to the government and the instruments at its disposal, there is a trade-off between the tax revenue R that the government can extract from the population for its own purposes, and the utility u that a citizen derives from his private after-tax consumption. This is shown as the downward-sloping frontier (the curvature is irrelevant to this analysis). A benevolent government needs to raise at least R_b of revenue for its legitimate administrative and related functions, but wants to maximize the citizens' utilities. This optimum occurs at the point B in the figure. A predatory or kleptocratic government wants to maximize its own take from the economy, but must provide the citizens some floor level of utility u_k to keep them alive or to prevent a revolution. This optimum occurs at the point K in the figure. The policies of the two types of government obviously differ in their details. Provided only that the best utility u_b that the benevolent government can provide is more than the u_k that is needed for subsistence or quiescence, the kleptocratic government will provide less utility and extract more revenue than the benevolent government. The marginal rates of substitution along the frontier at K and B will also differ in magnitude. But the two constrained maximization problems will have a very similar structure, and their solutions will share many qualitative properties. A more formal statement of the parallel between these problems is in the mathematical appendix to this chapter (Section 5.6.2).

The standard theory of optimal income taxation by a benevolent government comes from Mirrlees (1971). Its fundamental and realistic assumption is an information constraint on the government. The population has a continuous distribution of skills or productivities. Each citizen knows his own skill, but the government cannot directly or costlessly observe the skill of any individual. If the government could identify high-skilled individuals, it would try to extract more effort from them: a benevolent government would do this to help the less well-off people, and a kleptocratic government would do this to increase its own take. Therefore the high-skilled people will try to conceal or understate their skills. The government will anticipate such behavior, and will find it optimal to commit itself to giving the high-skilled people enough incentives to induce them to reveal the information. This means promising people of successively higher skills successively and sufficiently higher utility levels, by keeping the marginal tax rates sufficiently low. Of course the promise has to be credible, and in practice such credibility is likely to depend on the longevity of the government. The theory assumes credibility; in the case of a kleptocratic government this means assuming a stationary bandit.

To maximize its own take, the kleptocratic government would ideally like to drive everyone down to the subsistence or quiescence utility level u_k. But such a government, provided it is rational, will recognize the need to give the higher-skilled people sufficient marginal incentives to reveal their skills, because this increases its net extraction from the economy. Therefore it will keep only the least-skilled person at the lowest utility level, and allow the successively higher-skilled people to enjoy successively higher utility levels. Casual observation confirms that predatory governments do indeed treat the poor most harshly. (A benevolent government will also have to tolerate some inequality in the interests of revelation of high skills, but it will keep even the worst-off person above the subsistence level. In fact a government with an extremely egalitarian—so-called Rawlsian—objective function, such as the one in the formal model of the mathematical appendix (Section 5.6.2), wants to maximize the utility of the least-well-off person, to the extent permitted by the information and resource constraints.)

Next consider two people in the skill distribution, with skills n_1 and $n_2 > n_1$. The n_2 person needs a differential incentive, namely the promise of a level of well-being sufficiently higher than that of the n_1 person, to offset his temptation to pretend to have the lower skill level n_1. If the marginal tax rate on the n_1 person is lowered, then the total tax for the n_2 person must be lowered also, to preserve the needed differential incentive. Thus lowering the marginal tax rate on any one person reduces the revenue that the government can get from all those with skills higher than this person's. This is costly to the government: directly so for the kleptocratic government, and indirectly for the benevolent government because that tightens its revenue constraint and makes it harder to deliver utilities to the citizens. The calculation of the optimal tax schedule balances, at each skill level, the incentive effect of lowering the marginal tax rate for people at that skill level and the revenue loss from the people with skill levels higher than that. But the trade-off disappears at the highest skill level that exists in the population, because then there is no higher skill level and therefore no revenue loss. Therefore the incentive effect dominates at the top skill level, and the optimal marginal tax rate is zero there.

Benevolent governments usually have regard for equality and fairness. Therefore they are reluctant to lower the marginal tax rates on the most well-off people. They will let the marginal rate go to zero only at the very end, or may even choose to disregard this aspect of optimality in the interests of fairness. But a kleptocratic government does not care about equality or fairness. Therefore we should expect such a government to treat the richest people in society especially well. They will have to contribute to the government's coffers, to be sure, but at the margin they will be allowed to earn more income and keep it. Again casual observation supports the result that predatory dictators are often best buddies with their richest citizens.

The above analysis is merely one example of modeling a predatory government in a mechanism-design framework. The idea offers numerous possibilities for further research; here I merely mention some of them.

The optimal tax problem is one where the agent has advance private information. In the terminology of the theory, this is a situation of adverse selection. There are two other kinds of asymmetric information situations: moral hazard and costly state verification. In neither case does the agent have any advance information advantage when entering into the contract with the principal; such an advantage develops later.

In the case of moral hazard, the agent takes some action not observable to the principal, and *a fortiori* not verifiable to outsiders. Then the principal has to improve the technology of observation or verification, or offer the agent some material incentives based on some observable or verifiable magnitude. This theory of incentives is well developed; Gibbons (1997) and Prendergast (1999) offer excellent surveys. Some applications were modeled in Chapter 2. Similar models can be constructed for the case of a predatory government. Such a government has an advantage over the principal usually studied in this branch of theory: it will not bother with proofs of a standard high enough to satisfy an impartial court; therefore it needs only observability, not verifiability.

The case of costly state verification arises when the agent can conceal some outcome such as his crop output or his income. The principal can obtain this information at a cost, and its problem is to design an optimal auditing scheme. This theory, developed by Townsend (1979) and Mookherjee and Png (1989), can also be applied to a predatory government.

The basic theory of mechanism design has been extended to cover dynamics, hierarchical agencies, and other complexities. These are important for the reality of a predatory government just as they are in cases of firms and agencies of a benevolent government. Modeling of dynamics seems essential for a more satisfactory treatment of the distinction between roving and stationary bandits than the simple ad hoc procedures adopted in the discussion of this section. Hierarchical agencies are important in practice because a government has to use middle-level administrators to implement its policies, and these can have their own objectives and information advantages. Thus a top-level government may be more or less benevolent while its middle-level agents are predatory, or both may be predatory and the middle-level agents may be trying to keep some of the extorted sums for themselves. McMillan (2002, p. 95) describes how the agricultural reforms in China in the late 1970s eventually won the approval of the top-level government, overcoming initial resistance by local bureaucrats. Much of the theory of hierarchical agencies has been developed, and applied to the case of procurement contracts, by Laffont and Tirole (1993). These techniques can be used to model multi-tier governments, both benevolent and predatory.

Finally, Shleifer and Vishny (1998, Chapter 5) emphasize the especially harmful consequences when a citizen needs permissions from several officials of a predatory government to conduct his productive activities, and each of them can demand a bribe. They model this using the concept of double marginalization in microeconomic theory. However, the argument can benefit by being reformulated in information-theoretic terms as a situation of common agency. All the officials are simultaneously principals, and the citizen is their common agent. The equilibrium of such a game is characterized by very poor incentives (Dixit 1997).

5.5 Assessment and Prospects

This chapter contains a variety of models, each addressing a different question. The accomplishments of each model, the gaps or deficiencies of each, and the resulting opportunities for further research, were discussed in the sections above. But some matters that were found to be important in reality in the overview of Section 5.1 were not addressed in any of the models.

The most important of these is the multidimensionality of property rights that was emphasized by Barzel (1989). The games between private or governmental predators and citizens attempting to protect their property should also recognize this aspect. Some techniques for handling multidimensional agency relationships were developed in Chapter 2. They could be used for modeling such games in the principal–agent framework. The interaction between the definition of property rights and the information needed for the resolution of disputes about property, which emerged from Ellickson's (1989) study, is also worth modeling.

The choice of occupation—production, predation, or protection—was mentioned in the context of private protection in Section 5.3. It remains important in other contexts also. A citizen may try to become an official of a predatory government, instead of attempting to produce or invest and protect what he can of his output and assets. The competition for these lucrative positions will require some rent-seeking expenditures, making the economic inefficiency under a predatory government even worse. Shleifer and Vishny (1998, Chapter 4) have considered this issue.

5.6 Mathematical Appendix

5.6.1 *Production and Protection under Anarchy*

Here I sketch the algebraic details of the model of Section 5.2

Start with the expression for Player 1's payoff, and write it in a somewhat better form for differentiation:

$$
\begin{aligned}
\Pi_1 &= (X_1)^\alpha \frac{(Y_1)^\beta}{(Y_1)^\beta + \theta\,(Z_2)^\beta} + (X_2)^\alpha \frac{\theta\,(Z_1)^\beta}{(Y_2)^\beta + \theta\,(Z_1)^\beta} \\
&= (X_1)^\alpha \left[1 - \frac{\theta\,(Z_2)^\beta}{(Y_1)^\beta + \theta\,(Z_2)^\beta} \right] + (X_2)^\alpha \left[1 - \frac{(Y_2)^\beta}{(Y_2)^\beta + \theta\,(Z_1)^\beta} \right].
\end{aligned}
$$

Player 1 chooses X_1, Y_1, and Z_1 to maximize this, subject to the resource constraint

$$
X_1 + Y_1 + Z_1 \leqslant 1,
$$

and for given choices X_2, Y_2, and Z_2 of Player 2.

Let λ_1 denote the Lagrange multiplier for the resource constraint. Then the first-order conditions are

$$
\alpha\,(X_1)^{\alpha-1} \frac{(Y_1)^\beta}{(Y_1)^\beta + \theta\,(Z_2)^\beta} - \lambda_1 = 0,
$$

$$
(X_1)^\alpha \frac{\theta\,(Z_2)^\beta}{[(Y_1)^\beta + \theta\,(Z_2)^\beta]^2}\,\beta\,(Y_1)^{\beta-1} - \lambda_1 = 0,
$$

and

$$
(X_2)^\alpha \frac{(Y_2)^\beta}{[(Y_2)^\beta + \theta\,(Z_1)^\beta]^2}\,\theta\,\beta\,(Z_1)^{\beta-1} - \lambda_1 = 0.
$$

The restrictions on the parameters ensure the second-order conditions; see Hirshleifer (2001, pp. 110, 127) for analysis of this in a very similar model.

Similar first-order conditions hold for Player 2. A Nash equilibrium is a solution to the six first-order conditions and the two resource constraints, yielding the six allocation variables and the two Lagrange multipliers. To search for a symmetric equilibrium, set $X_1 = X_2 = X$, $Y_1 = Y_2 = Y$, and $Z_2 = Z_2 = Z$. Then the first-order conditions become

$$
\alpha\,X^{\alpha-1} \frac{Y^\beta}{Y^\beta + \theta\,Z^\beta} = \lambda,
$$

and

$$\frac{\beta \theta X^\alpha Y^{\beta-1} Z^\beta}{[Y^\beta + \theta Z^\beta]^2} = \lambda = \frac{\beta \theta X^\alpha Y^\beta Z^{\beta-1}}{[Y^\beta + \theta Z^\beta]^2}.$$

The second of these gives $Y = Z$. Substituting back and simplifying, the conditions become

$$\frac{\alpha X^{\alpha-1}}{1 + \theta} = \lambda = \frac{\beta \theta X^\alpha}{(1 + \theta)^2 Y}.$$

This further simplifies to

$$\alpha (1 + \theta) Y = \beta \theta X.$$

Finally, using $X = 1 - 2Y$, we get the solution stated in the text.

5.6.2 Taxation by a Predatory Government

Here I give a more formal treatment of the parallel between the optimal income tax schedule designed by a benevolent government and the optimal extortion policy of a kleptocratic government.

The classic and standard formulation of the optimal income tax problem by Mirrlees (1971) is as follows. The population consists of a continuum of people indexed by their productivity n; the cumulative distribution function is $F(n)$. A person of type n has a utility function $U(C, L, n)$, where C is consumption and L is labor supply in efficiency units; this has all the usual properties plus $U_n > 0$. (The usual reason is that a more skilled person needs to expend fewer clock hours to supply a given quantity of labor in efficiency units, and disutility of labor depends on clock hours.)

I assume that the economy's total output Y is a functional $Y(L(\cdot))$, that is, a function of the labor supply profile $(L(\cdot))$ of the whole group, where labor is measured in efficiency units. This encompasses many special cases.

The government does not know the productivity of any individual. In these circumstances, the best the government can do is characterized by the revelation principle of mechanism design (see Mas Colell, Whinston, and Green 1995, p. 868). This says that the government can be considered to be acting as if asking each individuals to report his productivity, and committing itself to a publicly announced rule as to how it will use this information. The rule can be stated in the form of functions $C(n)$ and $L(n)$, such that an individual who reports his productivity to be n will be directed to supply $L(n)$ efficiency units of labor and given $C(n)$ units of consumption. The rule has to be such that it is privately optimal for each individual to report his productivity truthfully. This is called the incentive compatibility constraint. In addition, the usual condition of material balance must be satisfied: the total output should be enough to meet the consumption commitments plus the government's requirements.

Formally stated, the incentive compatibility condition requires that for each n in the distribution of productivities,

$$n' = n \text{ maximizes } U(C(n'), L(n'), n). \qquad (5.9)$$

This condition, which captures the information limitation of the government, is the essence of the optimal income tax problem, and it generates many of the complexities of its analysis as well as its interesting new results. However, all of these considerations are irrelevant to my immediate concern, because they apply equally to the optimization problems of the benevolent and kleptocratic governments and therefore do not affect the comparisons between the two. Therefore I will omit the detailed treatment of (5.9), and merely summarize the constraint in the form

$$G(n) = 0$$

for all n, where $G(n)$ is a complicated function whose exact form I do not need.

Let $V(n) = U(C(n), L(n), n)$ be the maximized utility of a person of type n in the resulting allocation.

I will assume that the benevolent government is also extremely egalitarian: it wishes to maximize the utility of the least-well-off person in the society, as in the Rawlsian criterion of justice. That will make the parallel between such a benevolent government and a kleptocratic government even more remarkable.

The benevolent government needs to raise a specified amount of revenue R_b for its administration or other exogenous purposes. It wants to maximize the utility of the least-well-off person; we can express this as a set of constraints requiring the utilities $V(n)$ to be at least equal to u_b for all n and then maximizing this u_b. The other constraints of resource sufficiency and incentive compatibility are of course present. Therefore the benevolent government's optimization problem can be stated as

$$\text{maximize } u_b$$

subject to the constraints

$$V(n) \geqslant u_b \quad \text{for all } n, \qquad (5.10)$$

the incentive compatibility constraints

$$G(n) = 0 \quad \text{for all } n, \qquad (5.11)$$

and the resource constraint

$$Y(L(\cdot)) - \int C(n)\, dF(n) \geqslant R_b. \qquad (5.12)$$

Let $\lambda_b(n)$, $\mu_b(n)$ and θ_b be the Lagrange multipliers on the respective constraints. (The subscript "b" reminds us that this is the benevolent government's problem.)

The Lagrangian is

$$\mathcal{L}_b = u_b + \int \lambda_b(n) \left[V(n) - u_b \right] dF(n)$$

$$+ \int \mu_b(n) G(n) dF(n) + \theta_b \left[Y(L(\cdot)) - \int C(n) dF(n) - R_b \right]$$

$$= u_b \left[1 - \int \lambda_b(n) dF(n) \right] - \theta_b R_b + \int \lambda_b(n) V(n) dF(n)$$

$$+ \int \mu_b(n) G(n) dF(n) + \theta_b \left[Y(L(\cdot)) - \int C(n) dF(n) \right]. \quad (5.13)$$

Contrast this with a kleptocratic government, but one with a sufficiently long horizon (Olson's "stationary bandit") that its commitments are credible. The government wants to maximize the amount it can extract from the economy, subject to leaving people with a specified subsistence utility u_k (to keep them alive or to stop them from revolting). It faces the same information limitations. Its problem can be formulated mathematically as

$$\text{maximize } R_k$$

subject to the same constraints (5.10), (5.11), and (5.12) but with u_k instead of u_b on the right-hand side of (5.10) and R_k instead of R_b on the right-hand side of (5.12). Then the new (5.10) becomes the participation constraint in the kleptocratic government's optimization problem. The auxiliary choice variable R_k is introduced merely to make the parallel with the previous problem more obvious; the constraint (5.12) ensures that the maximized revenue will indeed equal the amount the government extracts from the people.

Using the subscript "k" for the Lagrange multipliers in the kleptocratic government's problem, the Lagrangian is

$$\mathcal{L}_k = R_k + \int \lambda_k(n) \left[V(n) - u_k \right] dF(n)$$

$$+ \int \mu_k(n) G(n) dF(n) + \theta_k \left[Y(L(\cdot)) - \int C(n) dF(n) - R_k \right]$$

$$= R_k (1 - \theta_k) - u_k \int \lambda_k(n) dF(n) + \int \lambda_k(n) V(n) dF(n)$$

$$+ \int \mu_k(n) G(n) dF(n) + \theta_k \left[Y(L(\cdot)) - \int C(n) dF(n) \right]. \quad (5.14)$$

Comparing (5.13) and (5.14) shows that the two problems have an almost identical mathematical structure. The only difference is that in the benevolent government's problem, R_b is given and u_b is a choice variable, leading to the first-order condition

$$\int \lambda_b(n) dF(n) = 1,$$

whereas in the kleptocratic government's problem, u_k is given and R_k is a choice variable, leading to the first-order condition

$$\theta_k = 1 \, .$$

Thus the two problems differ essentially only in the way the Lagrange multipliers are normalized. (This is a formalization of the heuristic idea in Figure 5.1, namely the different marginal rates of transformation between u and R along the transformation frontier at B and K.) Of course the actual values of the optimum choices and the multipliers will differ between the two problems, because the optimum u_b of the benevolent government's problem will be bigger than the specified subsistence u_k in the kleptocratic government's problem, and conversely the kleptocrat's optimum R_k will be bigger than the R_b that the benevolent government needs for its given expenditure commitments. But the qualitative properties of the solutions will be the same.

6
Conclusion

The study of non-state institutions to underpin economic activity is a lively research subject that spans several traditional disciplines—economics, law, politics, sociology, and anthropology. It merits recognition as a field in its own right, or perhaps as a subfield of the New Institutional Economics or Organizational Theory. I hope this book makes some useful contributions to the field and earns it better recognition. First, I bring together several strands that had previously been distinct: case studies and theoretical models, analyses of informal social networks and norms, and of more formal legalistic or profit-motivated organizations for governance, and so on. Second, I provide new theoretical analyses of the phenomena observed in several case studies. Third, these theoretical models yield some new results that go beyond the empirical observations, and therefore provide suggestions for further research, and if supported, for potential application.

The name I chose for the field, Lawlessness and Economics, was a deliberate ploy to attract attention. I am sure it will not survive long; a duller but more accurate name, perhaps simply "governance", will soon replace it. But I am confident that the field itself will remain important, both as a scholarly endeavor and as an important input to thinking about policy.

Each of Chapters 2–5 contains several suggestions for research, and some tentative ideas concerning institution design and reform, each pertaining to its topic. In this short concluding chapter I collect and expand some of these remarks.

6.1 Implications for Institutions and Policies

Of all the policy contexts where issues of governance arise, none are more important than those of growth in less-developed countries and transition in former socialist countries. This importance is widely recognized. A Google search for "governance" produced approximately 6.2 million web pages—three times the huge number cited for "cheating" in Chapter 3. Of course the word has many different connotations. One of these—namely corporate governance, which is about incentives and organization within a firm—is only indirectly connected to issues of protection of property rights and enforcement of contracts that are the theme of this book. A search for "governance without corporate" reduces the number to about 2.69 million. Many political and social commentators are concerned with governance-related but broader questions of human rights, of which property and contracts are only one aspect. It proved difficult to narrow the search accurately to exclude the other aspects. But narrower searches closer to my subject matter still yielded large numbers—"governance and transition economies" had 339 000 web pages, and "governance and less-developed countries or LDCs" yielded 61 400. "Governance and World Bank" led to 1.24 million, and "Governance and IMF" to 253 000; these presumably include official pages emanating from these organizations as well as those created by their supporters and critics. The World Bank runs a major research and policy guidance effort focusing on governance; its official web page, http://www.worldbank.org/wbi/governance/, has numerous links to data sources, publications, news, and announcements.

Even within the narrow subset of scholarly articles and books, the numbers remain daunting. A search of the EconLit database produced 7028 hits for "governance," of which 2234 remained after excluding "corporate." Combining "governance" and "transition economies" yielded 125 hits; "less-developed countries or LDCs," 73. And there may be numerous other articles on the subject that did not happen to use the key words in their titles or abstracts. I hope these numbers help the readers understand my reference to "lemmings" in the preface and my need to apologize to those whose work I overlooked or judged to be too far from my concerns.

Despite this wealth of material, neither empirical nor theoretical research has yet advanced to the point of offering clear or confident policy recommendations for the process of institution-building or reform. Country case studies show important links between good governance institutions and economic success, but they also highlight special features of each country. The work of distilling general insights that are likely to remain valid for other countries is only just beginning (see, for example, Rodrik 2003). Statistical analyses likewise show positive cross-country correlations between various measures of good governance and the levels and growth rates of output, and broadly supports the causal interpretation that good governance causes economic success; some of this evidence was cited in Section 1.3. But many of the instrumental variables that identify the effect are deep historical ones, leaving us no good prescriptions for acquiring good governance today. Rodrik (1995) offered Taiwan and South Korea as exemplars of government. But he was speaking of their economic policymaking; the basics of governance in the sense of the state legal system were much more advanced in these countries than the ones that are the focus on Lawlessness and Economics.

On the theoretical side, we have several models of the operation of different methods of governance, and some of their interaction, but formal modeling of the dynamics of transition from one system of governance to another remains generally unsatisfactory. Dynamic games are far harder to analyze than repeated games played under stationary conditions. Therefore dynamic models in the literature, those of Young (1998) and Aoki (2001) for example, are cast at a relatively abstract level, sacrificing most of the specific issues of information—verification, transmission, etc.—that are my focus here. Richer models can be constructed in stationary states, and their comparative static analyses do sometimes yield some ideas for dynamics, but the proper use of these is as hypotheses for further investigation, not immediate policy advice.

At most, the combination of empirical and theoretical studies gives some cautious and tentative suggestions for practical implementation. But even that may be worth having, first because the problem of development is so large and urgent, and, more importantly, because the policy recommendations that are actually offered by many political leaders and public officials from Western countries, and sometimes even by those in transition economies and LDCs, are merely simplistic exhortations for these other countries to adopt Western institutions. With the hope of improving the quality of discussion and advice, I offer some speculations for discussion. Specifically, I focus on one phenomenon that seems to offer a clue to good policy design, and view it in the light of several theoretical models from previous chapters. This is an apparent nonlinearity or structural break in the effect of governance institutions on economic performance that was emphasized by Rodrik (2003, p. 17):

> The policies required to initiate a transition from a low-income equilibrium to a state of rapid growth may be qualitatively different from those required to re-ignite growth for a middle-income country.

According to Pritchett (2003, p. 148), "one does not in fact need a great deal of 'institutional capacity' to achieve [a semi-industrialized] level of income." However, "[i]n the transition to a new, better set of policies and institutions—that if they functioned well could support a much higher level of income—one can create deep uncertainty among both past and future investors." I recognize the importance of such uncertainty about the rules of the game, but want to point out some other issues to do with size and transition that are also pertinent.

The model of Chapter 3 offers one explanation of why it is easier to grow from a low level of income per head to a middle level than it is to break through to a high level. In the first phase of the growth or transition, economic activity is on a small scale, trade is localized, and economic transactions involve a relatively small group of people. In such a setting, networks of information flows, norms of behavior, and sanctions for deviants may already be present from the social environment, or can develop quickly as people interact economically among themselves. Therefore self-enforcing governance is feasible. No elaborate state institutions are needed. Some basic protection of property rights helps, but even that may be achievable privately or using social norms and sanctions. Indeed, as the model of Section 5.4 shows, even a corrupt state can permit reasonably efficient outcomes, if it has sufficient stability to act as a stationary bandit.

However, the model of Chapter 3 also points out the limitations of self-enforcing governance. At some middle level of economic activity, the information network weakens to a point where contract enforcement throughout the economy cannot automatically be sustained; in fact the extent of honesty begins to shrink. However, the scale of activity is not yet large enough to justify the costs of the system of state-supplied rule-based governance. This is true even in the stationary model; the dynamic problems of introducing a new system only make the problem worse. Its functionaries need experience to achieve sufficient expertise for their job. Until they have it, the system lacks credibility in the eyes of the traders; they prefer to continue using the traditional modes of governance. But the new system cannot acquire experience without actual practice. There are political obstacles, too: people with sunk stakes in the old system resist the introduction of the new one. This helps explain why the middle level constitutes a trap from which it is difficult for a country to break out. It also suggests that a premature top-down imposition of state governance of the kind that now functions in Western countries may not work.

The model of Section 2.3 points to an even worse possibility. An imperfect state system may worsen the outcome of the prevailing relation-based system, by providing the participants with better outside opportunities and thereby weakening their incentives to abide by the norms. Fortunately, other models suggest better alternative paths out of the middle-income trap.

Section 3.5 suggests a two-tier solution—tying together small self-enforcing networks at an upper level by a network of information exchange among representatives of the individual networks. This has the advantage of preserving the advantage of local information, and building on it with a tier of communication. Theoretical models as well as observations of case studies indicate that such a bottom-up approach stands a better chance of success than a top-down imposition of a state system of laws.

The model of Section 2.4 says that private arbitration may work better with other methods of governance. Its advantage comes from the development of specialized skill to interpret commercial information; this can complement the information used in other modes, and allow more complete contracting. The model also brings out the technical nature of information that would be most valuable to add to what is now available. In the appropriate sense that comes from the theory of statistical inference, this is information that is best aligned with the shortfall of previously available information from the state of full information.

Finally, the model of Chapter 4 tells us that private for-profit provision of information has some merit, and this may be a practicable route for some countries because it relies on the natural incentives of individuals. However, the same model also says that private provision of enforcement may do more harm than good, because the private enforcer can create the demand for his own services and extort more from society than any benefits he provides.

In Section 1.2, I summarized some findings from case studies of institutions and economic performance as follows.

> [I]t is not always necessary to create replicas of Western-style state legal institutions from scratch; it may be possible to work with such alternative institutions as are available, and build on them.

We now see how the theoretical models begin to give some specificity to this. First, copying Western-style institutions in their entirety may be not merely unnecessary, but sometimes actually inappropriate or harmful. Some institutions such as arbitration may work well with the existing ones; others like official courts may not, until they attain sufficiently high quality to replace traditional relation-based governance. Where small and disjoint networks of information and punishment provide local governance, a good way to proceed may be to link these into an upper-level network of communication.

Institution design or reform is often posed as a matter of binary choices—shock therapy versus gradualism, mimicking Western laws versus keeping national or local customs. But this is too simplistic. The best choices typically will be more subtle mixtures of speeds and features that work well in combination; the theory is starting to reveal the desirable complementarities.

I should reiterate that these suggestions, and others made above and in previous chapters, are only a small and tentative beginning on a large and difficult set of problems. But I think they are a useful start, and provide encouragement for continued research. I should also add that, even if future research confirms these suggestions, they are at a general level, and combining them with country-specific knowledge to generate policy prescriptions for any one country requires another large step, which is best left to country specialists.

I do not have one model that combines all aspects of the problem to provide a composite answer, but I do not regard this as a flaw. I believe that the strategy of developing separate models to focus on different aspects of the problems, and then combining their individual insights through some flexible and imaginative interpretation, is the best feasible. Of course this is a matter for debate, as are the specific ideas that follow from my arguments here.

6.2 Implications for Future Research

Academic research is a never-ending process. Any one article or even book can at best be one step. It constitutes progress, but also brings to light further terrain that needs to be explored. In the process of the research reported in this book, I have found several open research questions, and pointed out specific ones in each chapter. Here I highlight three themes that arise in many contexts.

The first is the issue of multiple dimensions. Many case studies found several interconnected facts and issues. In most deals, the parties' actions are multidimensional, and the products produced and exchanged have multiple attributes. When a contract specifies arbitration to resolve any dispute that may arise, the parties have a large number of forums and legal traditions from which they can choose. When property rights are insecure, people can choose between productive activities, predation (private or governmental), and protection against other predators for one's own property or that of others. Theory usually focuses on one of these dimensions at a time, and analyzes that in depth. Some insights can be gained from having a collection of results from the separate models and then combining them with some exercise of judgment. But more can be learned from jointly modeling several issues and interactions. This may require the sacrifice of some other aspect of the complexity of the problem; for example, linear functional forms may have to be assumed for tractability. I hope that the techniques developed in Chapter 2 will prove useful in such multidimensional modeling.

The second is the endogeneity of institutions. The models of the previous chapters show the workings of different institutions, and how one or the other may yield better outcomes depending on various underlying conditions—the actions and the payoffs in the basic game, and the technologies of information generation and communication. Here we have some common factors that influence economic outcomes as well as the institutions that govern economic interactions. Empirical research on the effect of institutions on economic performance has struggled to cope with the problem of inferring causation from correlation, and the existence of a third set of factors that cause both is a continuing concern. Some of the theories in this book may provide useful suggestions for this work.

The third general theme is dynamics. The process of transition from one system of governance to another is inherently dynamic. So is the interaction between two systems that coexist for some time until one of them comes to dominate. Individuals' choices during these processes involve the building or milking of reputations; both are essentially dynamic. To keep the analysis tractable while introducing many complex aspects of information, communication, and enforcement, I restricted the time dimension to stationary states. This showed the workings of each system of governance, or of a continued coexistence of two modes, under ongoing conditions. Inferences about institutional change were then drawn using comparative static methods and by interpretations that go beyond the formal models. Others have focused on the dynamics, using evolutionary game theory and some stochastic dynamics, but simplifying the underlying game to a schematic or stylized specification. Combining these two approaches may be a fruitful although daunting research challenge and opportunity for the future.

References

Abreu, Dilip. 1986. Extremal equilibria of oligopolistic supergames. *Journal of Economic Theory* 39:191–225.

Abreu, Dilip, David Pearce, and Ennio Stacchetti. 1990. Toward a theory of discounted repeated games with imperfect monitoring. *Econometrica* 59:1713–1733.

Acemoglu, Daron, Simon Johnson, and James Robinson. 2001. Colonial origins of economic development: an empirical investigation. *American Economic Review* 91:1369–1401.

Acemoglu, Daron, Simon Johnson, James Robinson, and Yunyong Thaicharoen. 2002. Institutional causes, macroeconomic symptoms: volatility, crises, and growth. Working paper, MIT, Cambridge, MA.

Alchian, Armen A. 1965. Some economics of property rights. *Il Politico* 50:16–29. (Reprinted in Armen A. Alchian. 1977. *Economic forces at work*. Indianapolis, IN: Liberty Press.)

Alston, Lee J., Thráinn Eggertson, and Douglass C. North. 1996. *Empirical studies in institutional change*. Cambridge, UK: Cambridge University Press.

Anderson, James E. and Oriana Bandiera. 2002. Private enforcement and social efficiency. Working paper, Boston College, Boston, MA and London School of Economics, London, UK.

Aoki, Masahiko. 2001. *Toward a comparative institutional analysis*. Cambridge, MA: MIT Press.

Axelord, Robert. 1984. *The evolution of cooperation*. New York: Basic Books.

Baird, Douglas G., Robert H. Gertner, and Randal C. Picker. 1994. *Game theory and the law*. Cambridge, MA: Harvard University Press.

Baker, George. 1992. Incentive contracts and performance measurement. *Journal of Political Economy* 100:598–614.

———. 2002. Distortion and risk in optimal incentive contracts. *Journal of Human Resources* 37:728–751.

Baker, George, Robert Gibbons, and Kevin J. Murphy. 1994. Subjective performance measures in optimal incentive contracts. *Quarterly Journal of Economics* 109:1125–1156.

———. 2002. Relational contracts and the theory of the firm. *Quarterly Journal of Economics* 117:39–84.

Bandiera, Oriana. 2003. Land reform, the market for protection and the origins of the Sicilian Mafia: theory and evidence. *Journal of Law, Economics, and Organization* 19:218–244.

Barzel, Yoram. 1989. *Economic analysis of property rights*. Cambridge, UK: Cambridge University Press.

———. 2002. *A theory of the state: economic rights, legal rights, and the scope of the state*. Cambridge, UK: Cambridge University Press.

Bearak, Barry. 2000. In India, the wheels of justice hardly move. *New York Times* June 1:A1.

Becker, Gary S. 1968. Crime and punishment: an economic approach. *Journal of Political Economy* 76:169–217.

Benoit, Jean-Pierre and Vijay Krishna. 1985. Finitely repeated games. *Econometrica* 53:905–922.

Berger, Helge. 1997. The Bundesbank's path to independence: evidence from the 1950s. *Public Choice* 93:427–453.

Bernheim, B. Douglas and Michael Whinston. 1990. Multimarket contact and business behavior. *Rand Journal of Economics* 21:1–26.

Bernstein, Lisa. 1992. Opting out of the legal system: extralegal contractual relations in the diamond industry. *Journal of Legal Studies* 21:115–157.

———. 2001. Private commercial law in the cotton industry: creating cooperation through rules, norms, and institutions. *Michigan Law Review* 99:1724–1788.

Bowles, Samuel and Herbert Gintis. 2002. Optimal parochialism: the dynamics of trust and exclusion in networks. Working paper, University of Massachusetts, Amherst, MA.

Calvert, Randall L. 1995a. The rational choice theory of social institutions: cooperation, communication, and coordination. In *Modern political economy: old topics, new directions*, ed. Jeffrey S. Banks and Eric A. Hanushek, pp. 216–267. Cambridge, UK: Cambridge University Press.

———. 1995b. Rational actors, equilibrium, and social institutions. In *Explaining social institutions*, ed. Jack Knight and Itai Sened, pp. 57–93. Ann Arbor, MI: University of Michigan Press.

Camerer, Colin F. 2003. *Behavioral game theory: experiments in strategic interaction*. New York: Russell Sage Foundation and Princeton, NJ: Princeton University Press.

Casella, Alessandra. 1996. On market integration and the development of institutions: the case of international commercial arbitration. *European Economic Review* 40:155–186.

Casella, Alessandra and James E. Rauch. 2002. Anonymous market and group ties in international trade. *Journal of International Economics* 58:19–47.

Chancellor, Edward. 1999. *Devil take the hindmost: a history of financial speculation*. New York: Farrar, Straus and Giroux.

Charny, David. 1990. Nonlegal sanctions in commercial relationships. *Harvard Law Review* 104:373–466.

Coase, Ronald. 1937. The nature of the firm. *Economica* 4:386–406.

———. 1960. The problem of social cost. *Journal of Law and Economics* 13:49–70.

———. 1988. *The firm, the market, and the law*. Chicago, IL: University of Chicago Press.

Conley, Timothy and Christopher Udry. 2001. Social learning through networks: the adoption of new agricultural technologies in Ghana. *American Journal of Agricultural Economics* 83:668–683.

Cooter, Robert D. 1994. Structural adjudication and the new law merchant: a model of decentralized law. *International Review of Law and Economics* 14:215–231.

Cooter, Robert D. and Daniel L. Rubinfeld. 1989. Economic analysis of legal disputes and their resolution. *Journal of Economic Literature* 27:1067–1097.

Dasgupta, Partha S. 1988. Trust as a commodity. In *Trust: making and breaking cooperative relations*, ed. Diego Gambetta, pp. 49–71. Oxford, UK: Basil Blackwell.

Demsetz, Harold. 1967. Toward a theory of property rights. *American Economic Review* 57:347–359.

De Soto, Hernando. 1989. *The other path: the invisible revolution in the third world*. New York: HarperCollins.

———. 2000. *Mystery of capital: why capitalism triumphs in the West and fails everywhere else*. New York: Basic Books.

Dezalay, Yves and Bryant G. Garth. 1996. *Dealing in virtue: international commercial arbitration and the construction of a transnational order*. Chicago, IL and London, UK: University of Chicago Press.

Dixit, Avinash. 1996. *The making of economic policy: a transaction cost politics perspective*. Cambridge, MA: MIT Press.

Dixit, Avinash. 1997. Power of incentives in public versus private organizations. *American Economic Review: Papers and Proceedings* 87:378–382.

———. 2003a. On modes of economic governance. *Econometrica* 71:449–481. (A longer working paper version is available at http://www.princeton.edu/~dixitak/home/wrkps.html.)

———. 2003b. Trade expansion and contract enforcement. *Journal of Political Economy* 111:1293–1317.

———. 2003c. Two-tier market institutions. Working paper, Princeton University, Princeton, NJ.

Dixit, Avinash and Susan Skeath. 2004. *Games of strategy*, 2nd edn. New York: W. W. Norton.

Djankov, Simeon and Peter Murrell. 2002. Enterprise restructuring in transition: a quantitative survey. *Journal of Economic Literature* 40:739–792.

Dower, John W. 1999. *Embracing defeat: Japan in the wake of World War II*. New York: W. W. Norton.

Dugatkin, Lee. 1999. *Cheating monkeys and citizen bees: the nature of cooperation in animals and humans*. New York: Simon and Schuster.

Eggertson, Thráinn. 1996. A note on the economics of institutions. In *Empirical studies in institutional change*, ed. Lee J. Alston, Thráinn Eggertson, and Douglass C. North, pp. 6–24. Cambridge, UK: Cambridge University Press.

Ellickson, Robert C. 1989. A hypothesis of wealth-maximizing norms: evidence from the whaling industry. *Journal of Law, Economics, and Organization* 5:83–97.

———. 1991. *Order without law: how neighbors settle disputes*. Cambridge, MA: Harvard University Press.

Ellison, Glenn. 1994. Cooperation in the prisoner's dilemma with anonymous random matching. *Review of Economic Studies* 61:567–588.

Ensminger, Jean. 1992. *Making a market: the institutional transformation of an African society*. Cambridge, UK: Cambridge University Press.

———. 1997. Changing property rights: reconciling formal and informal rights to land in Africa. In *The frontiers of the new institutional economics*, ed. John N. Drobak and John V. C. Nye, pp. 165–196. San Diego, CA: Academic Press.

Fafchamps, Marcel. 2002. Spontaneous market emergence. *Topics in Theoretical Economics* 2:1–33.

Fehr, Ernst and Simon Gächter. 2000. Cooperation and punishment in public goods experiments. *American Economic Review* 90:980–994.

Ferguson, Niall. 1998. *The house of Rothschild*, Vol. I. *Money's prophets 1798–1848*. New York: Viking Press.

Ferguson, Niall. 1999. *The house of Rothschild*, Vol. II. *The world's banker 1849–1999*. New York: Viking Press.

Friedman, Milton. 1962. *Capitalism and freedom*. Chicago, IL: University of Chicago Press.

Fudenberg, Drew and Eric Maskin. 1986. The folk theorem in repeated games with discounting or with incomplete information. *Econometrica* 54:533–554.

Gambetta, Diego. 1993. *The Sicilian Mafia: the business of protection*. Cambridge, MA: Harvard University Press.

Ghosh, Parikshit and Debraj Ray. 1996. Cooperation in community interaction without information flows. *Review of Economic Studies* 63:491–519.

Gibbons, Robert. 1997. Incentives and careers in organizations. In *Advances in economics and econometrics*, Vol. II, ed. David M. Kreps and Kenneth F. Wallis, pp. 1–37. Cambridge, UK: Cambridge University Press.

Granovetter, Mark. 1985. Economic action and social structure: the problem of embeddedness. *American Journal of Sociology* 91:481–510.

Greif, Avner. 1993. Contract enforceability and economic institutions in early trade: the Maghribi traders' coalition. *American Economic Review* 83:525–548.

———. 1994. Cultural beliefs and the organization of society: a historical and theoretical reflection on collectivist and individualist societies. *Journal of Political Economy* 102:912–950.

———. 1997a. Contracting, enforcement, and efficiency: economics beyond the law. In *Annual World Bank Conference on Development Economics*, ed. Michael Bruno and Boris Pleskovic, pp. 239–265. Washington, DC: The World Bank.

———. 1997b. On the interrelations and economic implications of economic, social, political and normative factors: reflections from two late medieval societies. In *The frontiers of the new institutional economics*, ed. John N. Drobak and John V. C. Nye, pp. 57–84. San Diego, CA: Academic Press.

———. 2000. The fundamental problem of exchange: a research agenda in historical institutional analysis. *European Review of Economic History* 4:251–284.

———. 2003. Institutions and impersonal exchange: the European experience. Working paper, Stanford University, Stanford, CA.

Grossman, Herschel I. 1995. Rival kleptocrats: the Mafia versus the state. In *The economics of organized crime*, ed. G. Fiorentini and S. Peltzman. Cambridge, UK: Cambridge University Press.

———. 2002. Make us a king: anarchy, predation, and the state. *European Journal of Political Economy* 18:31–46.

Grossman, Herschel I. and Minseong Kim. 1985. Swords or ploughshares? A theory of security of the claims to property. *Journal of Political Economy* 103:1275–1288.

Grossman, Sanford J. and Oliver D. Hart. 1983. An analysis of the principal–agent problem. *Econometrica* 51:7–45.

Guinnane, Timothy W. 2003. A failed institutional transplant: Raiffeisen's credit cooperatives in Ireland, 1894–1914. *Explorations in Economic History* 31:38–61.

Hall, Robert E. and Charles I. Jones. 1999. Why do some countries produce so much more output per worker than others? *Quarterly Journal of Economics* 114:83–116.

Hammett, Dashiel. 1930. *The Maltese falcon*. New York: Knopf.

Hay, Jonathan R. and Andrei Shleifer. 1998. Private enforcement of public laws: a theory of legal reform. *American Economic Review Papers and Proceedings* 98:398–403.

Hendley, Katherine and Peter Murrell. 2003. Which mechanisms support the fulfillment of sales agreement? Asking decision-makers in firms. *Economics Letters* 78:49–54.

Hendley, Katherine, Peter Murrell, and Randi Ryterman. 2001. Law works in Russia: the role of law in interenterprise transactions. In *Assessing the value of law in transition economies*, ed. Peter Murrell, pp. 56–93. Ann Arbor, MI: University of Michigan Press.

Hirshleifer, Jack. 2001. *The dark side of the force: economic foundations of conflict theory.* Cambridge, UK: Cambridge University Press.

Hirshleifer, Jack and John G. Riley. 1992. *The analytics of uncertainty and information.* New York: Cambridge University Press.

Johnson, Simon, John McMillan, and Christopher Woodruff. 2002. Courts and relational contracts. *Journal of Law, Economics, and Organization* 18:221–277.

Kali, Raja. 2002. Social embeddedness, modernization and markets: a small world approach to economic governance. Working paper, University of Arkansas, Fayetteville, AR.

Kandori, Michihiro. 1992. Social norms and community enforcement. *Review of Economic Studies* 59:61–80.

Kaufman, Daniel and Aart Kraay. 2002. Growth without governance. *Economia* 3:169–229.

Kaufman, Daniel, Aart Kraay, and Massimo Mastruzzi. 2003. Governance matters III: governance indicators for 1996–2002. Manuscript. Washington, DC: The World Bank.

Klein, Benjamin, Robert G. Crawford, and Armen A. Alchian. 1978. Vertical integration, appropriable rents, and the competitive contracting process. *Journal of Law and Economics* 21:297–326.

Kranton, Rachel. 1996. Reciprocal exchange: a self-sustaining system. *American Economic Review* 86:830–851.

Landes, William M. and Richard A. Posner. 1979. Adjudication as a private good. *Journal of Law and Economics* 8:235–284.

La Porta, Rafael, Florencio Lopez-de-Silanes, Andrei Shleifer, and Robert Vishny. 1998. Law and finance. *Journal of Political Economy* 106:1113–1155.

———. 1999. The quality of government. *Journal of Law, Economics, and Organization* 15:222–279.

Li, John Shuhe. 2003. The benefits and costs of relation-based governance: an explanation of the East Asian miracle and crisis. *Review of International Economics* 11:651–673.

Li, Shuhe and Peng Lian. 1999. Governance and investment: why can China attract large-scale FDI despite its widespread corruption? Working paper, City University of Hong Kong.

Liebcap, Gary D. 1989. *Contracting for property rights.* Cambridge, UK: Cambridge University Press.

Macaulay, Stewart. 1963. Non-contractual relationships in business: a preliminary study. *American Sociological Review* 28:55–70.

Marin, Dalia and Monika Schnitzer. 2002. *Contracts in trade and transition: the resurgence of barter.* Cambridge, MA: MIT Press.

Mas Colell, Andreu, Michael Whinston, and Jerry R. Green. 1995. *Microeconomic Theory.* New York: Oxford University Press.

Mattli, Walter. 2001. Private justice in a global economy: from litigation to arbitration. *International Organization* 55:919–947.

McMillan, John. 2002. *Reinventing the bazaar.* New York: W. W. Norton.

McMillan, John and Christopher Woodruff. 1999. Dispute prevention without courts in Vietnam. *Journal of Law, Economics, and Organization* 15:637–658.

———. 2000. Private order under dysfunctional public order. *Michigan Law Review* 98:2421–2458.

Milgrom, Paul R., Douglass C. North, and Barry R. Weingast. 1990. The role of institutions in the revival of trade: the law merchant, private judges, and the Champagne fairs. *Economics and Politics* 2:1–23.

Mirrlees, James A. 1971. An exploration in the theory of optimum income taxation. *Review of Economic Studies* 38:175–208.

Mookherjee, Dilip and Ivan Png. 1989. Optimal auditing, insurance, and redistribution. *Quarterly Journal of Economics* 104:399–415.

Murrell, Peter. 1996. How far has the transition progressed? *Journal of Economic Perspectives* 10:25–44.

North, Douglass C. 1990. *Institutions, institutional change, and economic performance*. Cambridge, UK: Cambridge University Press.

North, Douglass C. and Barry R. Weingast. 1989. Constitutions and commitment: the evolution of institutions governing public choice in seventeenth century England. *Journal of Economic History* 49:803–832.

Olson, Mancur. 1965. *The logic of collective action*. Cambridge, MA: Harvard University Press.

———. 1993. Dictatorship, democracy, and development. *American Political Science Review* 87:567–576.

Osborne, Martin J. and Ariel Rubinstein. 1994. *A course in game theory*. Cambridge, MA: MIT Press.

Ostrom, Elinor. 1990. *Governing the commons: the evolution of institutions for collective action*. Cambridge, UK, and New York: Cambridge University Press.

Pearce, David G. 1992. Repeated games: cooperation and rationality. In *Advances in Economic Theory: 6th World Congress*, Vol. I, ed. Jean-Jacqes Laffont, pp. 132–174. Cambridge, UK: Cambridge University Press.

Persson, Torsten and Guido Tabellini. 2000. *Political economics: explaining economic policy*. Cambridge, MA: MIT Press.

Platteau, Jean-Philippe. 2000. *Institutions, social norms, and economic development*. London: Routledge.

Polinsky, A. Mitchell and Steven Shavell. 2000. The economic theory of public enforcement of law. *Journal of Economic Literature* 38:45–76.

Posner, Richard A. 2002. *Economic analysis of law*, 6th edn. New York: Aspen.

Posner, Richard A. and Francesco Parisi, eds. 1997. *Law and economics*, Vols I–III. Cheltenham, UK: Edward Elgar.

Prendergast, Canice. 1999. The provision of incentives in firms. *Journal of Economic Literature* 37:7–63.

Pritchett, Lant. 2003. A toy collection, a socialist star, and a democratic dud? Growth theory, Vietnam, and the Philippines. In *In search of prosperity: analytic narratives on economic growth*, ed. Dani Rodrik, pp. 123–151. Princeton, NJ: Princeton University Press.

Putnam, Robert D. 2000. *Bowling alone: the collapse and revival of American community*. New York: Simon and Schuster.

Rasmusen, Eric. 2000. *Games and information*, 3rd edn. Malden, MA and Oxford, UK: Blackwell.

Rauch, James. 2001. Business and social networks in international trade. *Journal of Economic Literature* 39:1177–1203.

Rodrik, Dani. 1995. Getting intervention right: how South Korea and Taiwan grew rich. *Economic Policy* 20:53–101.

———. 2000. Institutions for high quality growth: what they are and how to acquire them. *Studies in Comparative International Development* 35:3–31.

————, ed. 2003. *In search of prosperity: analytical narratives on economic growth.* Princeton, NJ: Princeton University Press.

Rubin, Paul H. 1994. Growing a legal system in the post-communist economies. *Cornell International Law Journal* 27:1–47.

Sachs, Jeffrey and Warner, Andrew. 2001. The curse of natural resources. *European Economic Review* 45:827–838.

Schotter, Andrew. 1981. *The economic theory of social institutions.* Cambridge, UK: Cambridge University Press.

Schwartz, Alan. 1992. Relational contracts in the courts: an analysis of incomplete agreements and judicial strategies. *Journal of Legal Studies* 21:271–318.

Shavell, Steven. 1982. Suit, settlement, and trial: a theoretical analysis under alternative methods for the allocation of legal costs. *Journal of Legal Studies* 11:55–81.

Shelling, Thomas C. 1960. *The strategy of conflict.* Oxford, UK, and New York: Oxford University Press.

Shleifer, Andrei and Robert W. Vishny. 1998. *The grabbing hand: government pathologies and their cures.* Cambridge, MA: Harvard University Press.

Sobel, Joel. 2002. Can we trust social capital? *Journal of Economic Literature* 40:139–154.

Sokoloff, Kenneth L. and Stanley L. Engerman. 2000. History lessons: institutions, factor endowments, and paths of development in the new world. *Journal of Economic Perspectives* 14:217–232.

Solow, Robert M. 1974. The economics of resources or the resources of economics. *American Economic Review* 64 (Papers and Proceedings): 1–14.

Stigler, George. 1988. Law or economics? *Journal of Law and Economics* 35:455–468.

Strouse, Jean. 2000. *Morgan: American financier.* New York: HarperCollins.

Tornell, Aaron and Philip R. Lane. 1998. Are windfalls a curse? A non-representative agent model of the current account. *Journal of International Economics* 44:83–112.

Townsend, Robert. 1979. Optimal contracts and competitive markets with costly state verification. *Journal of Economic Theory* 22:265–293.

Varese, Federico. 2001. *The Russian Mafia: private protection in a new market economy.* Oxford, UK: Oxford University Press.

Whiting, Robert. 1999. *Tokyo underworld.* New York: Random House.

Williamson, Oliver E. 1979. Transaction cost economics: the governance of contractual relations. *Journal of Law and Economics* 22:233–261.

————. 1985. *The economic institutions of capitalism.* New York: Free Press.

————. 1996. *The mechanisms of governance.* New York: Oxford University Press.

————. 2000. The new institutional economics: taking stock, looking ahead. *Journal of Economic Literature* 38:595–613.

Wright, Robert. 2000. *Nonzero: the logic of human destiny.* Pantheon.

Young, H. Peyton. 1998. *Individual strategy and social structure: an evolutionary theory of institutions.* Princeton, NJ: Princeton University Press.

Index

The Gorman Lectures in Economics

Richard Blundell, Series Editor

Terence (W. M.) Gorman was one of the most distinguished economists of the twentieth century. His ideas are so ingrained in modern economics that we use them daily with almost no acknowledgement. The relationship between individual behavior and aggregate outcomes, two-stage budgeting in individual decision making, the 'characteristics' model which lies at the heart of modern consumer economics, and a conceptual framework for 'adult equivalence scales' are but a few of these. For over fifty years he guided students and colleagues alike in how best to model economic activities as well as how to test these models once formulated.

During the late 1980s and early 1990s Gorman was a Visiting Professor of Economics at University College London. He became a key part of the newly formed and lively research group at UCL and at the Institute for Fiscal Studies. The aim of this research was to avoid the obsessive labeling that had pigeon holed much of economics and to introduce a free flow of ideas between economic theory, econometrics and empirical evidence. It worked marvelously and formed the mainstay of economics research in the Economics Department at UCL. These lectures are a tribute to his legacy.

Terence had a lasting impact on all who interacted with him during that period. He was not only an active and innovative economist but he was also a dedicated teacher and mentor to students and junior colleagues. He was generous with his time and more than one discussion with Terence appeared later as a scholarly article inspired by that conversation. He used his skill in mathematics as a framework for his approach but he never insisted on that. What was essential was coherent and logical understanding of economics.

Gorman passed away in January 2003, shortly after the second of these lectures. He will be missed but his written works remain to remind all of us that we are sitting on the shoulders of a giant.

Richard Blundell, University College London and Institute for Fiscal Studies

Biography

Gorman graduated from Trinity College, Dublin, in 1948 in Economics and in 1949 in Mathematics. From 1949 to 1962 he taught in the Commerce Faculty at the University of Birmingham. He held Chairs in Economics at Oxford from 1962 to 1967 and at the London School of Economics from 1967 to 1979, after which he returned to Nuffield College Oxford as an Official Fellow. He remained there until his retirement. He was Visiting Professor of Economics at UCL from 1986 to 1996. Honorary Doctorates have been conferred upon him by the University of Southampton, the University of Birmingham, the National University of Ireland and University College London. He was a Fellow of the British Academy, an honorary Fellow of Trinity College Dublin and of the London School of Economics, an honorary foreign member of the American Academy of Arts and Sciences and of the American Economic Association. He was a Fellow of the Econometric Society and served as its President in 1972.